THE
DICTIONARY OF
FOREIGN TERMS
IN
THE ENGLISH
LANGUAGE

THE
Dictionary
OF
Foreign Terms
IN THE
English
Language

DAVID CARROLL

HAWTHORN BOOKS, INC.
Publishers / NEW YORK
A Howard & Wyndham Company

Library of Congress Catalog Card Number: 70-39281

ISBN: 0-8015-2053-3

1 2 3 4 5 6 7 8 9 10

Contents

INTRODUCTION   vii

ABBREVIATIONS USED IN THIS WORK   ix

FOREIGN TERMS IN THE ENGLISH LANGUAGE   I

ABBREVIATIONS OF FOREIGN TERMS COMMONLY USED IN
    ENGLISH   207

Introduction

This book is designed for the scholar, the teacher, the linguist; it is also meant for the casual reader who has occasional difficulty remembering the difference between *a priori* and *a posteriori* or who has often puzzled over the untranslated foreign quotations which so many authors sprinkle throughout their prose. It is, in fact, a book for anyone who has at one time or another been stopped in the middle of a passage by a foreign word.

To arm the reader against such interruptions, *The Dictionary of Foreign Terms in the English Language* contains a selection of words and phrases that represent a wide range of subjects and which are taken from more than thirty different languages. Included are foreign terms from medicine, philosophy, psychology, law, the culinary arts, science, history, politics, religion; included also are ancient proverbs and modern quotations, familiar mottos and literary aphorisms, famous exclamations and infamous oaths, titles of nobility, entrees from a menu, musical terminology; words used in the office, in the classroom, in reference libraries, all are here. Abbreviations are listed, as are popular slang expressions, the names of dances and festivals, terms from the fine arts, colors, articles of clothing, rooms in a house, liqueurs, and—in short—a majority of the foreign words and phrases one is likely to run across are included in these pages.

In using this dictionary the following facts should be noted. First, certain words included have been assimilated into English and are now part of the language proper. Words such as "sabot," "raja," "factotum," "allegro," and "materia medica" are but a few examples. In these cases, when naturalized words are listed, they are set in roman type; consequently, all italicized listings are foreign words and should be kept in italics during textual usage. Also, where one word has more than one meaning, these meanings are numbered in sequence, beginning with the definition most commonly intended; when the meanings of a word differ only slightly, these meanings are divided by the word "also" or by a semi-colon. Furthermore, those words and phrases which customarily begin with an article (such as *l'amour* or *l'état, c'est moi*) have that article placed in parenthesis. The word or phrase itself is then alphabetized according to the first letter following the article. Thus *l'amour* is listed under the letter "A," *l'état, c'est moi* is listed under the letter "E," and so on. Finally, where interesting or appropriate, etymologies are briefly presented. For further information on the etymology of a particular word consult a good dictionary on the subject such as Eric Partridge's *Origins: A Short Etymological Dictionary of Modern English.*

Abbreviations Used in this Work

Am.	American English	Jap.	Japanese
Ar.	Arabic	L.	Latin
Chi.	Chinese	M.E.	Middle English
Czec.	Czechoslovakian	Norw.	Norwegian
Dan.	Danish	O.F.	Old French
Dut.	Dutch	Pers.	Persian
Eng.	English	Pol.	Polish
F.	French	Port.	Portuguese
G.	German	Russ.	Russian
Gael.	Gaelic	Sc.	Scottish
Gr.	Greek	Skr.	Sanskrit
Heb.	Hebrew	Sp.	Spanish
Hung.	Hungarian	Sw.	Swedish
It.	Italian	Turk.	Turkish
		Yidd.	Yiddish

Foreign Terms in the English Language

A

ab absurdo [L.] From absurdity; from an absurd standpoint. (*His reasoning was* ab absurdo *and incomprehensible.*)

ab actu ad posse valet consecutio [L.] From what has been to what may be.

ab antiquo [L.] From the old days; from ancient times.

à bas [F.] Down with! (As in "Down with the king.")

abat-jour [F.] (1.) A skylight. (2.) A reflective device used to shine sunlight into a dark chamber. (3.) An awning or shutter used to exclude daylight.

abattoir [F.] A slaughterhouse.

abbé [F.] A title given to secular ecclesiastics in the French Roman Catholic Church. This title was once reserved for the highest ranking member of a monastery, but today is used to describe any secular cleric.

abeja [Sp.] Bee.

abends wird der Faule fleissig [G.] In the evening the lazy man turns diligent.

Aberglaube [G.] Superstition; popular fancy.

abeunt studia in mores [L.] Studies become habits. What a man learns, so he shall become.

ab extra [L.] From without; exter-nally; on the outside. (*Nothing* ab extra *could disturb his poise.*)

ab identitate rationis [L.] From an identity of reasons; for the same reason.

abi in pace [L.] Go in peace; de-part peacefully.

ab imis ad summa [L.] From the depths to the heights.

ab imo pectore [L.] From the bot-tom of the heart.

ab incunabilis [L.] From the cra-dle; from birth.

ab initio [L.] From the beginning; from the start. (*If the proposition had been well defined* ab initio, *this difficulty would not have originated.*)

ab intra [L.] From within; on the inside; internally. (*Although public opinion raged,* ab intra *all was calm.*)

à bis ou à blanc [F.] In one way or another.

abnormis sapiens [L.] A wise man without rule, i.e., a sage inde-pendent of any sect or dogma.

à bon compte [F.] Inexpensively; reduced in price.

à bon droit [F.] Of or with good reason; justifiably.

abonnement [F.] Subscription, as to magazines, journals, theater, etc.

ab origine [L.] From the origin; from the beginning. (*Here is the entire tale* ab origine.)

à bouche ouverte [F.] With gaping mouth; thus, enthusiastically; without pause to discriminate.

a bove majori discit arare minor [L.] The older ox teaches the younger how to plow.

ab ovo [L.] From the egg; from the very beginning.

ab ovo usque ad mala [L.] From the eggs even to the apples; hence, from the first course to the last; from the beginning through to the end.

à bras ouverts [F.] With open arms; with friendliness and hospitality.

abrazo [Sp.] An embrace, used as a cordial greeting.

abri [F.] A shelter, usually dug into the ground or side of a hill; a recess; a cave.

absit omen [L.] May no ill omen befall; an oath like "knock wood" or "heaven help us," used to negate the possibility of a calamity.

absque ulla conditione [L.] Without conditions; unconditionally.

abundans cautela non nocet [L.] Abundant cautions cause no harm. One can never be too careful.

abundant dulcibus vitiis [L.] They abound in delightful faults.

ab uno disce omnes [L.] From one learn of all, i.e., from a single case know every other.

abusus non tollit usum [L.] Abuse does not do away with use, i.e., the misuse of a thing does not negate its potential value.

a capite ad calcem [L.] From head to heel.

a cappella [It.] In music, a term indicating that no instrumental accompaniment takes place.

a capriccio [It.] In music, a direction indicating that the interpretation is up to the performer's discretion.

a cattiva vacca, Dio da corte corna [It.] To a cursed cow God gives short horns. Our fate is determined by our endowments.

accès de colère [F.] A fit of passion; a great rage.

accouchement [F.] Confinement; childbirth.

accoucheur [F.] One who delivers babies; an obstetrician.

accoucheuse [F.] Midwife.

accusare nemo se debit nisi coram Deo [L.] No one is obliged to accuse himself, except before God; in law, the basis of the Fifth Amendment to the United States Constitution.

acequia [Sp.] An irrigation canal; a drain.

acerrima proximorum odia [L.] The hatred of those nearest kin is fiercest.

acervatim [L.] In heaps.

acharné [F.] Fierce; implacable; intense.

achcha [Hindi] Yes; yes, indeed; certainly; it is so.

acheruntis pabulum [L.] Food for death.

à cheval [F.] On horseback; mounted on a horse.

a chi la riesce bene, è tenuto per savio [It.] He who succeeds is held to be wise.

Achtung [G.] Attention; take heed; also, a command to attention.

acierta errando [Sp.] He blunders into the right, i.e., he finds the right path unwittingly.

à compte [F.] On account; in partial payment.

à contre coeur [F.] Against one's

heart; thus, unwillingly; against one's wishes.

à corps perdu [F.] With lost body; thus, without hesitation; with might and main; with all one's strength.

à coups de dictionnaire [F.] With the blows of a dictionary, i.e., with constant reference to the dictionary.

acta est fabula [L.] The play is over; the performance has come to a conclusion.

acte de naissance [F.] A birth certificate.

actum est de republica [L.] It is all over with the republic.

actus Dei nemini facit injuriam [L.] Acts of God harm no men.

actus ne agas [L.] Do not do what has already been done.

acustica [It.] Acoustics.

adagio [It.] (1.) In music, a direction calling for slow, careful rendering. (2.) In dance, a sequence of slow movements to show or develop grace and line; part of the classic pas de deux. (q.v.)

ad amussin [L.] According to the carpenter's level; hence, with perfect accuracy; to perfection; precise.

ad arbitrium [L.] At will; arbitrarily. (*He went down the line and* ad arbitrium *selected those for the mission.*)

ad arbor che cade, ognum grida—dagli, dagli [It.] When a tree is falling, all yell, "Down with it, down with it!" When a powerful man shows any sign of decline, his associates quickly demand his removal.

Ad arma, ad arma! [L.] To arms, to arms; used as a cry of battle.

ad astra per aspera [L.] To the stars through difficulties; used as the motto of the State of Kansas.

a datu [L.] From the date.

ad captandum vulgus [L.] For the purpose of winning the masses; in order to win popular favor.

ad clerum [L.] To the clergy; directed toward the clergy.

adde parvum parvo magnus acervus erit [L.] Add a little to a little, a great pile will accrue; step by step takes one a long way.

a Deo et rege [L.] From God and the king.

ad esse [L.] Here; in attendance.

à dessein [F.] On purpose; intentionally.

ad eundem [L.] To the same rank or degree; refers to admittance to one university or organization with the same rank earned at another. (*He was admitted to Harvard* ad eundem *and was thus not forced to take entrance examinations*).

à deux [F.] For two, as in a familiar relationship. (*The lovers ordered a quiet table* à deux.)

à deux fins [F.] For two ends; valuable for two purposes.

ad extremum [L.] To the extreme; to the utmost.

ad gloriam [L.] For the glory.

adhibenda est in jocando moderatio [L.] One should be moderate in one's jests.

ad hoc [L.] For this circumstance, case, or example only; for this instance alone. (*A commission was created ad hoc for the special hearing.*)

ad hominem. See *argumentum ad hominem.*

ad hunc locum [L.] On this passage; used for reference purposes.

adieu [F.] Good-bye; so long.

ad inferos [L.] To the inferno; to hell.

ad infinitum [L.] To infinity; without a limit; forever.

ad initium [L.] At the beginning.

ad interim [L.] For an interim period; in the meantime; provisionally. (*Waiting for guards, they made sure, ad interim, that the safe was locked.*)

ad internecionem [L.] To extermination.

adios [Sp.] Good-bye.

ad libitum [L.] At one's pleasure; as one desires.

ad majorem Dei gloriam [L.] For the greater glory of God; used as the Jesuit motto.

ad melius inquirendum [L.] After more thorough investigation.

ad modum [L.] After the mode; in the manner of; like.

ad nauseam [L.] To nausea; thus, to a degree that induces disgust; to the point of revulsion.

adorer le veau d'or [F.] To worship the golden calf; to value money and material objects above all else.

ad patres [L.] To the fathers, i.e., gathered to the fathers; thus, dead; deceased.

ad perpetuam rei memoriam [L.] To or for the perpetual memory of the thing.

ad placitum [L.] At pleasure; at will; voluntarily.

ad quem [L.] To which; the goal or extreme limit.

ad referendum [L.] To or for reference; under study. (*The treaty is taken* ad referendum *and results will be announced.*)

ad rem [L.] To the point; pertaining to the matter at hand.

à droite [F.] (1.) To the right, as in a direction. (2.) To or on the right hand.

adscriptus glebae [L.] A person who belongs to the soil; a serf; a peasant farmer.

adsiduus usus uni rei deditus et ingenium et ingenium et artem saepe vincit [L.] Constant devotion to one line of work often proves superior to genius and art.

ad sum [L.] I am here; I am present; used in response to a roll call in the British educational system.

a due [It.] In music, a direction indicating that two instruments should simultaneously play the same passage.

ad unum omnes [L.] To the very last man.

ad valorem [L.] According to the value. (*All possessions are taxed ad valorem.*)

ad verbum [L.] To the word; to the letter; verbatim.

adversae res admonent religionum [L.] Adversity reminds one of religion.

(l') adversité fait l'homme et le bonheur les monstres [F.] Adversity makes a man, and worldly success makes monstrosities.

ad vivum [L.] To life, to what is living; lifelike. (*His portraits were startlingly* ad vivum.)

advocatus diaboli [L.] The devil's advocate.

adytum [L.] A sacred chamber into which only priests or initiates may enter.

aeger [L.] Sick; in British universities, a leave of absence for sickness.

aegrescit medendo [L.] He grows worse because of the remedy.

aegri somnia vana [L.] The empty dreams of a sick man.

aequabiliter et diligenter [L.] Steadily and diligently.

aequam memento rebus in arduis servare mentem [L.] Remember to maintain a tranquil mind in difficult situations.

aequo animo [L.] With a calm mind; with unmoved feelings; coolly.

aetatis [L.] Aged; elderly.

aetatis suae [L.] Of his or her age.

aeternum servans sub pectore vulnus [L.] A wound ever rankling in the breast.

aeternum sub sole nihil [L.] Naught under the sun is eternal.

affaire d'amour [F.] An affair of love; a love affair.

affaire de coeur [F.] An affair of the heart; a love affair; a romance.

affaire d'honneur [F.] An affair of honor, usually a duel.

(les) affaires font les hommes [F.] The experiences make the man.

(l') affair marche [F.] The affair progresses.

affirmatim [L.] In the affirmative.

à fond [F.] To the bottom; totally; entirely.

a fonte puro pura defluit aqua [L.] From a pure fountain pure water flows.

a fortiori [L.] With greater reason; much more so. Said of a second conclusion that is deemed more important or logically correct than the first.

a fronte praecipitium, a tergo lupus [L.] In front a cliff, behind a wolf; between the devil and the deep blue sea.

à genoux [F.] On the knees; in a kneeling position; in a posture of prayer.

agent provocateur [F.] An agent who provokes, i.e., a secret agent who joins a group suspected of a particular crime and who, once accepted by its members, incites them into committing the illegal acts for purposes of entrapment.

age quod agis [L.] Do what you do carefully.

aggadah [Heb.] The nonlegal, moralistic portion of Rabbinic literature.

agitato [It.] In music, a direction calling for an agitated rendering.

Agnus Dei [L.] The Lamb of God, Jesus Christ; a popular late medieval Christian motif which appears in many paintings.

à gogo [F.] Aplenty; galore.

à grands frais [F.] At great expense.

agrémens [F.] Attractive refinements or embellishments; decorations of a charming and pleasing character.

agréments. See *agrémens.*

agri non omnes frugiferi sunt [L.] All fields are not fruitful.

agua de colonia [Sp.] Toilet water; cologne.

ahimsa [Skr.] In Hindu philosophy, the doctrine of harmlessness to all creatures, popularized in this century by Mahatma Ghandi.

à huis clos [F.] Behind closed doors; in secret.

aide-de-camp [F.] In the military, an officer who is a protégé (q.v.), secretary, or trusted adjunct attached to a general or superior officer.

aide-toi, le ciel t'aidera [F.] "Help yourself, heaven will help you": *La Fontaine.*

aîné [F.] Senior; elder; often used to differentiate two historical figures, usually father and son, bearing the same name.

aiquillette [F.] A decorative pendant, braid, or tag on a uniform.

à l'abandon [F.] To the abandon; thus, in a slipshod or untidy manner; with neglect.

à la belle étoile [F.] To the beautiful star; thus, under the stars; out in the starry night; al fresco (q.v.).

à la bonne heure [F.] At a good hour; thus, all right; fine; well done.

à la carte [F.] By or according to the menu; with a separate price for each dish listed on the menu.

à la dérobée [F.] By stealth; secretly; clandestinely. (He crept into the pantry à la dérobée.)

al agradecido más de lo pedido [Sp.] To the grateful man give more than he asked.

alam [Indonesian] Nature.

à la main [F.] In hand; at hand; available; also, by hand; done by hand.

à la mode [F.] (1.) In the mode; thus, chic; stylish; fashionable. (2.) Served with a scoop of ice cream, as in a banana cream pie à la mode.

à l'anglaisse [F.] In the English manner.

à la parisienne [F.] In the style of the Parisian; in the manner of an inhabitant of Paris.

á la paz de Dios [Sp.] God be with you.

à la Tartuffe [F.] In the fashion of Tartuffe, the hypocritical hero of Molière's play, Tartuffe; thus, in a deceiving manner; double-dealing; insincere.

alba lux [L.] The pale white light of dawn.

alborada [Sp.] Dawn; sunrise.

al buen pagador, no le duelen prendas [Sp.] An honest debtor makes sacrifices to pay his debts.

alentours [F.] The surrounding grounds.

al fine [It.] In music, a direction indicating that a passage be played to the end.

al fresco [It.] In the open air; outside.

alguacil [Sp.] A constable; an officer of justice.

al hijo y al mulo en el culo [Sp.] For a son and a mule, a slap on the backside.

alia tendanda via est [L.] Another way must be tried; find another method.

aliéné [F.] A madman; a lunatic.

alieni appetens, sui profusus [L.] Anxious to gain other's possessions, neglectful of his own.

alieni temporis flores [L.] Flowers of a bygone age.

aliis inserviendo, me consumo [L.] In serving others, I consume myself.

à l'improviste [F.] Without warning; suddenly.

alis volat propriis [L.] She flies with her own wings; used as the motto of the State of Oregon.

aliter catuli longe olent, aliter sues [L.] Puppies have one smell, pigs another.

aliter visum diis [L.] The gods have decided otherwise.

alitur vitium vivitque tegendo [L.] Vice feeds on and lives by concealment.

aliud est celare, aliud tacere [L.] To conceal is one thing, to remain silent is another.

Allahu akbar [Ar.] God is great.

all'alba [It.] At daybreak.

alla vostra salute [It.] To your health; used as a toast.

allée [F.] A walkway; a path through a park or garden; also, a narrow street; an alley.

allegro [It.] (1.) In music, a brisk, lively tempo. (2.) In dance, a fast dance or sequence of movements; leaps, jumps, and aerial turns, in ballet.

aller Anfang ist schwer [G.] Every beginning is difficult.

alliciunt somnos tempus, motusque, merumque [L.] Sleep is induced by time, movement, and wine.

all'occorrenza [It.] According to circumstances.

all'ottava [It.] In music, a term calling for a switch from a higher to a lower octave.

allzu klug ist dumm [G.] Too smart is dumb; too wise for one's own good.

alma mater [L.] The college or university one has attended, which presumably served as a "foster mother."

alme [Ar.] In Egypt, a skilled female musician.

al mondo mal non è senza rimedio [It.] In this world there is no evil without a remedy.

à l'occasion [F.] If the occasion presents itself; if the proper time comes.

à l'oeuvre on connaît l'ouvrier [F.] By his work one will know the workman.

aloha [Hawaiian] Love; friendship; good feelings; used as a term of greeting and farewell.

alta mente repostum manet [L.] It abides stored away in the depths of the mind.

alta moda [It.] High fashion; the world of society; the skill and art of designing clothes.

alter ego [L.] Another self; thus, a double or intimate companion; a close friend.

alter idem [L.] Another self; an alter ego (q.v.).

amabilis insania [L.] A pleasing madness.

à main armée [F.] By force of arms.

amari aliquid [L.] Something bitter; a slightly bitter taste.

a maximis ad minima [L.] From the greatest to the smallest; from the most to the least.

âme damnée [F.] A damned soul; someone who has given away his soul to another and is hence their hireling or lackey.

âme de boue [F.] A soul of mud; a dead soul.

âme d'élite [F.] An elite soul; an individual favored by the gods.

(l') âme n'a pas de sexe [F.] The soul has no sex.

à merveille [F.] Marvelous; wonderfully executed. (*His footwork was done* à merveille.)

amici fures temporis [L.] Friends are robbers of our time.

amico d'ognuno, amico di nessuno [It.] Everybody's friend is nobody's friend.

amicus certus in re incerta cernitur [L.] A real friend is known in adversity.

amicus curiae [L.] A friend of the court; a disinterested adviser at court who provides advice during a trial.

amicus usque ad aras [L.] A friend only up to the altar; thus, a friend with whom we can agree only on secular matters.

amore [It.] Love; affection.

amor in Deum [L.] Love of God.

amor in proximum [L.] Love of one's fellow man.

amor nummi [L.] Love of money.

amor omnia vincit [L.] Love conquers all.

amor patriae [L.] Love of one's country.

(l') amour passe le temps; le temps passe l'amour [F.] Love passes the time; time passes the love.

amour-propre [F.] (1.) Self-love; self-esteem. (2.) Self-respect.

amour, tu perdis Troie! [F.] Love, thou destroyedst Troy!

amrita [Skr.] In Hindu mythology, a nectar, the food of the gods.

ananda [Skr.] In Hinduism and Buddhism, the state of bliss.

anch'io son pittore [It.] I am also a painter; an enigmatic exclamation made by Correggio while looking at a work by Raphael.

ancien régime [F.] The old regime; pertains specifically to the monarchy existing before the French revolution.

ancipitis usus [L.] Useful in two ways.

andante [It.] In music, a direction calling for a tempo of moderate speed.

aniles fabulae [L.] Old wives' tales.

anima [L.] (1.) The human soul. (2.) In the psychology of Carl Jung, the feminine part of the male unconscious.

anima in amicis una [L.] One mind among friends.

anima mundi [L.] The spirit of the world.

anima rationalis [L.] The rational soul.

animis opibusque parati [L.] Prepared in spirit and wealth; used

as the motto of the State of South Carolina.

animositas [L.] Courage; bravery.

animus [L.] (1.) Mind; thus the spirit that empowers; the animating force; motivation. (2.) Hatred; animosity. (3.) In the psychology of Carl Jung, the male force active in the female unconscious.

ankh [Egyptian] The *crux ansata* (q.v.); an ancient cross formed of an elliptical loop on top of a T-shaped stem used in Egyptian hieroglyphics to symbolize, among other things, the life force.

ankusa [Skr.] An elephant goad.

Anlage [G.] (1.) A basic principle; a fundamental part. (2.) A proclivity; disposition; inclination toward something.

anno Domini [L.] In the year of our Lord; in a particular year of the Christian calendar; ordinarily abbreviated to A.D.

anno urbis conditae [L.] The year of the city's founding. A dating device, like B.C. and A.D., instituted by the Romans to count the passage of years from the founding of Rome in 753 B.C.

annuit coeptis [L.] He, i.e., God, has looked on our undertaking with favor; a passage from the *Aeneid* of Vergil; used as the motto on the great seal of the United States.

annus magnus [L.] The great year; a period of time, somewhat comparable to the Hindu *kalpa* (q.v.) which contains within itself approximately 15,000 sidereal years and which marks the completion of one year in the life of the Roman gods.

annus mirabilis [L.] A year of wonders; a year of awe-inspiring events or great catastrophe.

à nouvelles affaires, nouveaux conseils [F.] For new occasions, new advice.

anquis in herba [L.] A snake in the grass.

Anschluss [G.] A joining; used in reference to the German annexation of Austria in 1938.

anser, apis, vitulus populos et regna gubernant [L.] Pen, wax, and parchment govern the world.

ante-bellum [L.] Before the war; commonly used to characterize the period in the southern United States before the Civil War.

ante Christum [L.] Before Christ.

ante lucem [L.] Before light, i.e., before dawn.

antemeridian [L.] Before noon; commonly abbreviated as A.M.

ante-mortem [L.] Before death.

ante omnia [L.] Before all things; above and beyond everything; in the first place.

ante tubam trepidat [L.] He trembles even before the war trumpet sounds its call.

antevictoriam ne canas triumphum [L.] Before the victory do not sing the victory song.

antipasto [It.] The first course at the table, often a mixed salad of meats and raw vegetables; hors d'oeuvres (q.v.).

antwoorden [Dut.] An answer; response.

à nu [F.] Naked; bare; nude.

Août [F.] The month of August.

à outrance [F.] To the very end; to the final blow; to the ultimate conclusion, as in a duel to the death.

apage, Satanas! [L.] Get thee away, Satan!

à pas de geant [F.] A giant step.

aperçu [F.] A glance; a glimpse; a quick look. (*The novel is full of brilliant* aperçus *of Dutch life.*)

apéritif [F.] A light alcoholic beverage taken before a meal to increase the appetite.

à perte de vue [F.] As far as the eye can see.

a piacere [It.] At pleasure; at one's discretion.

à pobreza no hay verguenza [Sp.] Poverty has no shame.

a poco a poco [It.] Little by little; a little bit.

à point [F.] To the point; precisely.

apologia [L.] A formal defense or apology.

a posteriori [L.] Arriving at conclusion by experiment, observation, and experience rather than by use of theory or logical reasoning; basing determinations on empirical fact rather than on self-evident principles; the logical opposite of a priori (q.v.).

apparatus belli L.] The apparatus of war; weapons.

apparatus criticus [L.] Critical apparatus.

apparebit repentina dies [L.] Suddenly shall the day of judgment appear.

appetitus rationi obediant [L.] Let the appetites obey the reason.

appliqué [F.] A decorative art based on the application of one fabric or material on top of another, as in needlework.

appui [F.] A support; a stay or prop such as a buttress, post, or railing.

après moi le déluge [F.] After me the deluge; a phrase attributed to Louis XIV in reference to the future of the French government.

a prima vista [It.] At first sight.

a priori [L.] (1.) A manner of reasoning that derives conclusions from a hypothesis or from general principles rather than from observable facts; the logical opposite of a posteriori (q.v.). (2.) Based on theory rather than fact; stated without proper evidence or sufficient research.

à propos de bottes [F.] Concerning the subject of boots, i.e., not to the purpose; irrelevant.

à propos de rien [F.] Apropos of nothing; inapplicable; not to the point.

aqua [L.] Water.

aqua pura [L.] Pure water; drinking water.

a quatr'occhi [It.] To four eyes, i.e., face-to-face; close up; an intimate meeting.

aqua vitae [L.] (1.) The water of life. (2.) Liquor; a fortifying alcoholic drink such as cognac.

aquila non capit muscas [L.] An eagle does not catch flies; the great do not bother with the small.

arbiter bibendi [L.] The arbiter of drinking; one of great knowledge and impeccable taste in matters of alcoholic beverages; the toastmaster at a party or the person responsible for choosing the evening's wine.

arbiter elegantiae [L.] The arbiter of elegance; one who is considered to be the supreme judge of refinement and good taste.

arcades ambo [L.] Arcadians both; companions of similar type of motive, i.e., birds of a feather.

arcana caelestia [L.] Heavenly mysteries; celestial secrets.

arcana imperii [L.] Secrets of the government; state mysteries.

arc-boutant [F.] A flying buttress.

à rebours [F.] The wrong way; done in a backward or reversed manner; against the grain.

argent comptant [F.] Ready money; money on hand.

argumenti causa [L.] For the sake of argument. (*The assumption was made,* argumenti causa, *that we were right.*)

argumentum [L.] A logical argument; a proof designed to convince.

argumentum ad crumenam [L.] An argument to the wallet; an argument directed toward the monetary and economic interests of those who are being persuaded.

argumentum ad hominem [L.] An argument to the man; an argument that persuades by appealing to the emotions rather than to the reason or logical judgment; one that attacks the man rather than his arguments.

argumentum ad misericordium [L.] An argument aimed at persuasion by an appeal to pity and compassion rather than to intellect.

argumentum baculinum [L.] The argument of the stick, i.e., the persuasive powers of physical force.

arhat [Tibetan] In Lamaism, a man who has spiritually perfected himself; a great sage.

aria [It.] (1.) A song; an air; a melody. (2.) A vocal composition to be sung by a single voice with instrumental accompaniment, usually in an opera, operetta, or oratorio.

ariston metron [Gr.] Moderation is the finest way; temperance should be practiced in all things.

arrivederci [It.] Till we meet again; good-bye.

armes à feu [F.] Firearms; as opposed to *armes blanches* (q.v.).

armes blanches [F.] White arms; thus, hand weapons such as daggers and lances, as distinguished from firearms or *armes à feu* (q.v.).

armoire [F.] A large free-standing wardrobe, usually made of ornately decorated wood.

armonioso [Sp.] Harmonious; pleasing.

arpa [It.] A harp.

arrectis auribus [L.] Listening with ears perked up.

arrière-pensée [F.] A thought kept to oneself; a reservation; also, an ulterior motive.

arrivé [F.] A person who has very recently achieved success; a parvenu.

arrondissement [F.] In France, an administrative district of a department or city.

arroyo [Sp.] (1.) A natural watercourse or channel. (2.) An arid gully or dry riverbed. (3.) A small stream.

ars [L.] Art.

ars artium omnium conservatrix [L.] The art that preserves all other arts, i.e., printing.

ars longa, vita brevis [L.] Art is long, life is short.

ars pictoria [L.] The art of pictures, i.e., painting.

ars poetica [L.] The art of poetry.

ars politica [L.] The political art, i.e., politics; statecraft.

artis maxime proprium est creare et gignere [L.] It is above all the property of art to create and to bring into being.

asana [Skr.) In the practice of Yoga, a meditative posture or bodily position assumed for purposes of increasing the health or aiding in the process of contemplation.

Askenazi [Heb.] A Jew of Central or Eastern Europe.

ashram [Skr.] In Hinduism, a monastery; a place of retreat.

asinus ad lyram [L.] An ass at the lyre, i.e., one of no artistic ability and appreciation.

asperges [F.] Asparagus.

assentatio, vitiorum adjutrix, procul amoveatur [L.] Let flattery, the handmaiden of vices, be far from friendship.

assez bien [F.] Good enough; pretty good; OK.

assumpsit [L.] He undertook; in law, a lawsuit brought for breach of contract; cf. *non assumpsit*.

à tâtons [F.] Gropingly.

atelier [F.] An artist's studio; a workshop for craftsmen.

a tempo [It.] In music, in time; in tempo.

atman [Skr.] In the Hindu religion, the deeply-buried but omnipresent Self which, as a particle of the Divine, constitutes that which is eternal in man.

à tort et à travers [F.] Wrong and across; thus, by chance; haphazardly; without a definite reason, purpose, or goal.

à toute force [F.] With all force; absolutely; without any question; by all means.

à tout hasard [F.] At all hazards; no matter what.

(l')attrait de la nouveauté [F.] The charm of novelty.

attroupement [F.] A mob of people; a large crowd.

aubade [F.] A song at dawn; a musical composition written to be performed as the sun rises; also, morning music; music that melodically describes the dawn.

auberge [F.] An inn.

aubergiste [F.] An innkeeper; a hotel manager.

au bout de son Latin [F.] At the end of his Latin, i.e., at the end of his knowledge.

au contraire [F.] To the contrary.

au courant [F.] In the current; thus, well-informed; knowledge-able of current events; up with the times.

auctor opus laudat [L.] The author praises his work.

aucun chemin de fleurs ne conduit à la gloire [F.] No flowery road leads to glory.

aucun fiel n'a jamais empoissonné ma plume [F.] No gall has even poisoned my pen.

au désespoir [F.] In despair.

audi alteram partem [L.] Hear the other side; listen to both sides before you make a judgment.

audio sed taceo [L.] I hear but I am silent.

au fait [F.] Up to the mark; well-schooled; well-versed in something. (*He was* au fait *in Latin.*)

aufgeschoben ist nicht aufgehoben [G.] Postponed is not aban-doned.

au fond [F.] At bottom; essentially; basically.

auf Wiedersehen [G.] Till we see each other once more; farewell.

au grand serieux [F.] In great seri-ousness; in extreme earnest; often implies a seriousness not called for by the situation.

au gratin [F.] Cooked in a cover-ing of bread crumbs and grated cheese.

au jus [F.] With the juice; served with the natural gravies.

au lait [F.] With milk.

auld lang syne [Sc.] The old days long since passed.

au naturel [F.] Naturally; in na-ture's way; naked.

au pied de la lettre [F.] To the foot of the letter; something which is exact and precise to the last letter.

au plaisir de vous revoir [F.] Till I have the pleasure of seeing you again.

au premier abord [F.] At first sight.

aurea mediocritas [L.] The golden mean; the middle path between all extremes.

au reste [F.] For the rest; more-over; besides.

au revoir [F.] Till we meet again; good-bye.

auribus teneo lupum [L.] I hold a wolf by the ears, i.e., I have caught a traitor.

aurora [L.] The dawn.

au royaume des aveugles les borgnes sont rois [F.] In the valley of the blind the one-eyed men are kings.

aus celare autem [L.] The art to conceal art.

Ausgleich [G.] A mutual under-standing; an agreement, often po-litical.

auspicium melioris aevi [L.] An omen of a better age.

aut inveniam viam aut faciam [L.] I will find a way or I will make one.

Autobus [G.] A motor bus.

Autobahn [G.] A highway; turn-pike.

auto-da-fé [Port.] During the Span-ish Inquisition, the ceremony in which the members of the Holy Office and those accused of heresy met, listened to a sermon by the grand inquisitor, and heard a reading of the sentences allotted to the heretics, at the conclusion of which the accused were given over to secular officials for execution.

auto de fé [Sp.] See *auto-da-fé.*

autre temps, autres mores [F.] Other times, other ways.

au troisième [F.] On the third floor.

aut vincere aut mori [L.] Either conquer or die.

aux absents les os [F.] To those absent, the bones. Those not present receive the leavings.

aux armes! [F.] To arms! Used as a call to battle.

auxilia humilia firma consensus facit [L.] Unanimity makes humble help strong.

avaler les couleuvres [F.] To put up with indignities.

avant-coureur [F.] A herald; harbinger; forerunner.

avant-garde [F.] The vanguard; the most daring or innovative individuals in any practice, especially those in the field of art.

avant-propos [F.] A preface.

avatar [Skr.] In the Hindu religion, an incarnation of a deity in terrestrial form.

ave atque vale! [L.] Hail and farewell.

avec [F.] With.

avec impatience [F.] With impatience.

Ave, imperator! Morituri te salutant [L.] Hail emperor! Those of us who will die salute you; used as a gladiator's salutation to the emperor before a battle to the death.

Ave, Maria [L.] Hail, Mary; in the Roman Catholic Church, a prayer.

avidya [Skr.] In Hinduism, ignorance of one's real self.

avi numerantur avorum [L.] Ancestors of ancestors are counted up to me.

avion [F.] An airplane.

avise la fin [F.] Consider the end of things.

avoirdupois [F.] (1.) A system of weight measurement based on the sixteen-ounce pound and used in most of the English-speaking world. (2.) Colloquially, fat; over-weight; chubby.

à votre santé [F.] To your health; used as a toast.

Avril [F.] The month of April.

à vue d'oeil [F.] At a look of the eye; visibly; at a glance.

a vuestra salud [Sp.] To your health; used as a toast.

azan [Ar.] The Moslem call to prayer, called out five times a day from atop the minarets of the mosques.

azeite, vinho e amigo, o mais antigo [Port.] Of oil, wine, and friends, the oldest is the best.

B

babushka [Russ.] A triangularly folded kerchief worn by Russian women.

Babylonia undique [L.] Babylonia, or Babel, is everywhere, i.e., confusion reigns.

baccarat [F.] A French card game of chance, usually played in the great casinos of Europe, often for enormous stakes.

bacchanalia [L.] The festival of Bacchus, Roman god of wine, characterized by drunken revelry; thus, any festival or party that reaches an orgiastic or intoxicated frenzy.

Bachelier ès lettres [F.] Bachelor of Letters.

Bachelier ès sciences [F.] Bachelor of Sciences.

bacio di bocca spesso cuor non tocca [It.] Oft the heart is missed where the mouth is kissed.

badinerie [F.] Jesting; playful banter; silly but enjoyable joking.

badshah [Persian] In India and Persia, a title of royalty for a king or shah.

bagel [Yidd.] A donut-shaped hard-roll.

bagh [Hindi] A tiger.

bagh [Persian] A cultivated garden; a pleasure garden surrounding a gazebo, palace, or oasis.

baguettes de bois [F.] Wooden drumsticks.

bahadur [Hindi] Brave; bold; used as a common first or second name in India and Nepal.

Bahnhof [G.] Railroad station.

bain [F.] Bath; bathing place; bathtub.

bain d'eau de mer [F.] A saltwater bath.

bain de pied [F.] A foot bath.

bain de vapeur [F.] A steambath.

baïonette [F.] A bayonet.

baklava [Turkish] A honey pastry, popular in the Middle East and Russia.

baksheesh [Persian] (1.) Extra money given for services rendered; a gratuity. (2.) A plea of beggars for alms; also, the money given to beggars.

bal [F.] A ball; a dance.

balalaika [Russ.] A three-stringed instrument, native to Russia, with a triangular belly tapering up to a slender neck on which are located nineteen frets.

bal champêtre [F.] A country ball; a feast or festival held outdoors.

balcon [F.] Balcony.

bal costumé [F.] A costume ball; a fancy-dress party.

ballatore [It.] A male dancer.

ballet chanté [F.] A ballet that in-

15

volves the vocal participation of the dancers; a singing ballet.

ballet d'action [F.] A ballet that tells a story in pantomime.

ballon d'essai [F.] A test balloon; a small air-balloon used in France to ascertain the direction of the wind; hence, a feeler; a trial project; an idea, concept, or scheme tried out on a section of the public before mass release.

bal masqué [F.] A masked ball; a costume party.

balourdise [F.] A blunder; a stupid slip.

bambino [It.] A young child.

bambochade [F.] A droll or grotesque drawing; a caricature.

banco regis [L.] In law, on the King's bench.

Bancus Communium Placitorum [L.] The Court of Common Pleas.

bandera [Sp.] A flag; a banner.

bandera de paz [Sp.] A flag of truce.

banderilla [Sp.] A short pointed spear used to antagonize a bull in a bull fight before the matador has entered the arena.

banderole [F.] A small flag or banner; a streamer.

bandolero [Sp.] A brigand; a highwayman.

banlieue [F.] The outskirts of a town or city; the suburbs.

banni nuptiarum [L.] Matrimonial bands, i.e., wedding rings.

banshee [Gael.] In Ireland and Scotland, a female wraith who brings tidings of evil and death to all who perceive her.

banzai [Jap.] A Japanese cheer or war cry meaning "ten thousand years."

baragouin [F.] Gibberish; meaningless jargon; double-talk. (*He*

spoke in a bizarre baragouin *comprehensible only to himself.*)

barbae tenus sapientes [L.] Men as wise as the length of their beards, i.e., hypocritical philosophers; know-nothings masquerading as sages.

barbaris ex fortuna pendet fides [L.] The fidelity of barbarians depends on fortune.

barbouillage [F.] A scrawl; a dirty smear.

bardo [Tibetan] In Tibetan Lamaism, a plane visited by the human soul after death. There are three *bardos* through which the life-monad passes on its way either to a realization of its true self in the Absolute or toward a rebirth in a human or subhuman organism.

bar mitzvah [Heb.] In the Jewish religion, a male who has reached his thirteenth birthday, marking a transition into the responsibilities of manhood; also, the ceremony marking the occasion.

bas étage [F.] A lower story of a building.

bashi-bazouk [Turk.] Turkish mercenary soldiers, famous for their courage and feared for their barbarous and licentious behavior.

basis virtutum constantia [L.] The basis of all virtue is consistency.

basse naissance [F.] A low or mean birth; lowly born.

basso buffo [It.] In music, a singer with a deep bass voice who ordinarily sings the comic passages.

basso cantante [It.] In music, a bass with a well developed upper range.

basso continuo [It.] In music, a keyboard accompaniment, originally of a figured bass.

basso profundo [It.] In music, a deep bass singing voice; also, a singer capable of such a deep range.

basso-relievo [It.] A bas-relief; sculptural modeling slightly raised from its original plane; hence, low relief.

bastinado [Sp.] (1.) A club; a truncheon; also, a blow from such a weapon. (2.) A form of medieval torture, practiced in Spanish prisons for many years, consisting of pommelling applied to the soles of the feet until all the bones have been fractured.

bateau [F.] A boat; a ship; a seagoing vessel.

batterie de cuisine [F.] Implements of the kitchen, i.e., knives, spoons, pans, and various other cooking utensils.

battre à deux temps [F.] In music, a direction meaning two beats to a measure.

battre l'eau [F.] To beat the water, i.e., to struggle in vain.

battre le fer l'enclume [F.] To strike the iron on the anvil.

battue [F.] (1.) The act of thrashing in the woods and thickets to drive out game for hunters. (2.) Undiscriminating slaughter of animals on the hunt, or of men during times of war and riot.

(die) Baukunst ist eine erstarrte Musik [G.] "Architecture is frozen music": *Goethe.*

baum [G.] Tree.

bavardage [F.] Meaningless prattle or nonsense; silly gossip; the cackle of empty words.

bayer aux corneilles [F.] To gape at the crowd.

Bearbeitung [G.] A musical arrangement; a transcription.

beatae memoriae [L.] Of blessed memory.

Beata Virgo Maria [L.] The Blessed Virgin Mary.

beati [L.] The happy ones; those that are happy or blessed.

beau garçon [F.] A good looking young man; a fine fellow, often used ironically.

beau geste [F.] A noble and gracious gesture; also, a gesture which is impressive but essentially insincere.

beau idéal [F.] A beautiful ideal; the model of perfection. (*From the time she first saw him, Fairbanks became for her an eternal beau idéal.*)

beau monde [F.] The beautiful world, i.e., the world of fashion and high society.

beaux-arts [F.] The fine arts, i.e., painting, sculpture, engraving, etc.

bêche-de-mer [F.] (1.) A caterpillar of the sea, i.e., a species of sea-cucumber native to the East Indies, frequently used in oriental cuisine. (2.) A hybrid language, like pidgin English, spoken by natives of the South Pacific.

bedouin [Ar.] Nomadic tribesmen of the middle eastern deserts.

Begleitung [G.] In music, accompaniment.

bel canto [It.] In music, a vocal style characterized by its sparkling glibness rather than by its emotional profundity.

bel esprit [F.] An individual of brilliance and sparkling wit, capable of spirited, intelligent conversation on a variety of topics.

bella è il rossore, ma è incommodo qualche volta [It.] A blush is

beautiful but sometimes incon-
venient.

bella, horrida bella [L.] Wars, hor-
rid wars.

belle [F.] A lovely young lady of
many talents and genuine virtues.

belle amie [F.] Beautiful friend,
i.e., a mistress; a lover.

belle assemblée [F.] Beautiful assembly; a finely turned-out gathering; a fashionable crowd.

belle dame [F]. A pretty woman.

(la) belle dame sans merci [F.] The
beautiful woman without mercy;
title of Keat's famous poem and
a phrase descriptive of any beautiful man-hating woman.

belle parole non pascon i gatti [It.]
Beautiful words don't feed the
cats; actions speak louder than
words.

belles-lettres [F.] Artistic literature
such as poetry, drama, and the
novel, as opposed to academic or
purely informative writings.

belle-tournure [F.] A good figure;
a shapely form.

bellum [L.] War.

bellum omnium in omnes [L.] A
war of everyone against everyone.

*beltà e follia vanno spesso in com-
pagnia* [It.] Beauty and folly
often go together.

belua multorum capitum [L.] The
monster of many heads, i.e., the
masses; the public.

bem sabe o gato cujas barbas lambe
[Port.] The cat knows well whose
cheek she licks.

benedetto è quel male che vien solo
[It.] Blessed is the misery that
comes alone.

benedicite [L.] Bless you; blessings on you.

beneficium invito non datur [L.] A

boon cannot be handed to one
who will not accept it.

bene orasse est bene studuisse [L.]
To have prayed well is to have
studied well.

beneplacito a vostro [It.] At your
pleasure.

ben lo sai tu, che lo sai tutta quanta
[It.] "A man indeed who knew
all tricks that belong to the magic
art": *Dante.*

ben venuto [It.] Welcome.

berceuse [F.] A lullaby; a cradle-
song.

berger [F.] A shepherd; a sheep-
herder; a swain.

(das) Beste ist gut genug [G.] The
best is good enough.

bête [F.] A beast; a lowly animal;
a stupid or barbaric creature;
also, a bumbling fool; a boor.

bête noire [F.] A bugbear; an object of hatred; something that is
feared for the harm it may cause.
(*Men are the old maid's bête
noire.*)

bêtise [F.] Foolishness; stupidity;
silliness; an unthinking or blundering action.

beurre [F.] Butter.

beurre manié [F.] A creamy butter
sauce made by adding two parts
of butter to one part flour.

bhakti [Skr.] In Hinduism, devotion; the path of emotional dedi-
cation to one's duty in life and to
God.

Bhakti Yoga [Skr.] A form of Yoga
in which the devotee strives to
reach a higher understanding of
his life and the universe through
intense emotional devotion to
God.

bheesty [Hindi] A caste in India
whose function is to bear water
for the higher castes.

bhikku [Pali] A Buddhist monk who gains his livelihood by begging rice and coins each morning before his day's chores begin.

bibelot [F.] A trinket; an ornamental bauble.

bibendum est nunc [L.] Now is the time for drinking; used as the motto of many drinking establishments throughout the world.

bibere venenum in auro [L.] To drink poison from a cup of gold.

Bibliothek [G.] Library.

Bibliothekar [G.] Librarian.

bibliothèque [F.] Library.

bien-aimé [F.] Well-loved; beloved.

bien entendu [F.] Well understood; but of course; agreed.

(un) bienfait n'est jamais perdu [F.] A kind deed is never lost.

bien obligé [F.] Well obliged; delighted.

bien predica quien bien vive [Sp.] The man who lives the best life preaches the best sermons.

bienséance [F.] Etiquette; propriety; proper behavior for a social situation.

bienvenu [F.] Welcome.

bière [F.] Beer.

Bierhaus [G.] A beer house; a tavern.

bijou [F.] A jewel; a precious stone.

Bild [G.] Illustration; picture.

Bilderbuch [G.] A picture book; an album.

Bildergalerie [G.] A hall of pictures; a gallery.

billet-doux [F.] A sweet note, i.e., a love letter.

billig [G.] Cheap; inexpensive.

bis [L.] Twice; in music, a term used to call for an encore or the repetition of a refrain.

biscoti [It.] A hard, crisp biscuit containing anise and nuts.

bise [F.] A strong north wind native to the alpine regions of Europe.

bis peccare in bello non licet [L.] A second blunder in war is not allowed.

bis pueri senes [L.] Old men are boys twice.

bisque [F.] A creamy rich soup made from game or seafood.

bistro [F.] A small bar, tavern, or cafe.

bis vincit qui se vincit in victoria [L.] Twice conquers he who conquers himself in the victory.

bitte [G.] Please; also used as a response to a thank you.

bivouac [F.] A temporary encampment or hasty, improvised shelter.

blague [F.] Empty bragging; a prank or practical joke.

blagueur [F.] A hypocrite; a malicious practical joker; a prankster.

blanc [F.] The color white.

blanc-bec [F.] A greenhorn; a novice.

blanc comme neige [F.] White as snow.

blanc fixe [F.] Barium sulfate; $BaSo_4$, a chemical used in industry in the production of rubber and paper.

blanchi [F.] Blanched.

blandae mendacia linguae [L.] The lies of a bland tongue.

blasé [F.] A state of being bored with objects or experiences that most people consider stimulating.

Blasinstrument [G.] In music, a wind instrument.

Blech [G.] In music, a brass instrument.

Blechmusik [G.] The music played by brass instruments.

(la) blessure est pour vous, la douleur est pour moi [F.] You have received the wound, but it is I who suffer.

blitz [G.] (1.) Lightning. (2.) A shortening of blitzkrieg (q.v.).

blitzkrieg [G.] Lightning war; an unexpected and usually unprovoked military offensive designed, by the force of its sudden intensity, to destroy the enemy before he can mobilize.

blödsinnig [G.] Feeble-minded; stupid; giddy.

Blut [G.] Blood.

Blut und Eisen [G.] Blood and iron; used as the motto of Prince Otto Eduard Leopold von Bismarck, first chancellor of Germany.

bocage [F.] A grove of trees; a copse; a wooded area.

boche [F.] Colloquially, a German; used disparagingly as a nickname for German troops.

boeuf [F.] Beef; cooked beef.

boeuf bourguignon [F.] Beef stew.

(La) Bohème. [F.] The world of the Bohemians.

bois [F.] Wood; timber; also, a woods or forest.

bolero [Sp.] (1.) A Spanish dance in three-four time; also, the music for that dance. (2.) A vestlike jacket open in the front and usually without buttons or fasteners.

bon accueil [F.] A good welcome; a friendly reception. (*We received a* bon accueil *from our host.*)

bona fide [L.] In good faith; authentic; guaranteed.

bona pars [L.] A large portion; a goodly part; a sizeable section.

bona peritura [L.] Perishable property.

bona roba [It.] A beautiful robe, i.e., a prostitute; a harlot.

bona verba [L.] Words of good omen.

bonbon [F.] A small and delicate chocolate candy, usually having a cream or nut filling.

bon diable [F.] A good devil, i.e., a friendly rogue; a jolly dog.

bon goût [F.] Good taste.

bon gré, mal gré [F.] Good will, bad will; willy-nilly; willingly or not willingly.

bonheur [F.] Happiness.

(le) bonheur des méchants comme un torrent s'écoule [F.] The happiness of the wicked like a torrent flows away.

bonhomie [F.] An amiable and easy-going disposition; also, a good natured person; a friendly and affable individual.

boni judicis est ampliare jurisdictionem [L.] Part of being a good judge is to enlarge one's jurisdiction, i.e., a good judge should tend toward leniency to avoid convicting innocent men.

boni pastorie esse tondere pecus, non deglubere [L.] A good shepherd shears his sheep, he does not skin them.

bonis avibus [L.] With good birds, i.e., with good auspices, since certain Roman soothsayers, known as *haruspex*, based their prophecies on the flight of birds or on the configurations of their entrails.

bonitas non est pessimis esse meliorem [L.] It is not goodness to be better than the very bad.

bon jour [F.] Good day; used as a greeting.

bon marché [F.] Cheap; at a bargain price; a good buy.

bon mot [F.] A witticism; a clever phrase; a nimble or keen-witted observation.

bonne bête [F.] A good fool; a good natured idiot; a simpleton.

bonne bouche [F.] A tidbit; the very last tasty bite.

bonne compagnie [F.] Good company, i.e., a fashionable assembly; a refined collection of people.

bonne d'enfants [F.] A nursemaid.

bonne foi [F.] Good faith.

bonne raison [F.] Good reason.

(les) bons comptes font les bons amis [F.] Good accounts make good friends.

bon soir [F.] Goodnight; used as a farewell.

(le) bon temps viendra [F.] The good times are coming.

bon ton [F.] Polite manner; drawing room deportment; behavior of a refined but superficial nature.

bonum magnum [L.] A great good.

bonum omen [L.] A good omen; a sign from the heavens that all will be to one's advantage.

bonum publicum [L.] The public good.

bon vivant [F.] One who is devoted to the pleasures of high living and the fulfillment of sensuous appetites; cf. *bon viveur.*

bon viveur [F.] One who enjoys life; cf. *bon vivant.*

bon voyage [F.] A good voyage; used as a farewell to those leaving on a journey.

bonyata [Bengali] Savagery; barbarism; cruelty.

bordello [It.] A house of prostitution.

Borgen macht Sorgen [G.] Borrowing makes for sorrowing.

borné [F.] Bounded; hence, narrow-minded; confined; lacking a realistic perspective.

borsch [Russ.] A Russian soup made with beets or cabbage.

borzoi [Russ.] A Russian wolfhound.

bouche [F.] The mouth; also, the lips or the tongue.

bouffe [F.] In music, a descriptive term meaning comic or humorous.

bouillabaisse [F.] A soup made of fish and mixed vegetables.

boulanger [F.] A baker.

boulevardier [F.] A boulevardier, i.e., one commonly seen promenading on the boulevards.

bouleversement [F.] Overturning; revolution; destruction and ruin.

bourgeois [F.] A member of the bourgeoisie (q.v.)

bourgeoisie [F.] (1.) The middle class; a tradesman or businessman. (2.) A class of people with a conventional or purely economic outlook on life.

bourrée [F.] A kind of gavotte; a *pas de bourée* (q.v.).

boutade [F.] A whim; a caprice; also, a witty remark; a bright saying.

boutique [F.] A small store; a modest shop selling interesting gifts or clothing.

boutonniere [F.] A flower, usually a carnation, placed in the buttonhole of a man's jacket.

bouts-rimes [F.] Rhyming ends; rhyming words to which are written lines of verse.

Brahman [Skr.] The priest caste in Indian Hindu culture, considered to be the most advanced human incarnation to which a man can aspire. From this is derived the word "Brahmin," meaning (often disdainfully) an individual of aristocratic or high-born standing, as in the phrase "Boston Brahmin."

braisière [F.] A pan for holding pieces of burning charcoal.

bratwurst [G.] A pork sausage popular in Germany.

Brauer [G.] A brewer.

Brauhaus [G.] A brewery.

brassard [F.] An arm-badge.

bravissimo [It.] Splendid; superb; wonderful; used as an exclamation of great approval.

bravo [It.] Well done; used as an exclamation of approval.

bravura [It.] (1.) Bravery; a tremendous display of courage. (2.) In music, a florid, difficult passage.

brevet [F.] A certificate; an official paper.

brevet d'invention [F.] A certificate of invention; a patent.

brevi complector singula cantu [L.] I tell of the unique in a short song.

brevis esse laboro, obscurus fio [L.] In the attempt to be succinct I become obscure.

brevis oratio penetrat caelum [L.] Short prayers penetrate heaven.

bric-à-brac [F.] Miscellaneous objects, sometimes valuable, sometimes not; old, unsorted items and knickknacks.

brindisi [It.] A drinking song.

britska [Pol.] A carriage with a large hood over the passenger's seat which can be removed or folded down for riding in the open air.

brochette [F.] A small spit used for cooking meat over a fire.

broda [Pol.] Beard.

Brücke [G.] Bridge.

Bruder [G.] Brother.

bruder [Yidd.] Brother.

(le) bruit des armes l'empeschoit d'entendre la voix des loix [F.] "The noise of arms deafens the voice of the laws": *Montaigne.*

bruia [Sp.] (1.) A witch. (2.) A witchdoctor or sorcerer.

brun [F.] The color brown.

brut [F.] Dry; used to describe wine.

brutum fulmen [L.] A thunderbolt without force; a display of power without anything to back it up; a bark that is worse than the bite.

buen abogado mal vecino [Sp.] A good lawyer makes a bad neighbor.

bueno, bueno, bueno, mas guarde Dios mi burra de su centeno [Sp.] Good, good, good, but God keep my mule out of his rye.

Bühne [G.] A theatrical stage.

Bund [G.] (1.) An organization; an association. (2.) A group of German-Americans sympathetic to the Nazi regime.

buona notte [It.] Goodnight; used as a farewell.

buona sera [It.] Good evening; used as a greeting.

Büro [G.] Office; place of business.

Bushido [Jap.] A code of ethical principles developed by the Samurai warriors during the Kamakura Period (twelfth century) in Japan. This code, influenced by Zen Buddhism and the Confucian doctrine of the "Superior Man," was characterized by fearlessness and unswerving allegiance to one's lord.

byuró [Russ.] Office; place where business is conducted.

C

caballero [Sp.] A aristocratic gentleman; a man of courage, dash, and good breeding; a knight.

cabaña [Sp.] A small cabin on the beach, often with one side open and facing the ocean.

cabaret [F.] A nightclub or restaurant where live entertainment is provided for the customers; also, a live performance (with singing, dancing and comic routines) given in such a nightclub.

cabildo [Sp.] (1.) a meeting house attached to a cathedral. (2.) A town hall.

cabinet d'aisances [F.] A toilet.

cabob [Hindi] A piece of meat cooked on a spit over an open fire.

cabriole [F.] (1.) In furniture design, a leg with a gentle outward bow, found on lowboys, buffets, chairs, etc., and popular in the Queen Anne and Chippendale style. (2.) In dance, a ballet leap in which one leg beats against the other leg, which has been raised in the air.

cachot [F.] A cell in an underground dungeon; a prison.

cacoëthes [L.] A bad habit; a compulsion; a disease, usually of the spirit.

cacoëthes loquendi [L.] The habit of talking; the disease of words; prolixity.

cacoëthes scribendi [L.] The habit of writing; an uncontrollable mania to write.

cada uno sabe adonde le aprieta el zapato [Sp.] Everyone knows best where the shoe pinches him.

cada uno tiene su alguacil [Sp.] Every man has his own policeman; every man has his master.

cadeau [F.] A gift; present.

cadit quaestio [L.] The inquiry collapses; the question is closed; the case is dropped.

caeca invidia est [L.] Envy is blind.

caelitus mihi vires [L.] My strength is from heaven.

caelum non animum mutant qui trans mare currunt [L.] Those who go across the sea change their sky, not their souls.

caetera desunt [L.] The remainder is wanting; the rest is missing.

cafard [F.] A hypocrite; a charlatan; a sanctimonious pretender; also, hypocritical; false.

cafardise [F.] Something hypocritical; a falsehood; something that distorts the truth.

café [F.] Coffee.

café [F.] A coffeehouse; a small restaurant.

café au lait [F.] (1.) Coffee with

milk. (2.) Colloquially, a tan skin color, as on a mulatto.

café noir [F.] Black coffee.

cahier [F.] (1.) A notebook or manuscript composed of many loose sheets of paper held together with a binder. (2.) A collection of notes and records kept at a meeting; a report.

cahotage [F.] Jolting; jerking motions.

calabozo [Sp.] (1.) A jail; a prison. (2.) A knife used to trim branches; a gardener's blade.

calando [It.] In music, a gradual slowing of tempo and decrease in volume.

calembour [F.] A play on words; a pun.

caliche [Sp.] A deposit of sodium nitrate which tends to accumulate on rocks in desert regions.

camarade [F.] A comrade; a close friend.

camarade de classe [F.] A classmate; fellow pupil.

camarade de lit [F.] A bed-fellow.

camarade de voyage [F.] A fellow traveler.

camaraderie [F.] Comradeship; the good will and exchange of warm feelings that takes place between close friends.

camarilla [Sp.] A small group of unofficial but active political advisers; a cabal.

camera obscura [L.] A dark chamber; hence, by extension, any light-tight chamber, such as a photographic camera.

camino [Sp.] A road.

camisade [F.] In the military, a night attack.

camisole [F.] A woman's nightshirt or robe.

camorra [Sp.] A fight; a quarrel.

campagna [It.] Country; place.

campanajo [It.) A bell ringer; one who tolls the bell in a church.

campanile [It.] A belfry of a steeple.

campo [It.] In Italian towns, an open area in or near a village; a village square.

campo santo [It.] A holy field, i.e., a cemetery.

Campus Martius [L.] The Field of Mars; in ancient Rome, a place of assembly for civic and military affairs.

canaille [F.] The herd of common people; the lower classes; the dregs of society; from the Italian *canaglia* meaning "pack of dogs."

canapé [F.] A light delicacy such as crabmeat on toast, cream cheese on crackers, or anchovies on strips of bread, served before the main meal.

canard [F.] A hoax; a false story invented to deceive the public.

canard rôti [F.] Roast duck.

candelabrum [L.] A large candlestick, often of silver or brass, equipped with a sturdy base and a number of arms.

candide et caute [L.] With candor and caution.

canis in praesepi [L.] A dog in the manger.

cannabis sativa [L.] The hemp plant; marijuana.

canorae nugae [L.] Sweet-sounding trifles.

cantata [It.] In music, a composition to be performed by a large choral ensemble with elaborate instrumental accompaniment, including many solo, duet, and recitative sections.

cantatrice [F.] A female singer.

cantina [Sp.] A canteen; a tavern; an eating place.

canto funebre [It.] A funeral hymn.

cantus firmus [L.] A vocal motif,

part of the Gregorian musical tradition, found in medieval church music.

canzone [It.] A song; a lyric poem.

capistrum maritale [L.] The matrimonial halter; the binding ties of marriage.

capo d'anno [It.] New Year's Day.

cappita [It.] Great; wonderful; magnificent; used as an exclamation.

caput [L.] The human head.

caput mortuum [L.] A dead head, i.e., residue, especially the worthless leftovers from a chemical experiment.

caquet [F.] Cackle of geese; thus, chatter; empty gossip.

carabinier [F.] A mounted soldier armed with a rifle.

caracará [Sp.] A large carrion-eating hawk, native to Central and South America.

carafe [F.] A bottle-shaped glass container, used to hold water or to serve wine.

carambole [F.] In billiards, the red ball.

cara sposa [It.] Dear wife.

caravanserai [Per.] An overnight resting place for travelers and caravans in the middle east.

caravelle [F.] A small, sleek sailing ship.

carmina morte carent [L.] Songs are exempt from death.

carne [Sp.] Meat.

carottes glacées [F.] Glazed carrots.

carpere et colligere [L.] To pluck and gather.

carrefour [F.] A crossroads; the spot where four roads converge.

carte blanche [F.] A white paper, i.e., a blank sheet of paper bearing only an official signature, giving the recipient power to fill in the blank section; thus, full and unrestrained freedom; unlimited power and authority.

carte de visite [F.] Visiting card; calling card.

carte du pays [F.] A map of a country.

carte postale [F.] A postcard.

cartes sur table [F.] Cards on the table, i.e., nothing hidden.

cartouche [F.] (1.) A decorative scroll design, either drawn or carved, often containing an open space for inscription. (2.) A box for storing pyrotechnical equipment.

casaque tourner [F.] To turn one's coat, i.e., to be a turncoat; to desert one party for another; to be a traitor.

casarás y amansarás [Sp.] Marry and be tamed.

casus belli [L.] The occasion of the war, i.e., the series of events that caused a war.

casus conscientiae [L.] A case of conscience.

casus magister alius [L.] Chance is a second master.

casus major [L.] A major incident; an occurrence of great importance such as the death of a king or a vast natural disaster.

catalogue raisonné [F.] A descriptive catalogue.

causa causans [L.] The cause of causes, i.e., the Prime Mover; the Absolute.

causa causata [L.] The cause of the cause, i.e., the effect.

causa essendi [L.] The cause of being.

causa latet, vis est notissima [L.] The cause is hidden, the effect quite apparent.

causa mali [L.] The cause of the trouble; the heart of the difficulty.

causa sine qua non [L.] A cause

without which not, i.e., a cause which is imperative and indispensable; a necessary condition.

causa vera [L.] The true cause.

cause célèbre [F.] A well-publicized case, usually a popular scandal; a controversial subject or situation which arouses great excitement among the public.

causerie [F.] (1.) An informal conversation; a chat. (2.) A brisk and informal essay such as an article in a popular magazine or literary journal.

cavalero [Sp.] A dashing soldier; a cavalier (q.v.).

cavalier servente [It.] A gentleman platonically or romantically attached to a married woman; cf. *cicisbeo.*

cave [L.] Beware.

caveat actor [L.] Let the doer (i.e., the man of action) beware.

caveat emptor [L.] Let the buyer beware; used as a warning for the buyers that the seller is not responsible after the sale.

caveat viator [L.] Let the traveler beware.

cave canem [L.] Beware of the dog.

cave ignoscas [L.] Beware of forgiving.

cavendo tutus [L.] Safe through taking care.

cave ne cadas [L.] Beware lest you fall.

cave quid dicis, quando, et cui [L.] Beware what you say, when, and to whom.

cavetto [It.] An ornamental concave molding.

céad míle fáilte [Gael.] A hundred thousand welcomes; used as a common greeting in Ireland.

cedant arma togae [L.] Let arms yield to the toga, i.e., let the military establishment be subordinate to the civil community; used as the motto of the State of Wyoming.

cela ne fait ni chaud ni froid [F.] That is neither hot nor cold; that is neither here nor there.

cela ne me fait rien [F.] That makes no difference to me; that is of no account.

cela se laisse manger [F.] A thing fit to eat.

cela va sans dire [F.] That goes without saying; that is understood.

céleri [F.] Celery.

celui qui veut celui la peut [F.] The one who wishes is the one who is able; he who has the will has the skill.

Cena Domini [L.] The Lord's Supper.

c'en est fait [F.] It is finished.

ce n'est que le premier pas que coûte [F.] It is only the first step that costs.

censor morum [L.] Censor of morals.

cent [F.] One hundred.

central [Sp.] In Spanish American countries, a large sugar factory which provides employment for many surrounding districts.

cerealia [L.] The cereals.

certeris paribus [L.] Other things being equal.

certosina [It.] A method of decoration where small pieces of bone or ivory are inlaid into wood, forming symmetrical designs.

certum quia impossibile [L.] It is certain because it is impossible.

certum scio [L.] I know for certain.

certum voto pete finem [L.] Set a limit to your desire.

cessante causa, cessat effectus [L.]

The cause ceasing, the effect ceases.

c'est-à-dire [F.] That is to say.

c'est autre chose [F.] That's another thing; that's something different.

c'est double plaisir de tromper le trompeur [F.] It is double pleasure to deceive the deceiver.

c'est la guerre [F.] That's war; that's what war is like.

c'est la vie [F.] That's life, that's the way it goes.

c'est magnifique [F.] It is magnificent.

c'est magnifique mais ce n'est pas la guerre [F.] It's magnificent but it isn't war; phrase said by General Bosquet while watching the remarkably courageous but tactically absurd charge of the Light Brigade at Balaklava.

c'est plus qu'un crime, c'est une faute [F.] It's worse than a crime, it's a mistake; saying attributed to Tallyrand in speaking of Napoleon's execution of the Duc d'Enghien.

c'est selon [F.] That's according; that depends.

c'est toujours la même chanson [F.] It's always the same song, i.e., it's always the same old thing.

cestui que trust [L.] One to whom is made a trust; the beneficiary of a trust fund.

c'est une economie de bouts de chandelle [F.] That is a candle-end economy, i.e., that's pennywise and pound foolish.

c'est un faible roseau que la prosperité [F.] Prosperity is a feeble reed.

chabouk [Hindi] A rawhide whip used to punish offenders in the East.

chacun à son goût [F.] Each to his own taste.

chahar bagh [Pers.] In Persia, the four-fold design of a garden.

chaise longue [F.] A long comfortable couch.

chakra [Hindi] (1.) A wheel; a turning circle. (2.) In Hindu philosophy, one of the seven vital centers of the body located in the brain, above the eyes, in the throat, chest, stomach, base of the spine, and genital organs.

chalet [F.] A two-storied house with a projecting roof and decoratively modeled roof struts and windows, native to the alpine regions of Europe.

chamade [F.] In the military, a signal for a parley sounded on the drums or by bugle.

champignon [F.] A mushroom.

champlevé [F.] A method of enameling in which pulverized enamel is placed into raised cells on a decorative object, such as a vase, fused, smoothed with a pumice stone, and polished.

chanson [F.] A song; ballad.

chanson de geste [F.] An old French historic epic, originally written in 12-syllabled verse, telling the exploits of various heroes and saints.

chanson de route [F.] A marching song.

chansonnette [F.] A little song; a short ballad.

chansons que tout cela [F.] All songs, those, i.e., all idle stories; all just chitchat.

chant du cygne [F.] The swan song; the song allegedly sung by a swan the moment before it expires; hence, the last work of an artist before he dies.

chantefable [F.] A song story; a medieval epic or fable in which the major part of the narrative is in prose and the more delicate sections in verse.

chanter [F.] To sing.

chanteuse [F.] A female singer.

chant funèbre [F.] A funeral song; a dirge.

chaparajos [Sp.] Leather pants fitted to the front of the legs and worn in the Southwest and Mexico as protection against the prickly shrubs of the plains.

chapeau [F.] A hat.

chapeau à plumes [F.] A plumed hat; a hat with a feather.

chaqueta [Sp.] A heavy leather jacket worn by cowboys.

charas [Hindi] A narcotic drug made of the hashish resin, ox blood, and human fat.

char de triomphe [F.] The triumphal chariot.

chargé d'affaires [F.] (1.) A government official temporarily placed in a high diplomatic post. (2.) A low-ranking diplomat.

chargé de cours [F.] A substitute lecturer; an assistant to the professor.

charivari [F.] A burlesque serenade consisting of cacophonous noises made on the brass and percussion instruments; hence, clatter; noise; a mock serenade.

charka [Russ.] A small cup with a large handle, used for holding liquor.

charmante [F.] A thoroughly charming and fascinating woman.

chasser [F.] To hunt; chase; pursue.

chasseur [F.] (1.) A hunter; a sportsman. (2.) An infantry man; a foot soldier.

chat [F.] A cat.

château [F.] In France, a large castle usually built of stone and sur-rounded by a vast estate; also, a large private home; a showplace.

château en Espagne [F.] A castle in Spain, i.e., a fantasy, a dream, an illusion.

chattri [Skr.] In Indian architecture, a pointed umbrella-shaped dome or cupola.

chaud [F.] Warm; hot.

chauffeuse [F.] A female who drives a motor car; a woman chauffeur.

chaussure [F.] Footware; anything that is worn on the feet such as slippers, sneakers, boots, etc.

che cosa hai? [It.] What's wrong with you?

chef de cuisine [F.] The master chef; the head cook of a large commercial kitchen.

chef d'oeuvre [F.] A masterpiece; a great creation in any field, such as art, cooking, architecture, etc.

che'l perder tempo a chi più sa più spiace [It.] "Loss of time most grieveth him who knowest most": *Dante.*

chemin de fer [F.] (1.) A railroad. (2.) A card game.

chercher une aiguille dans une botte de foin [F.] To look for a needle in a haystack.

cherchez la femme [F.] Look for the woman; i.e., behind any trouble one will find a woman.

chéri [F.] Darling; dearest; beloved.

che sarà sarà [It.] What will be, will be.

cheval [F.] A horse; stallion.

cheval à bascule [F.] A rocking horse.

cheval de course [F.] A racehorse.

cheval-de-frise [F.] A protective device used to mark boundaries in warfare consisting of long horizontal cylinders covered with crisscrossed spikes and barbed wire.

chevalier [F.] A knight; a gentleman; a gallant.

Chevalier de la Legion d'Honneur [F.] A Knight of the Legion of Honor.

(le) Chevalier de la Triste Figure [F.] The Knight of the Sad Countenance; in literature, a title for Don Quixote.

chevalier d'industrie [F.] One who lives by his cunning and shrewdness; an opportunist.

chevelure [F.] A thick head of hair.

chez [F.] At the house, place, or establishment of. (*He resided* chez *Jean.*)

chia [Chi.] In China, an ancient bronze ritual cup used for drinking and sacrifice.

chi ama, crede [It.] He who loves, trusts.

chiaroscuro [It.] (1.) Any strong contrast of dark and light. (2.) A style of painting introduced by the Italian painter Caravaggio in which emphasis is given to strong contrasts of dark and light, intense shadows and deeply modeled contours are used at every opportunity, and color is at times reduced to an almost monochromatic scale.

chi dici i fatti suoi, mal tacerà quelli d'altrui [It.] He who talks about his own affairs will scarcely keep silent about the affairs of others.

chignon [F.] A tight knot of hair pulled behind or piled on top of the head.

chi non esce dal suo paese, vive pieno di pregiudizi [It.] The one who never leaves his country is filled with prejudices.

chi non fa, non falla [It.] The man who does nothing makes no mistakes.

chi non s'arrischia non guadagna [It.] Nothing ventured, nothing gained.

chintamani [Skr.] In Lamaism, the jewel that satisfies all desires.

chi tace acconsente [It.] Silence gives consent.

chi t'ha offeso, non ti perdona mai [It.] He who has wronged you never forgives you.

chose jugée [F.] A thing judged, i.e., something already decided upon; a closed case.

chose qui plaît est à demi vendue [F.] A thing which pleases is half sold.

(les) choses valent toujours mieux dans leur source [F.] "The stream is always purest at its source": *Pascal.*

chou [F.] Cabbage.

Christenheit [G.] Christendom.

Christi crux est mea lux [L.] Christ's cross is my light.

chronique scandaleuse [F.] A scandalous chronicle; a report that makes a point of emphasizing sordid or sensational details.

chutzpa [Yidd.] Gall; impudence; a fearless and pushy insistence on having one's way.

ciao [It.] A greeting or word of farewell.

cicatrix manet [L.] The scar remains, i.e., pain leaves its mark.

cicerone [It.] A guide; one who leads a tour.

cicisbeo [It.] The knightly attendant or clandestine lover of a married lady.

ci-devant [F.] Former; formerly.

ci-gît [F.] Here lies; the first words of an epitaph.

cimarrón [Sp.] Wild; savage; untamed.

cinéma [F.] Film; cinema; motion pictures.

cinq [F.] The number five.

cinquecento [It.] In Italy, the sixteenth century; also, in art, the painting, sculpture, and literature practiced in Italy during this period.

cinquefoil [F.] (1.) A design copied after the pattern of the cinquefoil flower. (2.) A design having five symmetrical parts.

circa [L.] About; around; used with dates to show an approximate period of time. (*The clock dates circa 1850.*)

citoyen [F.] Citizen.

civilitas successit barbarum [L.] Civilization succeeds barbarism; used as the motto of the State of Minnesota.

civitas magna, magna solitudo [L.] A great city, a great solitude.

clair-obscur [F.] Light and shade.

clarum et venerabile nomen [L.] Illustrious and venerable name.

(la) classe ouvrière [F.] The working class; the laboring class.

clausis januis [L.] With closed doors.

clinique [F.] A clinic, especially one connected to a hospital.

cloacina [L.] The purifier; the cleanser; a surname of Venus.

cloisonné [F.] A technique of applying enamel in which bands of metal are shaped into patterns and soldered onto the surface of an object, such as a vase; enamel is then placed in these areas, fused, smoothed, and polished.

clou [F.] A nail; a spike.

cocotte [F.] A tart; a cheap tease; a young girl whose morals are but a few degrees less wanton than those of a prostitute.

código [Sp.] A code of law; a set of rules.

coeur [F.] The heart.

(le) coeur a ses raisons que la raison connaît pas [F.] The heart has its reasons, which reason does not know.

cogito ergo sum [L.] I think, therefore I am; a famous philosophical maxim from Descartes' *Discourse on Method.*

cognitionis via [L.] The way or path to enlightenment.

cognosca occasionem [L.] Know the opportunity.

cognoscente [It.] An individual capable of making authoritative judgments on a particular subject; a connoisseur (q.v.).

cohue [F.] A wild crowd; a pushing, excited mob; a throng of angry people.

coiffeur [F.] A hair style; a way of wearing one's hair; also, a hairdresser.

col [F.] The human neck.

collectanea [L.] A compendium of passages and excerpts collected from many different authors.

col rabuttu [F.] A turned-down collar.

col raide [F.] A stiff collar.

comandante [Sp.] A commander; a commandant.

camarista [Sp.] A maid of honor.

cambio non è furto [It.] An exchange is not robbery.

combien [F.] How much? How many?

comedia [Sp.] A comedy; a farce.

comédie de moeurs [F.] A comedy of manners or morals; a play lampooning social mores.

comelón [Sp.] A big eater; a gourmand.

come va? [It.] How's it going?; how are you?

comme ci, comme ça [F.] Not bad; passable; so-so; *là, là* (q.v.).

comme deux gouttes d'eau [F.] Like two drops of water; like two peas in a pod.

commedia al'improviso [It.] The comedy of improvisation, so named because the actors improvised through each performance; another title for the *commedia dell'arte* (q.v.).

commedia dell'arte [It.] Comedy of craft; a type of improvised comedy played by traveling professional actors which originated in Italy during the Renaissance, and in many forms, including the English Punch and Judy, lasted in Europe up to the nineteenth century.

commedia erudita [It.] The academic theatre; a form of intellectual comedy, meant for royalty and the aristocracy, which originated in Europe in the fifteenth century as a break from the traditional religious theatre.

comme il faut [F.] As it should be.

commencement de la fin [F.] The beginning of the end.

comment allez-vous? [F.] How are you?

commis-voyageur [F.] A commercial traveler; a traveling salesman.

commune periculum concordiam parit [L.] Common danger produces accord.

communibus annis [L.] Common years; in a yearly average.

como lo pasa? [Sp.] How do you do?

cómo no [Sp.] But of course; naturally.

compos mentis [L.] Of sound mind; sane. (*The psychologists found him to be* compos mentis.) Cf. *non compos mentis.*

compte rendu [F.] (1.) In economics, an account rendered. (2.) In law, a record of a legal procedure; also, a record of any transaction in general.

con affectto [It.] With affection.

con amore [It.] (1.) With love; with genuine involvement and enthusiasm. (2.) In music, a direction to play a passage tenderly.

con anima [It.] (1.) With soul; with deeply felt spirit. (2.) In music, a direction calling for a serious and soulful rendering.

con brio [It.] In music, a direction to play a passage with zest and spirit.

con calore [It.] In music, a direction to play a passage with warmth and ardor.

concha [L.] Shell-shaped; any object shaped like a shell, such as the human ear.

concierge [F.] A doorman; a janitor; one who guards the entrance to a building.

conciliatrix [L.] A match-maker; a "madame" at a house of prostitution; a procuress.

concordia discors [L.] Inharmonious harmony, i.e., a quiet situation with overtones of discord; a tense friendship or alliance.

concordia res parvae crescunt [L.] Through concord small things grow great.

condition de l'homme, inconstance, ennui, inquietude [F.] The condition of man is changeableness, boredom, anxiety.

condottiere [It.] (1.) The leader of a band of mercenary soldiers. (2.) The mercenary soldiers themselves, who from the thirteenth to the fifteenth century in Italy were famous for their ferocity, licentious behavior, and loyalty to the highest bidder.

confer [L.] To compare.

confrère [F.] A fellow member of an organization, society, brotherhood, or profession; a close associate.

con fuoco [It.] In music, a direction to play a passage with fire, with great excitement, and animation.

congé [F.] An official note or formal permission to take leave of a location.

con grazia [It.] In music, a direction to play a passage with grace.

conjunctis viribus [L.] With united powers.

connaître les dessous des cartes [F.] To know the bottom card.

connoisseur [F.] An expert in a specific field; one whose tastes and knowledge in a particular subject qualify him to make definitive judgments in that subject.

con prestezza [It.] In music, a direction to the performer to play a passage with a quickness.

conquistador [Sp.] A conqueror, especially the Spaniards who conquered the New World; a great leader.

conscientia sana, muras aereus [L.] A sound conscience, a wall of brass.

consensus facit auxilia humilia firma [L.] Concord makes feeble assistance strong.

con sensus omnium [L.] The agreement of everyone; universal accord.

consilio melius vincas quam iracundia [L.] You conquer better by prudence than by passion.

consommé [F.] A clear broth made from chicken or beef.

consuetudo quasi altera natura [L.] Habit is almost a second nature.

consummatum est [L.] It is consummated.

contadina [It.] A peasant girl.

contra bonos mores [L.] Against good morals.

contra pacem [L.] Against the peace.

contre-coup [F.] The return blow, i.e., a repercussion; reaction; reverberation.

contredanse [F.] A country dance.

contretemps [F.] Against the times; thus, an unpleasant or embarrassing incident which causes a change in plans or policy.

convenance [F.] (1.) Conventional usage. (2.) Convenience; expediency.

conversazione [It.] A group of literate persons gathered to exchange opinions on the arts and sciences.

coolie [Hindi] In the East, a laborer who works long hours at menial tasks for extremely low wages; a bearer; a runner or temporary servant.

copia verborum [L.] Copious talk; many words.

coq [F.] A rooster; a cock.

coq au vin [F.] Chicken cooked in a wine sauce and usually garnished with onions and mushrooms.

coq de bruyère [F.] A grouse.

coq de combat [F.] A gamecock;

a rooster groomed to fight other roosters.

coquette [F.] A woman well-versed in the arts and ploys of flirtation; a tease.

coram [L.] Before; in front of.

coram domino rege [L.] Before the lord sovereign.

coram judice [L.] Before a judge.

coram populo [L.] In public; publically.

corbeau [F.] A crow; a raven.

corbeille [F.] A small basket.

corbie [Sc.] A crow or raven.

cordon bleu [F.] (1.) A blue ribbon; a medal or decoration. (2.) A cook of great expertise in all areas of cuisine.

corimagistro [It.] The director of a choir; a choirmaster.

cornet-à-pistons [F.] A horn similar to the French horn.

corps céleste [F.] A heavenly body.

corps de ballet [F.] The ensemble dancers of a ballet company or ballet.

corps de bâtiment [F.] The main part of a building.

corps d'élite [F.] An elite corps; a group of highly-qualified men hand-picked to perform a certain job.

corps de reserve [F.] In the military, reserve troops; reinforcements.

corps diplomatique [F.] The diplomatic corps.

corps expéditionnaire [F.] An expeditionary force.

corps glorieux [F.] A glorified body.

corps mort [F.] A dead body.

Corpus Christi [L.] (1.) In Christianity, the Body of Christ. (2.) A church festival, instituted by Pope Urban IV in 1264 to honor the miracle of blood appearing on the Host in the Italian town of Bolsena. The festival was observed on the Thursday after Trinity Thursday and was marked by a grand procession, which at one time was joined by kings and lords, after which a series of miracle plays and mysteries were performed by members of the pageant.

corpus delicti [L.] The body of the crime, i.e., the facts proving that a crime has been committed, such as the discovery of a dead body in a case of murder. It does not, however, pertain specifically to a corpse but may be any evidence that a crime has taken place.

corpus juris [L.] The body of law, i.e., the laws and statutes adhered to by a town or nation.

Corpus Juris Canonici [L.] The body of canon law.

corregidor [Sp.] A magistrate common to most towns in Spain.

correio [Port.] Mail.

corrida [Sp.] A bullfight.

corruptissima republica plurimae leges [L.] When the state is most corrupt, the laws are most numerous.

corso [Sp.] A race field for horses.

cortège [F.] A long line of servants and followers; a retinue; a parade or caravan.

cortesias engendran cortesias [Sp.] Politeness begets politeness.

corvée [F.] (1.) A feudal agreement between a lord and his vassal, binding the vassal to a fixed number of days of unpaid labor for the lord. (2.) Enforced labor; labor without pay.

cosa ben fatta è fatta due volte [It.] A thing well done is twice done.

costumé [F.] All dressed up; formally attired.

côte [F.] A sea-coast; a shore.

côtelette [F.] A cutlet; chop.

côtellette de porc [F.] Pork chop.

côtelette de veau [F.] Veal cutlet.

côtes de veau [F.] Veal chops.

couloir [F.] A steep gorge found in the upper alpine regions of Europe.

coup [F.] A blow; a stroke; a fast and effective action.

coup de grâce [F.] A compassionate stroke to relieve the sufferings of death agony; thus, the final blow; the last and most decisive act.

coup de hasard [F.] A lucky chance.

coup de main [F.] A blow of the hand; thus, an unexpected attack; a sudden and surprising change of tactics.

coup de maître [F.] A master stroke.

coup de malheur [F.] A stroke of bad luck.

coup de plume [F.] A stroke of the pen, i.e., a scathing literary attack; a pointed satire.

coup de soleil [F.] A blow of the sun, i.e., sunstroke.

coup d'essai [F.] An attempt; a try; an experiment.

coup d'état [F.] A surprise maneuver designed to overthrow the existing political state.

coup de théatre [F.] A theatrical stroke; a prearranged trick designed to produce a dramatic effect; a stunt.

coup de vent [F.] A strong wind; a gale.

coup d'oeil [F.] A glance of the eye; a fast look; a quick glimpse.

coupé [F.] (1.) A four-wheeled carriage drawn by horses, with a cab for seating two people and an external platform for the driver. (2.) A two-door, as opposed to a four-door, automobile.

cour de derrière [F.] The backyard.

cour d'honneur [F.] The court of honor; the forecourt of a palace or castle.

courreur de bois [F.] A French trapper in North America, especially in French Canada.

couteau [F.] A dagger; a hunting knife.

coûte que coûte [F.] Cost what it costs; cost what it may; no matter the cost.

(le) coût fait perdre le goût [F.] The cost makes one lose the taste.

couturière [F.] A dress designer; a dressmaker.

cravat [F.] A scarf; an ascot; a man's necktie.

credenza [It.] A buffet or table copied after an Italian Renaissance credence.

crede quod habes, et habes [L.] Believe that you have, and you have.

crede ut intelligas [L.] Believe so that you may understand.

credo quia impossible [L.] I believe that which is impossible.

crème [F.] Cream.

crème de la crème [F.] The cream of the cream; the cream of the crop; the best of a good lot.

crescens aetas [L.] Increasing age.

crescite et multiplicamini [L.] Increase and multiply; used as the motto of the State of Maryland.

crescit eundo [L.] It grows as it goes; used as the motto of the State of New Mexico.

crier famine sur un tas de blé [F.]

To cry famine over a pile of grain.

critique est aisée, et l'art est difficile [F.] Criticism is easy and art is difficult.

(la) Croix de Guerre [F.] The Cross of War, a medal awarded for military heroism in France.

crouton [F.] A piece of dried toast or bread, used to garnish a salad or a soup.

crux ansata [L.] An ancient T-shaped cross symbolizing the divine spirit.

crux criticorum [L.] The puzzle of the critics; an enigma.

cual el cuervo [Sp.] As the crow, so the egg; like father, like son.

cui bono? [L.] To whose advantage?; who makes the profit?

cujus vulturis hoc erit cadaver? [L.] To what vulture will this carcass fall?

culbute [F.] A somersault.

cul-de-jatte [F.] One whose legs have been amputated; a paraplegic.

cul-de-sac [F.] A blind alley; a road, plan, or passage that leads only to an impasse with no means of escape.

culpam poena premit comes [L.] Punishment presses close upon crime; crime does not pay.

cum feriunt unum, non unum fulmina terrent [L.] Though the thunderbolt strikes only one, it is not only one that it alarms.

cum grano salis [L.] With a grain of salt.

cum laude [L.] With praise; used to designate an honor awarded for distinctive scholastic achievement.

cum multis aliis [L.] With many other things.

cunctando restituit rem [L.] By delaying he retarded the affair.

curae leves loquuntur, ingentes stupent [L.] Small problems talk much, great ones remain silent.

cur ante tubam tremor occupat artus? [L.] Why should fear seize the limbs before the war trumpet is played?; do not fear things until they come to pass.

curiosa felicitas [L.] Felicity of expression; used to describe a particular precise and mannered style of Roman literature.

currente calamo [L.] With a running pen; thus, glibly written; dashed off; carelessly penned.

curriculum vitae [L.] A biographical resumé (q.v.) that is presented to a potential employer.

custos [L.] A keeper; custodian.

custos morum [L.] A guardian of morals; a controller of public morality; a censor.

D

dabit qui dedit [L.] He who gave will give again.

d'accord [F.] In accord; agreed upon; allowed.

da capo [It.] In music, a direction to return to the beginning of a piece and play it again.

Dada [F.] A school of artists active in the first part of the twentieth century which used disjointed and accidental effects in its work.

da dextram misero [L.] Give the right hand to the miserable, i.e., give help to those who need it.

daimio [Jap.] In feudal Japan, a lord who owned vast sections of land.

dal [Hindi] In India, a lentil bean served with or on top of cooked rice.

da locum melioribus [L.] Give place to your superiors; honor those higher than yourself.

dame de compagnie [F.] A woman employed to serve as a companion.

dames de la halle [F.] Ladies of the marketplace; female shopkeepers.

Dämmerschlaf [G.] Twilight sleep.

damnant quod non intelligunt [L.] They damn what they do not understand.

damné [F.] Damned; condemned.

damnosa hereditas [L.] A harmful inheritance; a legacy which does more harm than benefit.

damoiselle [F.] A young lady of good manners and fine breeding.

danke [G.] Thank you.

danke schön [G.] Thank you very much.

danse macabre [F.] Dance of death; a medieval didactic theme, popular in literature and art, in which death, represented by a skeleton, is seen taking part in events of everyday life, reminding the viewer of the inevitability of his death.

danseur [F.] A male ballet dancer.

danseur noble [F.] The male ballet dancer who partners the ballerina in a pas de deux (q.v.) or plays a princely role.

danseuse [F.] A female dancer; a ballerina.

dare fatis vela [L.] Give the sails to fate, i.e., let fate decide the circumstances; let matters progress as they will.

das ist [G.] That is.

data et accepta [L.] Expenditures and receipts; expenses and profits in an economic venture.

Daten [G.] Actual facts; data.

date obolum Belisario [L.] Give a penny to Belisarius; once a powerful commander of Byzantium who fell into ruin, went blind, and was reduced to beggarhood, thus becoming a symbol of those who have fallen from the heights of fame.

Davus sum, non Oedipus [L.] I am Davus, i.e., a simple man, not Oedipus.

dea certe [L.] A goddess, assuredly; often said ironically.

de auditu [L.] By hearing; by word of mouth.

de bon augure [L.] Of good augury; auspicious for any undertaking; hopeful.

de bonis asportatis [L.] In law, of goods or property that has been taken away.

de bonis propriis [L.] From his own property, i.e., from his own resources; out of his own pocket.

de bonne grâce [F.] Of or with good grace; gladly; without hesitation or resentment.

Décembre [F.] The month of December.

deceptio visus [L.] An optical illusion.

decies repetita placebit [L.] Though ten times repeated it will still please.

decimo [It.] A tenth; a tenth part of something.

decipimur specie recti [L.] We are led astray by the semblance of what is right; the road to hell is paved with good intentions.

decipit frons prima multos [L.] The first appearance fools many people.

Decke [G.] A heavy quilted blanket stuffed with down.

déclassé [F.] Declassed; hence, ostracized from polite society; struck from the social records; no longer recognized in certain social circles.

décolletage [F.] That part of a low-cut gown or dress that exposes the shoulders and sometimes part of the breasts; also, the low-cut dress itself.

décolleté [F.] Exposing the upper shoulders and sometimes part of the breasts.

décoré [F.] Decorated; knighted; honored with an award or title; wearing the medallion of some legion or order.

décousu [F.] Unsewn; unstitched; rambling; usually said of a desultory literary style.

decrescendo [It.] In music, a direction to decrease the volume.

décret [F.] (1.) Decree; order; proclamation. (2.) In law, a writ or warrant.

decretum [L.] A decree; an authoritative order; an official command.

dedans [F.] The area of a tennis court reserved for the spectators; also, the spectators themselves.

de die in diem [L.] From day to day.

de dolo malo [L.] Of evil intent; with intent of fraud; from dishonesty.

de facto [L.] From the fact; actually; in actuality.

défense de fumer [F.] Do not smoke.

défense d'entrer [F.] Do not enter.

deficit omne quod nascitur [L.] Everything comes to an end which has a beginning.

de fide [L.] Of the faith; of a revealed church doctrine.

de fiéndame Dios de mi [Sp.] May God defend me from myself.

definitum [L.] That whch is being defined; the object of a definition.

de fond en comble [F.] From the ground to the roof; thus, from bottom to top; from head to toes.

dégagé [F.] At liberty; unconstrained; unencumbered with responsibility; free and easy, sometimes to the point of being flip.

de gustibus non est disputandum [L.] Of tastes there is no disputing; each his own.

de haut en bas [F.] From bottom to top; from head to toe. (*She stared at him* de haut en bas.)

deificatio [L.] Deification; union with God.

Dei gratia [L.] By the grace of God.

Dei memor, gratus amicis [L.] Mindful of God, grateful to friends.

de integro [L.] Over again; anew; from the start.

dei plena sunt omnia [L.] Filled with divinity are all things.

déjà vu [F.] Already seen; hence, an inexplicable sensation that what is now happening has happened before.

déjeuner [F.] Breakfast.

de jure [L.] By proper right of law; by authority of the existing legal system.

délabrement [F.] Collapse; a state of dilapidation and decay.

dele [L.] Erase; delete; used as a direction to printers.

delenda est Carthago [L.] Carthage must be destroyed; the oft-repeated demand made by Cato the Elder before the Roman senate.

délicat [F.] Delicate; dainty; fragile; pleasing the senses; exquisite.

délice [F.] Delight; happiness.

deliciae humani generis [L.] The delight of humanity; a title of the Roman Emperor Titus.

délicieux [F.] Delicious; wonderful; delightful.

delineavit [L.] He has drawn or painted it; used after a signature or attribution.

delirant reges plectuntur achivi [L.] The kings rage and the Greeks suffer, i.e., the people must pay for the folly of their leaders.

delirium tremens [L.] A trembling delirium; a state of frenzy characterized by violent shaking and bizarre hallucinations brought on by excessive use of alcohol.

de lunatico inquirendo [L.] In law, a writ to allow research into the life of an individual to determine his sanity.

de mal en pis [F.] From bad to worse.

de mal grado [Sp.] Unwillingly.

démarche [F.] An attempt; a definite step; a mode of procedure, usually political, which causes a shift in course or a change of program.

de mauvaise goût [F.] Of or in bad taste.

demi-jour [F.] Half-day; thus, twilight.

demi-lune [F.] The half-moon.

demimondaine [F.] A prostitute; a woman of the streets; a woman from the demimonde (q.v.).

demimonde [F.] The half-world; thus, the world of the streets; the riffraff; also, the type of woman who frequents such an area; a woman of low morals; a harlot.

demi-savant [F.] A half-scholar; thus, a superficial scholastic; a pseudointellectual.

démodé [F.] Old-fashioned; out of vogue; no longer in style.

de mortuis nil nisi bonum [L.] Of the dead nothing but good should be spoken.

denaro [It.] Money; cash.

de nihilo nihil fit [L.] From nothing, nothing is made.

dénouement [F.] An uncovering; the final revelation of a fact that clarifies the plot of a story. (*The dénouement of Poe's story comes when we learn that the murderer was not a man but an orangutan.*)

de novo [L.] From the beginning; anew.

de nuit [F.] By night; at night; taking place during the evening.

Deo date [L.] Give unto God.

Deo favente [L.] With the favor of God; with God approving of the enterprise.

Deo gratias [L.] Thanks to God.

Deo, non fortuna [L.] From God, not from chance.

Deo, Optimo, Maximo [L.] God, the Best, the Greatest; used as the motto of the order of Benedictines.

deorum cibus est [L.] It is food for the gods.

deos placatos pietas efficiet et sanititas [L.] Piety and holiness will propitiate the gods.

Deo volente [L.] God willing; an expression used after a statement of intent.

dépêche [F.] A dispatch; an important official message; a letter or telegram.

deperdit numerus [L.] There is ruin in numbers.

déporté [F.] A deportee; one deported from a country.

de profundis [L.] From the depths; thus, a heartfelt cry of pain from the depths of the soul.

de proprio motu [L.] Of its own movement; hence, of its own accord; by its own momentum; spontaneously.

de règle [F.] Of the rule; hence, after the proper rules; done with correct form and protocol.

de retour [F.] Back again; returned; on the way home.

de rigueur [F.] Of strictness; hence, according to a set of rules and manners strictly required by etiquette.

dernier cri [F.] The latest cry; the latest fashion; the popular mode of the day. (*Bernoldi's pocket bags were judged by public response to be the* dernier cri *in handware for 1971.*)

dernier ressort [F.] The last resort; the final opportunity; the last chance.

dertro tempore [L.] A lucky moment.

dervish [Ar.] A wandering Moslem mendicant connected with the order of the Sufi, an esoteric branch of Islam.

déshabillé [F.] Undressed; scantily clothed; also, dressed poorly or carelessly.

desideratum [L.] That which is needed or deemed desirable but not yet possessed.

desipere in loco [L.] To unbend on occasion; to relax at times; to drop formalities when the situation is appropriate.

des Lebens Mai [G.] The May of life; the springtime of life; youth.

désoeuvré [F.] Unoccupied; lazy; without work.

désorienté [F.] Disoriented; having lost one's balance or bearings.

dessous des cartes [F.] The underside of the cards, i.e., the part which is hidden and unknown; the secret details of a situation.

destin [F.] Destiny; fate; a man's pathway through life.

de te fabula narratur [L.] The story is told of you.

détente [F.] An easing of a tense situation, as between two political forces.

détourné [F.] Unfrequented; off the beaten track.

de trop [F.] Too much; too many; said especially of an unnecessary person or one whose company is not desired.

Deus det! [L.] God grant it.

deus ex machina [L.] A god from a machine; hence, an unlikely force or improbable agency that intervenes to aid human affairs. In drama this phrase applies where difficult situations are cleared up by an artificial plot device. The phrase originated in Greek theater when gods were lowered on stage by mechanical cranes at the last moment to rescue the characters from difficulties.

Deus nobis haec otia fecit [L.] A god has granted us this case.

Deus, vindex, cernit omnia [L.] God the avenger sees everything.

Deus vult [L.] God wills it; used as a slogan of the first Crusade.

deutsch [G.] German; of German origin or characteristics.

Deutsches Reich [G.] The German Empire.

Deutschland, Deutschland über alles [G.] "Germany, Germany above all"; words of a German national song.

deux [F.] The number two.

deux à deux [F.] Two-by-two.

deux demis valent un entier [F.] Two halves make a whole.

deux fois [F.] Two times; twice.

deux-points [F.] A colon.

deva [Skr.] In Hindu mythology, a god or diety.

de visu [L.] From or by sight.

devoir [F.] A service; a necessary duty; an expected courtesy; a polite attention.

dewan [Ar. and Pers.] (1.) In India or Persia, a prime minister; a high minister of finance. (2.) In India, a native superintendent or overseer of a foreign business.

dharana [Skr.] In the Buddhist and Hindu religions, concentrations on a single thought or image during meditation.

dharma [Skr.] (1.) In the Hindu and Buddhist religions, individual religious duty; religious obligation that must be performed daily; also, right conduct; proper moral behavior. (2.) A man's rightful occupation; his true life's calling. (3.) A man's individual fate and proper place in relation to other men and all forms of life in the universe.

dhobi [Hindi] In India, a caste of launderers; also, a launderer himself.

dhoti [Hindi] In India, a long white loincloth worn by Hindu men.

dhyana [Skr.] In the Buddhist and Hindu religions, the state of thoughtless concentration arrived at during meditation.

dia [Port.] Day.

diable [F.] The devil; Satan; a terrible man.

diablerie [F.] Devilry.

diablo [Sp.] The devil; Satan; a hideous individual; a wretch.

diabolo [It.] The devil; a man of perverse temper.

diamanté [F.] Sparkling like a diamond; glittering.

Diaspora [Gr.] A scattering; used specifically to describe the dispersion of the Jews.

dibbuk [Heb.] In Hebrew lore, a spirit that possesses and controls a living being.

di buon'ora [It.] Early.

Dichtung [G.] Poetry; a poem.

dictum ac factum [L.] Said and done; no sooner is it said, then it is done.

dictum de dicto [L.] A saying of a saying, i.e., a hearsay report; information that arrives second-hand; a rumor.

dictum quod non dictum sit prius nullum est iam [L.] Nothing is said today that has not been said before.

dictum sapienti sat est [L.] A word to the wise is sufficient.

Die Mater [G.] The Madonna, i.e., the Virgin Mary.

diem perdidi [L.] I have lost a day.

Dienstag [G.] Tuesday.

dies [L.] Day.

dies faustus [L.] An auspicious day; a day when all omens are favorable to an enterprise; cf. *dies infaustus.*

dies infaustus [L.] An inauspicious day; a day of bad omens; cf. *dies faustus.*

Dies Irae [L.] Day of Wrath; the opening words of a Christian hymn performed at Mass for the dead.

dies non juridicus [L.] A day, but not a court day, i.e., a day on which the courts do not convene.

Dieu avec nous [F.] God with us; used after making a statement of intent.

Dieu défend le droit [F.] God defends the right.

Dieu est toujours pour les gros bataillons [F.] God is always on the side of big batallions.

Dieu et mon droit [F.] God and my right; used as the motto on the royal arms of Britain.

Dieu le veuille [F.] God grant it.

Dieu vous garde [F.] God watch over you.

difficultatis patrocinia praeteximus segnitiae [L.] We make a pretext of difficulty to rationalize our sloth.

di grado in grado [It.] Step-by-step; by degrees; one at a time.

di il vero e affronterai il diavolo [It.] Speak the truth and you will shame the devil.

dii majores [L.] The greater gods, i.e., the supreme gods, as opposed to the lesser angels or nymphs; thus, greatly eminent men; individuals far above the level of normally talented men; cf. *dii minores.*

dii minores [L.] The lesser gods, i.e., lesser dieties as compared to the archangels or to a god such a Jove; thus, men of real but uninspired talent; second-rank greatness; cf. *dii majores.*

Dimanche [F.] Sunday.

dimidium facti, qui coepit, habet [L.] What's well begun is half done.

diminuendo [It.] In music, a direction to decrease the volume.

dîner [F.] Dinner.

dîner de garçons [F.] A men's dinner; a stag party.

di novello tutto par bello [It.] Everything new is fair to view.

Dios me libre de hombre de un libro [Sp.] God deliver me from a man of one book, i.e., from a narrow man or man of superficial learning.

Dios, que da la llaga, de la medicina [Sp.] God who sends the wounds sends the cure.

dipinto [It.] A painting; a picture.

dirigo [L.] I direct; used as the motto of the State of Maine.

dis aliter visum [L.] The gods have decreed otherwise; the best laid schemes of mice and men oft times go astray.

discordia fit carior concordia [L.] Discord makes concord more precious.

discours d'enfant [F.] The speech of a child; baby talk.

diseur de bon mots [F.] A sayer of good words, i.e., a wit; a jolly wag; a joker.

diseur de bonne aventure [F.] A soothsayer; a fortune teller.

disjecta membra [L.] The scattered parts or remains; scrambled sections of a body; in literature, usually said of random and unconnected phrases.

disjecta membra poetae [L.] The scattered members of a poet, i.e., hopelessly mistranslated or misquoted lines of poetry that held merit before they were mangled by careless usage.

dis-june [Sc.] Breakfast.

distinctio boni et mali [L.] The distinction between good and evil.

distingué [F.] Distinguished; of noble and impressive bearing; elegant.

dit [F.] Called; known as. (*The work was by Jean Baptiste Poquelin* dit *Molière*.)

Ditat Deus [L.] God enriches; used as the motto of the State of Arizona.

divertissement [F.] (1.) Pleasant diversion; light and enjoyable entertainment. (2.) A short interim performance between the acts of a play. (3.) In music, a cheerful and light composition.

divide et impera [L.] Divide and rule.

divina particula aurae [L.] The divine particle of spirit; the spirit of life within a living being.

divisum sic breve fiet opus [L.] Thus divided, the work will become short.

divorcé [F.] A divorced man.

divorcée [F.] A divorced woman.

divus [L.] (1.) A god or goddess; a divine man. (2.) Title of a dead and deified king, especially a Roman emperor.

dix [F.] The number ten.

docendo discimus [L.] We learn by teaching.

dolce [It.] (1.) Sweet; soft. (2.) In music, a direction to play sweetly and softly.

dolce far niente [It.] It is sweet to do nothing; hence, pleasant leisure; sweet laziness; sublime indolence.

dolce vita [It.] The soft life; the easy existence.

dolendi modus, timendi non item [L.] There is an end to sorrow but none to fear.

doli capax [L.] In law, capable of criminal behavior.

doli incapax [L.] In law, incapable of criminal behavior.

dolmen [F.] In archaeology, a prehistoric table-shaped megalith, usually part of a burial chamber, found, with more or less similarity in size and shape, in the ruins of Neolithic civilizations throughout the world.

dolore che ricordarsi del tempo felice nella nessun maggior [It.] There is no greater sorrow than to re-call happiness in misery.

Dom [G.] Cathedral; a large church.

Domine, dirige nos [L.] Lord, di-rect us; used as the motto of the City of London.

Domingo de Resurrección [Sp.] Eas-ter Sunday.

Dominus vobiscum [L.] The Lord be with you; the blessing be-stowed by the priest at the close of the Mass.

domus [L.] A house; a home; a private dwelling.

domus et placens uxor [L.] A good and pleasing wife.

Dona [Port.] Lady; madame; used as a title of respect for a lady.

Doña [Sp.] Lady; madame; used as a title of respect for a lady.

don de la nature [F.] A gift of na-ture.

donec eris felix multos numerabis amicos [L.] As long as you are fortunate you will number many friends.

donna [It.] Lady; madame; used as a title of respect for a lady.

Donnerstag [G.] Thursday.

Donnerwetter [G.] A thunder-storm; a violent spell of rain and lightning.

dood [Dutch] Death; demise.

dopo [It.] After; afterwards; next.

Doppelgänger [G.] A double; an unearthly second self, especially one that haunts or harasses his human twin.

dos-à-dos [F.] (1.) Back-to-back. (2.) Any piece of furniture built so that the seated parties are placed facing opposite directions.

dos pou sto kai kosmen kineso [Gr.] Show me where to stand, and I will move the earth; a phrase at-tributed to Archimedes who maintained that with the proper fulcrum any object in the uni-verse could be levered.

dossier [F.] A file of information; a notebook containing records of a particular individual or case history.

douanier [F.] A customs officer; a nickname of Henri Rousseau, nineteenth-century French primi-tive painter.

double-entendre [F.] A double meaning; a play on words in which a word or expression car-ries two meanings, one of which is often off-color.

doublure [F.] The internal side of a book cover, often, in fine bind-ings, covered in decoratively tooled leather.

douceur [F.] (1.) Sweetness of character; kindness; friendliness. (2.) A tip; a gratuity; sometimes a bribe.

(la) douleur qui se tait n'en est que plus funeste [F.] Silent anguish is only that much more danger-ous.

doux yeux [F.] Sweet eyes; soft and amorous glances; romantic looks.

doyen [F.] A dean; the oldest member of an organization; one who holds power or position be-cause of seniority.

dragée [F.] (1.) A sugar-almond; a piece of candy. (2.) A sugar-coated pill.

dramatis personae [L.] The cast of characters appearing in a play.

drame [F.] Drama.

dramma lirico [It.] In theatre, a lyric drama.

dramma per musica [It.] In music, a musical drama; a play with musical accompaniment.

drap d'or [F.] A cloth of gold.

drapeau [F.] A flag; banner.

drei [G.] The number three.

(le) droit commun [F.] Common law.

droit d'aînesse [F.] Primogeniture; the right of the first son to inherit the father's estate; also, a birthright.

droit des gens [F.] The right of the people; the law of nations; a law common to all countries.

droit divin [F.] Divine right; sanction from the heavens.

droit du plus fort [F.] The right of the stronger; the power of the most capable; might makes right.

droit du seigneur [F.] The supposed right of a feudal lord to deflower the brides of his vassals.

droits d'admission [F.] Right of admission, i.e., entry price; fare.

drôle de corps [F.] A droll fellow; a wag.

drôlerie [F.] Something droll or oddly humorous; a bizarrely comic thing or situation.

duce [It.] The chief; the commander; used as an appelation for Benito Mussolini.

duecento [It.] In Italy, the thirteenth century.

duello [It.] In Italy, the art and practice of dueling.

dueña [Sp.] Mistress; a married lady; an older woman who acts as a chaperone for a young lady.

dueño [Sp.] Master; proprietor; the landlord of an estate or owner of a rented home.

dulce bellum inexperto [L.] War is sweet for the one who has not yet experienced it.

dulce domum [L.] Sweet home.

dulce est desipere in loco [L.] It is pleasant to act like a fool in the right place.

dulce et decorum est pro patria mori [L.] It is sweet and proper to die for one's country; a phrase popular in Europe in the nineteenth century as a rationale for war.

dum casta [L.] While chaste, i.e., while still a virgin.

dumm [G.] Stupid; dense; dumb.

dummodo sit dives, barbarus ipse placet [L.] Provided he is rich, even the barbarian pleases.

dum spiro, spero [L.] While I breathe, I hope; used as the motto of the State of South Carolina.

dum vita est, specs est [L.] While there is life, there is hope.

dum vivimus, vivamus [L.] While we live, let us live.

duodecimo [L.] In twelfths; a large book page folded into twelve leaves in preparation for binding; also, a book of that size measuring approximately 5 x 8 inches.

duolo [It.] Grief; sorrow; pathos.

duomo [It.] A cathedral.

dura lex sed lex [L.] A hard law yet still a law.

durante viduitate L.] During widowhood.

durante vita [L.] During life; while life occurs.

du sublime au ridicule il n'y a qu'un pas [F.] From the sublime to the ridiculous there is only one step; a phrase said by Napoleon during his flight from Russia.

du vieux temps [F.] Of the old times; old-fashioned.

dux gregis [L.] The leader of the flock.

E

---

eadem, sed aliter [L.] The same, but different; the same thing but done in a different manner.

eau bénite [F.] Holy water.

eau bénite de cour [F.] Holy water of the court, i.e., courteous but empty words.

eau de cologne [F.] Cologne water; perfumed toilet water.

eau de source [F.] Water from a source; spring water.

eau-de-vie [F.] The water of life; thus, cognac; brandy; spirits.

eau potable [L.] Drinking water.

eau salée [F.] Salt water.

eau sucrée [F.] Sugar water.

ébats [F.] Games; pleasant pastimes; frolics.

ébauche [F.] A rough sketch or preliminary draft of an artistic project, such as a painting or work of literature, that serves as an outline for the entire plan.

ébranlement [F.] A great shock; violent shaking; trembling.

ebrii gignunt ebrios [L.] Inebriates beget inebriates.

ebuccinator [L.] A trumpeter; one such as the Angel Gabriel, who sounds the call of the trumpet.

è buon orator chi a se persuade [It.] He is a good orator who persuades himself.

ecce [L.] Behold.

ecce homo [L.] Behold the man; words of Pilate (John 19:1–5) as he presented Christ to the people.

ecce iterum Crispinus adest [L.] Look, here comes Crispinus again, i.e., here comes that pest once more to bother us.

eccellentissimo [It.] Highest; most excellent; used as a title of honor.

ecce signum [L.] Behold the sign; witness the proof of the case.

ecco [It.] Here; here is; there is; look here.

écervelé [F.] Hair-brained; thoughtless; rash.

échange de politesses [F.] An exchange of compliments; mutual politeness.

éclair [F.] A chocolate-covered pastry with a cream fill.

éclaircissement [F.] A solution to a problem; the answer to a mystery; an explanation that enlightens.

éclat [F.] (1.) A great noise; a noise; a bursting forth; an explosive effect. (2.) Great success; universal fame; great distinction.

école [F.] A school; university; also, a political or cultural circle, such as the Renaissance school of painters.

école de droit [F.] A college of law.

e contrario [It.] On the contrary; to the contrary.

écorcher les oreilles [F.] To irritate the ears; to grate.

écrasé [F.] Crushed; thoroughly defeated; destroyed; put to shame.

écrasez l'infâme [F.] Crush the infamous thing; said by Voltaire about the Roman Catholic Church.

écrin [F.] A box for jewels; a casket.

écriture [F.] Handwriting; script.

écroulement [F.] A crumbling to pieces; disintegration; collapse; also, a landslide; a breaking apart of the earth.

edax rerum [L.] Devourer of everything; Ovid's name for time.

Edelweiss [G.] A small white-flowering alpine flower, national symbol of Austria.

edite, bibite [L.] Eat, drink.

éditeur [F.] Publisher.

édition de luxe [F.] A specially printed and bound limited edition, geared for sale to libraries and wealthy collectors.

editiones expurgatae [L.] Expurgated editions; censored works.

editio princeps [L.] The first edition, especially of a book.

edo, ergo sum [L.] I eat, therefore I am; used as a pun on *cogito, ergo sum* (q.v.).

effectus sequitur causam [L.] The effect follows the cause.

effendi [Turkish] Sir; master; a title of respect; also, a title of an official or officer of the law.

effusio sanguinis [L.] Flowing blood; bloodshed.

égalité [F.] Equality.

ego et rex meus [L.] I and my king.

eheu! Fugaces labuntur anni! [L.] Alas, the fleeting years slip by.

eigner Herd ist Goldes wert [G.] One's own hearth has the worth of gold.

Eile mit Weile [G.] Make haste slowly.

Ein' feste Burg ist unser Gott [G.] A mighty fortress is our God; the first verse of Martin Luther's famous hymn.

einmal, keinmal [G.] Just once counts not at all.

ein Volk, ein Reich, ein Führer [G.] One people, one state, one ruler; used as the slogan of the German Third Reich.

Eisenbahn [G.] A railroad.

ejusdem farinae [L.] Of the same flour, i.e., of the same make-up; similar in character.

ejusdem generis [L.] Of the same class; similar in character. (*These delinquents were all* ejusdem generis, *brothers of the truncheon and club.*)

ejus nulla culpa est, cui parere necesse sit [L.] He who is forced to comply is not responsible for his deeds.

ekka [Hindi] A small two-wheeled carriage built of bamboo and drawn by a single horse.

élan [F.] Spirit; drive; great energy and readiness for action.

elapso tempore [L.] The time having elapsed.

el deseo vence al miedo [Sp.] Strong desire conquers fear.

elenchus [L. from Gr.] A wrong conclusion; a principle arrived at by fallacious reasoning.

elephantus non capit murem [L.] Elephants don't bother to catch mice; cf. *aquila non capit muscas.*

élévation [F.] In ballet, a leap in which the dancer seems to hang motionless in the air.

élève [F.] A pupil; a student.

eli, eli, lamma sabacthani [Aramaic] "My God, my God, why hast thou forsaken me"; the words of Christ on the cross.

elixir vitae [L.] The elixir of life.

éloge [F.] A speech of praise; a eulogy.

éloignement [F.] Distance; estrangement; a remoteness caused by aversion.

el tiempo corre, y todo tras el [Sp.] Time runs on, and all run after it.

emax faemina [L.] A woman who is always buying.

embarcadero [Sp.] A pier; wharf.

embarras de choix [F.] An embarrassment of choices; a vast number of attractive possibilities from which to choose.

embarras de richesse [F.] Embarrassment of riches; an overabundance of wealth of possessions; too much of a good thing.

embassatrix [L.] A female ambassador.

emboscada [Sp.] An ambush; a sneak attack.

embrasement [F.] A great blaze; an illumination.

embrassade [F.] A warm embrace; a hug.

éméché [F.] Slightly intoxicated; tipsy.

emeritus [L.] Title of one released or resigned from an office.

émeute [F.] A riot; an outbreak of violence; an insurrection.

émigré [F.] An emigrant; an ex-patriot.

eminente [Sp.] Eminent; high ranking; lofty.

empennage [F.] The tail of an airplane.

emperador [Sp.] An emperor; a ruler.

Empfindung [G.] Perception; feeling; sensation.

(l') empire c'est la paix [F.] "The empire, it is peace": *Napoleon III*.

empoignade [F.] An argument; spirited dispute; a fight.

empressé [F.] Eager; anxious; obsequiously attentive.

empressement [F.] A warm show of hospitality; a spirited expression of cordiality.

empta dolore docet experientia [L.] When purchased with sorrow, experience teaches.

emptor [L.] A buyer; shopper; cf. *caveat emptor.*

e multis paleis paulum fructus collegi [L.] From much chaff I have gathered a bit of grain.

en arrière [F.] In the rear; behind; also, in arrears; in debt.

en attendant [F.] In or while waiting; meanwhile. (*We shall soon eat, but,* en attendant, *let us talk.*)

en avant [F.] Forward; into the coming times ahead; also, used as a command to move forward.

en beau [F.] As handsome; presented as attractive. (*Sargent was thus forced to paint his subject* en beau, *with broad smile and pleasing exterior.*)

en bloc [F.] In a block; all in one large group. (*His prejudice forces him to judge all people en bloc.*)

en bonne foi [F.] In good faith. (He swore en bonne foi *on the Bible.*)

enbonpoint [F.] Plumpness; a hearty and well-fed appearance; used as a euphemism for fat.

en caballo [Sp.] On horseback; mounted on a steed.

en cache [F.] In hiding; secretly placed; hidden. (*We put the instruments* en cache *and locked the door.*)

enceinte [F.] (1.) A wall or line of defense encircling a palace or fortress. (2.) Pregnant; with child.

en clair [F.] Written clearly; written in words rather than in a cipher.

en compagne [F.] In the field, i.e., at work; busy. (*Some were at their desks but most were* en compagne, *interviewing prospects.*)

en congé [F.] On a leave of absence; on vacation.

en cueros [Sp.] Naked.

en cuerpo y en alma [Sp.] In body and soul.

encuesta [Sp.] An inquest; an investigation of a crime or problem.

en déshabillé [F.] In a state of undress; carelessly clothed. (*For her to be seen* en déshabillé *was akin to ruin.*)

endimanché [F.] Dressed in one's Sunday best; formally attired.

en échiquier [F.] Arranged like the squares of a chess board.

en effet [F.] In effect; actually; really.

energico [It.] Energetic; full of vitality.

en évidence [F.] In evidence; apparent; obvious.

en faction [F.] On duty; at work.

en famille [F.] In the family; accepted as a member of the family; also, quietly alone with the family; at home.

enfant de miracle [F.] A child of a miracle, i.e., a child born unexpectedly, especially one whose birth has been long in coming.

enfant gâté [F.] A spoiled child; a problem child.

enfant perdu [F.] A lost child, i.e.,

an exile; a soldier sent to a distant and dangerous front.

enfants perdus [F.] Lost children, i.e., lost hopes; plans that have come to ruin.

enfant terrible [F.] A terrible child; a child who by his misbehavior or imprudent tongue is a cause of continuous trouble and embarrassment. (*Dennis the Menace might be termed the archetypical* enfant terrible.)

enfant trouvé [F.] A found child; an orphan.

en fête [F.] In festivity; in merrymaking.

en fin [F.] Succinctly; briefly; in a word.

en garçon [F.] Like a bachelor; as a single man.

en garde [F.] On guard; a term used to warn a fencer that the duel has begun.

engourdi [F.] Dulled; languid; apathetic.

en grande toilette [F.] Fully dressed; dressed to the hilt.

en masse [F.] In mass; in one large group; all together. (*His children arrived en masse.*)

ennuyé [F.] A state of boredom or ennui; also, an individual who is habitually bored.

en paix [F.] At peace; in a state of restfulness.

en partant [F.] In parting; in taking one's leave. (En partant *we were reconciled.*)

en passant [F.] (1.) In passing. (*I noticed him only* en passant.) (2.) In chess, a maneuver of capture by opposing pawns.

en plein air [F.] In the open air; outside.

en plein jour [F.] In plain day; thus, without disguise; openly.

en prise [F.] In chess, a term to designate that a piece is being threatened.

en queue [F.] In a line; standing in line.

enragé [F.] Enraged; furious; mad with anger.

en rapport [F.] In rapport; in accord; relating harmoniously.

en retiré [F.] In retirement; secluded; out of reach.

en revanche [F.] In return; in revenge; in retribution for a wrong.

en route [F.] On the road; on the way.

ens [L.] Being; existence.

ense petit placidam sub libertate quietem [L.] With the sword she seeks calm repose under liberty; used as the motto of the State of Massachusetts.

ens rationis [L.] A rational being.

Ens Supremum [L.] The Supreme Being; God.

en suite [F.] Following; in series; attached to each other.

entbehre gern was du nicht hast [G.] Willingly renounce what you do not possess.

entente [F.] An understanding; an agreement, especially between governments or political forces.

entente cordiale [F.] A cordial understanding; especially between governments or political forces.

entête [F.] Infatuated; obsessed with an idea; stubbornly nursing an opinion or attitude.

en tout cas [F.] In any case.

en tout chose il faut considérer la fin [F.] "In all things it is necessary to consider the end": *La Fontaine.*

en toutes lettres [F.] In full letters; totally presented; unmistakably.

entr'acte [F.] The interact; the period of time between two acts of a play; also, a performance given between the acts.

en train [F.] In progress; occurring at this moment; on-going. (*The project is* en train.)

entre [F.] Between; in between, among.

entre autres [F.] Among others.

entrechat [F.] In ballet, a leap during which a dancer repeatedly touches or crosses his feet.

entrecôte [F.] A piece of steak carved from the ribs of the cow.

entre deux âges [F.] Between two ages, i.e., middle-aged.

entremets [F.] A side dish, usually served after the main meal.

entre nous [F.] Between us; just between ourselves.

entrepôt [F.] A warehouse; a depot; a distribution center.

entrez [F.] Enter; come in.

en vérité [F.] In truth.

(les) envieux mourront, mais non jamais l'envie [F.] The envious will die, but envy never.

eo loci [L.] At that exact place.

eo nomine [L.] Under the name; by the name.

épanchement [F.] An unburdening of the soul; an outpouring of emotions and thoughts in which all details of a problem are revealed.

épatant [F.] Fantastic; amazing; surprising.

epea pteroenta [Gr.] Winged words.

epée [F.] A sword used in fencing.

éperdu [F.] Distracted; confused; in a state of extreme bewilderment.

epimythium [Gr.] The moral of a story; the allegorical lesson contained in a fable.

epistola non erubescit [L.] A letter does not blush.

e pluribus unum [L.] One out of many; used as the motto of the Great Seal of the United States of America.

époque [F.] Epoch; era; long period of time.

épris [F.] Taken with someone; in love.

eppure si muove! [It.] "And yet it does move"; reputedly said by Galileo after being forced by the church to gainsay his theory that the earth moves around the sun.

equi et poetae alendi, non saginandi [L.] Horses and poets are to be fed not made fat.

erba mala presto cresco [It.] A noxious weed grows quickly.

e re nata [L.] From the thing or circumstances arising; according to the present situation.

ergo [L.] Thus; therefore; hence.

Erin go bragh [Gael.] Erin, i.e., Ireland, go free; used as a nationalistic slogan of Ireland.

Erinnerung [G.] A remembrance; recollection.

eripitur person, manet res [L.] The mask is torn off, and the reality is seen.

errare est humanum [L.] To err is human.

ersatz [G.] A replacement or cheap imitation; a shoddy substitute.

es bildet ein Talent sich in der Stille, sich ein Charakter in dem Strom der Welt [G.] Talent is built up in solitude, character in the stream of the world.

escalier de dégagement [F.] The back stairs.

escalier dérobé [F.] A secret staircase.

escamotage [F.] Juggling; sleight of hand.

escapada [Sp.] An escape; a flight from a dangerous situation.

escargot [F.] A snail.

esclandre [F.] A great scandal; an exposé (q.v.).

escritório [Port.] Office; office building; location of business.

es de vidrio la mujer [Sp.] Woman is made of glass: Cervantes.

espalier [F.] A fence or trellis on which trees, especially pear trees, are trained to grow in decorative configurations.

espiègle [F.] Playful; roguish; in the manner of a wag.

espièglerie [F.] A playful trick; also, playfulness; roguish behavior.

espresso [It.] A rich black coffee.

esprit de corps [F.] The spirit of the group; a feeling of unity or of common aim that inspires members of a group.

esprit dérangé [F.] A sick mind; a mentally deranged person.

esprit d'escalier [F.] A wit on the staircase, i.e., the witty and devastating retorts one thinks up after having just left the scene of an argument.

esprit fort [F.] A strong spirit; a free thinker; one who is free from the prejudices of his contemporaries.

esse [L.] Being; existence.

Essenz [G.] The essence; the essential part.

esse quam videri [L.] To be rather than to seem; used as the motto of the State of North Carolina.

estafette [F.] A mounted chevalier; a knight on horseback.

estaminet [F.] A small tavern or restaurant; a coffee house.

est in aure ima memoriae locus, quem tangentes attestamur [L.] The lobe of the ear is the seat of the memory, and we touch it when calling someone to witness.

esto perpetua [L.] May it be perpetual; used as the motto of the State of Idaho.

est quaedam flere voluptas [L.] In weeping there is a certain form of pleasure.

estque pati poenas, quam meruisse, minus [L.] It is less to be punished than to have deserved punishment.

esurienti ne occurras [F.] Do not oppose a hungry man.

es verdad [Sp.] It's the truth.

et alibi [L.] And elsewhere.

étape [F.] (1.) A warehouse; a depot for the storage of goods. (2.) A military campsite; a place of lodging for soldiers on the march; also, the march itself.

(l') état, c'est moi [F.] "The state, it is I"; a statement allegedly spoken by Louis XIV of France, often quoted to show the extent of monarchical power in seventeenth century Europe.

état militaire [F.] The military service.

et cetera [L.] And others; commonly abbreviated as "etc."

e tenebris lux [L.] Light out of darkness.

et hoc genus omne [L.] And all that sort of thing.

etiam capillus unus habet umbram suam [L.] Even a single hair casts its shadow.

etiam fera animalia, si clausa teneas, virtutis obliviscuntur [L.] Even savage animals, if kept shut up, forget their courage.

etiam periere ruinae [L.] Even the ruins have now perished.

etiam stultis acuit ingenium fames [L.] Hunger sharpens the wits even of fools.

et in Arcaria ego [L.] I, too lived in Arcadia; an inscription found on a tomb by shepherds in a famous pastoral painting by Poussin, the theme of the work being the ephemeral quality of life, even when lived in the paradise of Arcadia. Another interpretation of this phrase claims it to mean that one will find death even dwelling in Arcadia.

étoile [F.] Star.

étonnement [F.] Great astonishment; amazement; wonder.

étourderie [F.] A thoughtless blunder; a heedless act; a stupid mistake.

et quis non causas mille doloris habet [L.] And who has not a thousand causes of grief.

étranger [F.] A stranger; an alien.

et sequens [L.] And the following; commonly abbreviated as "et seq."

et tu Brute [L.] And you too, Brutus; the exclamation made by Caesar in Shakespeare's *Julius Caesar* when he sees that his friend Brutus is also a member of the party that will assassinate him.

étude [F.] In music, a practice piece of music; also, a musical composition based on a single motive.

euge, poeta! [L.] Bravo, poet!

e vestigio [L.] Instantly; immediately; at once.

Ewigkeit [G.] Eternity.

(das) Ewig-Weibliche zieht uns hinan [G.] The eternal feminine draws us on.

ex abrupto [L.] Abruptly; without warning; suddenly.

ex abundanti cautela [L.] From or because of excessive caution.

ex accidenti [L.] By accident; accidentally.

(l') exactitude est le sublime des sots [F.] Exactness is the sublimity of fools.

ex aequo et bono [L.] According to that which is fair and good.

ex animo [L.] From the heart; of the spirit; with sincerity. (*The gift was* ex animo.)

ex auctoritate mihi commissa [L.] By the authority vested in me.

ex cathedra [L.] From the throne; by virtue of one's position and authority. (*The Pope speaks ex cathedra on matters of faith, that is, from the power of his office instead of through his authority as an individual.*)

excelsior [L.] Ever higher; higher still; used as the motto of the State of New York.

exceptis excipiendis [L.] Excepting that which is to be excepted; with allowance made for obvious exceptions.

excerpta [L.] Excerpts; words or phrases taken from passages of literature.

ex comitate [L.] Out of courtesy; from etiquette.

ex concessis [L.] From that conceded; from that which has been admitted.

ex confesso [L.] Confessedly; admittedly.

ex consequenti [L.] As a logical consequence; as an expected result. (*Since the law could furnish no evidence it could not, ex consequenti, furnish a trial.*)

ex contractu [L.] From contract.

excrementum [L.] Excrement; residue; waste materials; that which is left over from a process of refinement.

ex curia [L.] Out of court; not done through litigation.

ex dono [L.] As a gift; as a present; often precedes the name of a contributor. (Ex dono *David Hobler.*)

ex dono Dei [L.] By the gift of God.

exempli gratia [L.] For the sake of example.

exemplis non judicandum sed legibus [L.] One should judge not by actions, but by principles.

exeunt [L.] They leave the scene; they exit; used as a stage direction.

exeunt omnes [L.] Everyone leaves; used as a stage direction.

ex facto jus oritur [L.] The law arises from the fact.

ex improviso [L.] Suddenly; without warning.

exitus acta probat [L.] Outcome justifies methods; the ends justify the means.

ex lege [L.] From or of the law; arising from judicial matters.

ex libris [L.] From the library of; used as an inscription on a bookplate preceding the owner's name. (*Ex libris Fred Hamburg.*)

ex mero motu [L.] From its own accord; of its own volition.

ex more [L.] From the mores; from the local habits; according to the customs practiced.

ex necessate rei [L.] From the necessity of the thing.

ex necessitate [L.] Of necessity; without choice. (*They were forced, ex necessitate, to eat what was put before them.*)

ex nihilo [L.] From or out of nothing; from nowhere. (*The little creation sprang up* ex nihilo *without an apparent creator.*)

ex nihilo nihil fit [L.] Out of nothing, nothing comes.

ex nudo pacto non oritur actio [L.] In law, from a mere verbal agreement no legal action can be brought.

exoriare aliquis nostris ex ossibus ultor [L.] May one who will take revenge come up from my bones.

ex oriente lux, ex occidente lex [L.] From the East, light and from the West, law.

ex parte [L.] From one side only; in the interests of one side only.

experientia docet [L.] Experience teaches.

experimentum crucis [L.] A crucial experiment; a critical test that proves or disproves the validity of an enterprise.

experto crede [L.] Believe he who has had the experience.

exposé [F.] A revelation of previously hidden facts or information; the disclosure of scandalous information or the popularization of a scandal.

ex post facto [L.] After the fact; retroactive. (*His attempt to prosecute him for a crime declared illegal after it was committed was clearly judged by all to be ex post facto.*)

ex propriis [L.] From one's own property.

ex quocunque capite [L.] From whatever source.

externe [F.] An external person; a person outside, especially said of a day student at a boarding school.

extortor bonorum legumque contortor [L.] An extorter and contorter of the laws.

extrait [F.] An extract; certificate.

extrait de baptême [F.] A certificate of baptism.

extrait de mariage [F.] A certificate of marriage.

extrait mortuaire [F.] A certificate of death.

extra muros [L.] Outside or beyond the walls.

(les) extrêmes se touchent [F.] Extremes meet.

ex ungue leonem [L.] From a claw, the lion, i.e., from the claw the entire lion can be made; an entity can be reconstructed from a study of any of its separate parts.

ex usu [L.] Of use; capable of being used. (*He found the small library* ex usu.)

ex vita ita discedo tanquam ex hospitio, non tanquam e domo [L.] "I leave this life as I would leave an inn, not as from my home": *Cicero.*

ex vi termini [L.] By force of the term.

ex vitio alterius sapiens emendat suum [L.] When he sees the faults of others a wise man corrects his own.

ex voto [L.] Of a vow; done because of a vow; a gift made in gratitude for an answer to a prayer. (*The curéd cripple hung his cane on the altar as an* ex voto *for all to witness.*)

Exzellenz [G.] Excellence; eminence; used as a title of rank.

F

fabas indulcat fames [L.] Hunger sweetens beans.

faber est quisque fortunae suae [L.] Every man is the architect of his own fortune.

fable convenue [F.] A fable agreed upon; used by Voltaire regarding history.

fabliau [F.] A short medieval poem, popular in France in the thirteenth and fourteenth centuries, written in rhymed couplets and dealing with contemporaries in a burlesque and occasionally bawdy manner.

fabricando fit faber [L.] One is turned into a craftsman only by laboring at his craft.

facetiae [L.] Witty sayings; humorous aphorisms.

facette [F.] A facet; a face.

facies non omnibus una [L.] All do not look alike.

facies tua computat annos [L.] Your face betrays your years.

facile est inventis addere [L.] It is easy to add to things that have already been invented.

facile largiri de alieno [L.] It is easy to be lavish with what is not your own.

facile princeps [L.] Easily the best; unquestionably the finest.

facilis descensus Averno [L.] The descent to Avernus, i.e., hell, is easy; the path of evil is easily followed.

facilius crescit dignitas quam incipit [L.] Dignity increases more easily than it begins.

facinus quos inquinat aequat [L.] Crime reduces to the same level all those it corrupts.

facit indignatio versum [L.] Anger makes verses; indignation finds its outlet in poetry.

facito aliquid operis ut semper te diabolus inveniat occupatum [L.] "Keep thyself always occupied lest the devil find thee idle": *St. Jerome.*

façon [F.] Fashion; manner; style of the period.

façon de parler [F.] A manner of speaking; a way of speech.

facta, non verba [L.] Deeds, not words.

factotum [L.] A worker capable of performing many tasks in an efficient manner; a servant used in multiple capacities by his employer or master; a jack-of-all-trades.

factum est [L.] It is done.

facula [L.] In astronomy, a spot on the surface of the sun brighter than the rest of the photosphere; a sun spot.

faculté ([F.] Ability; skill; faculty.

facultés intellectuelles [F.] Intellectual faculties; mental abilities.

fadaise [F.] Tomfoolery; twaddle; silly nonsense.

fade [F.] Dull; stale; ordinary.

faenum habet in cornu, longe fuge [L.] He has hay on his horns, i.e., he is dangerous; the phrase recalls that in ancient Rome tufts of hay were tied to the horns of dangerous bulls.

faex populi [L.] The dregs of the people; the lower orders of society.

faïence [F.] Pottery or stoneware that has been glazed and painted, originating in a type of pottery manufactured in the Italian town of Faenza.

fainéant [F.] Slothful; lazy; also, a lazy man; an idler.

faire accueil [F.] To make welcome; to give a warm reception.

faire antichamber [F.] To take attendance.

faire attention [F.] To pay attention; to take heed.

faire bonne chère [F.] To live the good life; to eat much and drink well.

faire de la prose le savoir [F.] To speak prose without knowing it.

faire de l'esprit [F.] To make of the light spirit, i.e., to be witty or keen.

faire d'une mouche un éléphant [F.] To make an elephant from a fly; to make a trifle seem important.

faire la belle [F.] To act like a beauty; to play at being handsome.

faire l'aimable [F.] To talk elegantly; to speak in a refined manner.

faire la sourde oreille [F.] To turn a deaf ear.

faire le malade [F.] To pretend to be sick; to feign an ailment.

faire le roi [F.] To play the king; to act like an important man.

faire les yeux doux [F.] To make sweet eyes, i.e., to look lovingly at someone.

faire l'homme d'importance [F.] To play the man of importance; to act the bigshot.

faire l'innocent [F.] To affect innocence; to behave as if one were guiltless.

faire mon devoir [F.] To do my duty.

faire pattes de velours [F.] To make feet of velvet, i.e., to be all smiles; to fawn.

faire sans dire [F.] To act without talking.

faire ses choux gras [F.] To make one's cabbages fat; hence, to look out for one's own welfare; to be ambitious for gain.

faire son devoir [F.] To do his duty; to do what is expected of him.

faire suivre [F.] To be forwarded; used on a letter that is to be sent to another address.

faire une promenade [F.] To take a walk; to stroll.

faire un esclandre [F.] To cause a commotion; to make a scene.

faire venir l'eau à la bouche [F.] To make the mouth water.

(il) faisoit de nécessité vertu [F.] "He made a virtue of necessity": *Rabelais.*

fait accompli [F.] An accomplished fact; an act or situation that is irreversibly concluded. (*The destruction of the Goya painting was a fait accompli.*)

fait à peindre [F.] Made to be

painted; highly paintable; also, an artist's model.

faits divers [F.] Diverse facts, i.e., trivial bits and pieces of information; news flashes.

fakir [Ar.] An ascetic who performs physical austerities and mortifications to attain self-mastery; also, someone skilled in magic and spiritual achievement or, conversely, a charlatan or spiritual quack.

fallentis semita vitae [L.] The narrow path of an obscure life.

falsetto [It.] A voice pitched unnaturally high; also, one who sings in such a voice.

falsi crimen [L.] The crime of forgery.

falsitas [L.] Deceit; treachery.

falsus in uno, falsus in omnibus [L.] False in one thing, false in everything.

fama clamosa [L.] A noisy rumor, i.e., a rumor that is spread quickly in all directions.

famam extendere factis hoc virtutis opus [L.] To gain fame through deeds is the work of virtue.

fama nihil est celerius [L.] Nothing is swifter than a rumor.

(la) fama non ha leggi [It.] Hunger has no laws.

fama semper vivat [L.] May his fame live forever.

fames optimum condimentum [L.] Hunger is the best condiment.

famille [F.] Family; kin; kindred.

famoso [Sp.] Famous; well-known; popular.

fandango [Sp.] A Spanish folk dance played in triple-time.

fandi mollia tempora [L.] Favorable opportunities for speaking.

fanfaronnade [F.] Great bragging; bombast; puffery; braggadocio.

fantastico [It.] Fantastic; wonderful.

fantoccini [It.] In Italy, a puppet show, often animated by mechanical devices; also, the puppets themselves.

farceur [F.] A practical joker; a humorist; also, one who writes or performs in farces.

farina [It.] Flour; cereal.

fari quae sentiat [L.] To speak what one thinks.

farouche [F.] Fierce; untamed; shy.

fas est ab hoste doceri [L.] It is proper to be taught even from an enemy.

fasti et nefasti dies [L.] Lucky and unlucky days.

fata morgana [It.] A mirage; an illusion.

fata obstant [L.] The fates oppose; the gods are against us.

fata viam invenient [L.] The fates will discover a way.

fata volentem ducunt, nolentem trahunt [L.] Fate leads those who are willing, drags those who are not.

Fatiha [Ar.] The first chapter of the Moslem holy book, the Koran.

(un) fat quelquefois ouvre un avis important [F.] A fool sometimes gives important advice.

fatras [F.] A jumble; medley; confusion.

fatti maschii, parole famine [It.] Deeds are men, words are women; used as the motto of the State of Maryland.

fatto storico sagro [It.] A reference from a religious history.

faubourg [F.] The area immediately surrounding a French metropolis; a suburb.

faute [F.] A fault; a failing.

faute de mieux [F.] For lack of

something better; for want of a more attractive alternative.

fauteuil [F.] An armchair; an easy chair.

faux pas [F.] A false step; thus, an obtuse blunder; an insensitive slip of diplomacy; a social error.

fax mentis incendium gloriae [L.] The fire of glory is a torch to the mind.

fazer bem a velhacos, é deitar agua no mar [Port.] To be kind to scoundrels is to throw water into the sea.

fecit [L.] He or she made it; used on works of art preceding the name of the creator.

felice ritorno [It.] Happy return.

felicitas multos habet amicos [L.] Prosperity has many friends.

felicitas nutrix est iracundiae [L.] Prosperity is the nurse of ill-temper.

felix, heu, nimium felix [L.] Happy, alas, too happy.

felix qui nihil debet [L.] Happy he who nothing possesses.

felix qui potuit rerum cognoscere causas [L.] Happy he who is able to ascertain the causes of things.

felix se nescit amari [L.] As long as one is prosperous he will never know whether he is loved.

fellah [Ar.] In middle eastern countries, a peasant; a laborer or field hand.

felo-de-se [L.] In law, one who takes his life; a suicide.

femme [F.] A woman; a lady.

femme de lettres [F.] A woman of letters; an authoress.

femme fatale [F.] A siren; a woman who leads men to their undoing.

femme publique [F.] A prostitute.

fer [F.] Metal; iron.

ferae naturae [L.] Of a wild nature; untamed.

fer forgé [F.] Wrought iron.

feriunt summos fulgura montes [L.] Lighting strikes the highest peaks.

fermez la bouche [F.] Close your mouth; shut up.

ferto, fereris [L.] Bear, and you shall be born with.

fervens difficili bile tumet jecur [L.] The soul raging with fierce anger.

(Ein') feste Burg ist unser Gott [G.] A mighty fortress is our God; the first verse of Martin Luther's famous hymn.

festina lente [L.] Make haste slowly.

fête [F.] A feast; a celebration; a great banquet.

fête champêtre [F.] A rural feast; a festival or celebration held outdoors and in the country.

feu [F.] Fire; flames.

feu de joie [F.] (1.) A fire of joy, i.e., a bonfire; a large, merry conflagration. (2.) A rifle salute commemorating an important occasion.

feu d'enfer [F.] Fire of hell; a scorching fire.

feu de paille [F.] A flash in the pan.

feuille-morte [F.] The color of a dead leaf; light brown.

(la) feuille tombe à terre, ainsi tombe la beauté [F.] The leaf falls to earth and so does beauty.

feuilleton [F.] That part of a newspaper devoted to light literary entertainment.

feux d'artifice [F.] A display of fireworks; hence, a great show of wit; a dazzling display of quick thinking and mental agility.

Février [F.] The month of February.

fez [Turkish] A cylindrical felt hat crowned with a tassle.

fiacre [F.] A small four-wheeled public carriage.

fiat justitia ruat caelum [L.] Let justice be done though the heavens fall.

fiat lux [L.] Let there be light.

fide et amore [L.] With faith and love.

Fidei Defensor [L.] Defender of the Faith; used as a title of the king of England.

fideli certa merces [L.] For the faithful, a certain reward.

fide, non armis [L.] By faith, not by arms.

fide, sed cui vide [L.] Trust, but watch whom you do.

fides Punica [L.] Punic faith, i.e., an undependable trust, since the Romans believed the Poeni to be treacherous and dishonest.

fidus Achates [L.] Faithful Achates, i.e., the loyal companion of Aeneas who was the personification of a trustworthy friend.

fiel, pero desdichado [Sp.] Faithful but unlucky.

fiera [Sp.] (1.) A wild beast; an animal; (2.) colloquially, a go-getter; a hustler.

fieri facias [L.] Order it to be done; in law, a writ specifying that the belongings of a debtor be sold in order to cover the amount of the judgment against him.

fiesta [Sp.] A holiday; a feast; also, a religious holiday.

filet [F.] A piece of meat from which the bones have been removed; a fillet.

filius nullius [L.] Son of nobody, i.e., a bastard.

filius terrae [L.] Son of the soil.

fille [F.] A daughter; also, a young girl.

fille de chambre [F.] A chambermaid; a female servant.

fille de joie [F.] A woman of joy, i.e., a lady of easy virtue; a courtesan.

fille d'honneur [F.] A maid of honor.

fils [F.] Son; used to differentiate between a father and a son bearing the same name. (*The book was written by Alexandre Dumas* fils.)

fin contre fin [F.] Cunning matched against cunning; wits against wits.

fin de siècle [F.] The end of the century, specifically the close of the nineteenth century.

fine [It.] In music, the end, indicating a stopping point after the repeat of a phrase.

finem respice [L.] Regard the end; keep the whole picture in view.

fines herbes [F.] Fine herbs, i.e., kitchen herbs; herbs for seasoning, such as parsley, sage, tarragon, etc.

finis [L.] The end; the conclusion.

finis coronat opus [L.] The end crowns the work.

finis ecce laborum [L.] Behold the ends of our labors.

fisc [F.] A public treasury.

flacon [F.] A flask; a bottle-shaped container.

flagellum Dei [L.] The scourge of God, i.e., God's righteous anger.

flagrante bello [L.] While the war is blazing, i.e., during the battle; as the fight is occurring.

flagrante delicto [L.] While the crime blazes, i.e., in the act; while occurring. (*The scandal began when they were apprehended in flagrante delicto.*)

flânerie [F.] Purposelessness; aimlessness.

flâneur [F.] A saunterer; one who lounges around without purpose; also, an intellectual idler; a dilettante.

flèche [F.] (1.) A spire, especially one at the intersection of a nave and transept. (2.) A triangular field fortification with an open gorge.

fleur [F.] A flower; a blossom.

fleur-de-lis [F.] (1.) In heraldry, a three-pointed flower design, popular as a decorative motif. (2.) The iris.

fleur de mai [F.] A flower of May.

fleurs d'arbre [F.] Flowers from a tree; tree blossoms.

flosculi sententiarum [L.] The flowers of wisdom.

flos juventutis [L.] The flower of youth.

Flöte [G.] A flute.

fluctuat nec mergitur [L.] She is tossed in the waves but she does not sink; used as the motto of the city of Paris.

flux de bouche [F.] A flow of the mouth; drool; also, a flood of words; prolixity.

foehn [G.] A south wind native to the alpine regions of Europe.

foie gras [F.] The bloated livers of geese, eaten as a delicacy.

folâtre [F.] Playful; full of fun; flirty.

folio verso [L.] On the back of the page.

fonctionnaire [F.] A public official; a functionary.

fond [F.] The basis of any matter; the essential ground-work; the foundation.

fonda [Sp.] A hotel; a wayside inn.

fondre en larmes [F.] To dissolve into tears; to break down crying.

fons et origo [L.] Source and origin.

fons et origo malorum [L.] The fountain and source of misery.

fons omnium viventium [L.] The fountain of all living beings.

foramen magnum [L.] The great opening, i.e., an opening at the base of the skull where the spinal column and the medulla oblongata join.

force d'âme [F.] Strength of spirit; courage; bravery.

(la) force de la verité [F.] The power of truth.

(la) force des choses [F.] The force of circumstances.

force gens veulent être dévots; mais personne ne veut être humble [F.] Everyone wishes to be pious; but nobody wants to be humble.

force majeure [F.] A major power; an irresistible or superior force.

forensis strepitus [L.] The frenzy of the forum.

forma bonum fragile est [L.] Beauty is a frail good.

forma flos, fama flatus [L.] Beauty is a flower, fame a breath.

formes libres [F.] Free forms; in art, nonrepresentational designs and images.

foro conscientiae [L.] Before the tribunal of conscience.

forsan et haec olim meminisse juvabit [L.] Perhaps someday there will be pleasure in remembering even these unpleasant things.

forte [It.] In music, a direction calling for a forceful rendering.

fortes fortuna juvat [L.] Fortune favors the brave.

fortissimo [It.] In music, a direction meaning very loud.

fortis cadere, cedere non potest [L.] The brave man may fall, but he shall never yield.

fortiter et recte [L.] Bravely and uprightly.

fortiter in re [L.] Firmly in deed.

fortuito quodam concursu atomorum [L.] By a fortuitous concourse of atoms.

fortuna [L.] Fortune; destiny; luck.

fortuna favet fatuis [L.] Fortune favors the fools.

fortuna multis dat nimium, nulli satis [L.] To many fortune gives too much, but none she gives enough.

fortuna rerum humanarum domina [L.] Fortune rules human affairs.

(la) fortune et l'humeur gouvernent le monde [F.] Fortune and caprice govern the world.

fósforo [Sp.] A match.

fosso [It.] A ditch; a trench.

fossoribus orti [L.] Arising from ditch diggers, i.e., of lowly beginnings.

fou [F.] Mad; insane.

fou à lier [F.] Mad as a March hare.

fourche [F.] A fork; a pitchfork.

fourgon [F.] A van used to transport luggage and supplies; also, in the military, a truck used to move arms and ammunition.

fourragère [F.] In the military, a decoration awarded to the members of an entire troop for gallantry in the field and worn by each on his left shoulder.

fragola [It.] The strawberry plant.

franco [It.] Post-free.

franc-tireur [F.] A sharpshooter; a sniper.

frangas, non flectes [L.] You may break, you shall not bend.

frappé [F.] Frozen; iced; also, a drink made with milk and ice cream.

frate [It.] Brother; also, a friar; monk.

Frau [G.] Lady; used as a title of respect for a married woman.

Fräulein [G.] Young lady; used as a title of respect for an unmarried woman; a young lady.

fraus est celare fraudem [L.] It is a fraud to conceal a fraud.

fraus pia [L.] A pious fraud.

fredaine [F.] A frolic; a game; a prank.

freddamente [It.] In music, a direction indicating that a passage be played coldly.

Freitag [G.] Friday.

frère [F.] Brother.

frère d'armes [F.] A brother in arms; a fellow soldier.

(das) freut mich [G.] I am glad of it.

friandise [F.] Daintiness; also, a small candy; a tidbit.

Fridubarn [G.] The peace-child, i.e., Christ.

frijole [Sp.] A black bean popular in Mexico and the Southwestern United States.

fripon [F.] Swindler; a cheater; a rascal.

friseur [F.] Hairdresser.

froid [F.] Cold; cool.

froides mains, chaudes amours [F.] Cold hands, warm heart.

Frokost [Dan.] Breakfast.

fromage [F.] Cheese.

fromage de chèvre [F.] Goat's cheese.

fromagerie [F.] A farm where cheese is produced and processed; a dairy.

frondeur [F.] Fault-finder; a mud-slinger; a carper.

frons est animi janua [L.] The forehead is the gate of the mind.

front à front [F.] Face to face.

fronti nulla fides [L.] Trust not to appearances.

fructu non foliis arborem aestima [L.] Judge a tree by its fruits, not by its leaves.

fruges consumere nati [L.] Born only to eat.

fruit sec [F.] Dried fruit.

frustra laborat qui omnibus placere studet [L.] The man who attempts to please all labors in vain.

fu [Chi.] In Chinese art, the motif of the bat, said to symbolize luck and good fortune.

Fuchs [G.] Fox.

fuga [It.] In music, a fugue.

fugit hora [L.] The hour flies.

Führer [G.] Leader, used especially as epithet of Adolf Hitler.

fumeur [F.] A room where smoking is allowed.

functus officio [L.] Having functioned in his office, i.e., retired.

(il) fuoco non s'estingue con fuoco [It.] Fire is not put out by fire.

fuori le mura [It.] Outside the walls (of Rome).

furari litoris arenas [L.] To steal the sand from the seashore.

furore [It.] Furor; a state of great excitement; a frenzy.

furor loquendi [L.] A rage for speaking; cf. *cacoëthes loquendi.*

furor scribendi [L.] A rage for writing; cf. *coëthes scribendi.*

Fürst [G.] Prince.

(der) Fürst ist der erste Diener seines Staats [G.] The Prince is the first servant of the state.

G

gabelle [F.] In France, a salt tax common before the Revolution.

gabionnade [F.] A fortification built with large cone-shaped baskets that are filled with stones and debris.

gaffe [F.] A stupid blunder; a thoughtless mistake.

gage d'amour [F.] A promise of love; a token of faith between lovers.

gageur [F.] Better; one who places bets; a gambler.

gai [F.] Gay; merry.

gai comme un pinson [F.] Gay as a lark.

gaieté [F.] Gaiety; happiness; great joy.

gaieté de coeur [F.] Gaiety of heart; joy.

gaio [It.] Gay; sprightly; merry.

gajamente [It.] In music, a direction calling for a merry interpretation of a musical passage.

galantuomo [It.] A gallant; a noble; a man of faith and honor.

galerie [F.] Gallery; a lobby; a long corridor.

galerie de tableaux [F.] Picture gallery.

Gallia est omnis divisa in partes tres [L.] "Gaul is divided into three parts": opening words of Caesar's *Gallic Wars*.

Gallice [L.] In Gaulish, i.e., in the manner of the French.

gambado [Sp.] An unorthodox or surprising movement made in dancing; thus, an antic; a trick.

gamin [F.] Urchin; a boy of the streets; a young beggar.

ganga [Hindi] A potent form of marijuana found in India, known biologically as *Cannabis Indica*.

gaon [Heb.] Rabbinic title of honor.

garbanzo [Sp.] Chick-pea.

garçon [F.] (1.) Young boy; a youth; a lad. (2.) Waiter.

garçon d'honneur [F.] The man of honor, i.e., the best man at a wedding.

garde à cheval [F.] A guard on horseback; the mounted guard.

garde-chasse [F.] Gamekeeper.

garde d'enfants [F.] A children's guard; a nurse.

garde du corps [F.] Bodyguard.

garde-feu [F.] Fire-guard; a screen to prevent the escape of flames and stray embers from a firebox.

(la) garde meurt, et ne se rend pas [F.] The guard dies, it does not surrender.

garde nationale [F.] National guard.

garde royale [F.] Royal guard.

gardez [F.] Take care; be careful; watch yourself.

gardez bien [F.] Take good care; guard yourself well.

gardez la foi [F.] Keep the faith.

gare [F.] Railroad station; depot.

garni [F.] (1.) Garnished with; sprinkled with. (2.) Furnished, as in a furnished room.

garrote [Sp.] A form of capital punishment in which the victim is strangled to death by an iron collar.

gasconnade [F.] A great boast; bragging.

Gasthaus [G.] Inn; a guesthouse.

gâté [F.] Spoiled; damaged; tainted.

gâteau [F.] Cake; a small piece of pastry.

Gaucho [Sp.] In South America, a cowboy; a range rider.

gaudeamus, igitur, juvenes dum sumus [L.] Let us rejoice, then, while we are young.

gaudet tentamine virtus [L.] Virtue rejoices in trial.

gaudium certaminis [L.] The joy of battle.

gavage [F.] Forced-feeding, as in the fattening of geese for *foie gras* (q.v.).

gavotte [F.] A dance in double-time, popular for many years with French peasants.

gazette [F.] A weekly journal; a newspaper.

Geburtsschein [G.] Birth certificate.

geflügelte Worte [G.] Winged words.

(die) Gegenwart ist eine mächtige Göttin [G.] "The present is a mighty goddess": *Goethe.*

geisha [Jap.] A Japanese serving lady, trained in the arts of entertainment and skilled in feminine accomplishments.

Geist [G.] The animating force; psyche; spirit.

Geländeläufer [G.] In skiing, a skier making a cross-country run.

Geländesprung [G.] In skiing, a jump over an obstacle, executed in a crouching posture.

gelasma anerithmon [Gr.] Endless laughter, said of the waves of the ocean.

Geld [G.] Money; revenue; gold.

Geld oder Tod [G.] Gold or death, i.e., your money or your life.

Geld regiert die Welt [G.] Money rules the world.

gelée [F.] Jelly; jelly filling.

gemütlich [G.] Comfortable; cozy; snug.

gendarme [F.] A policeman; one who keeps the peace.

(la) genie c'est la patience [F.] Genius is patience.

genius loci [L.] The genii of a location; thus, the invisible spirit that watches over a place.

genossen habe ich, das irdische Glück, ich habe gelebt und geliebet [G.] I have tasted the good of the earth, I have lived and loved.

genouillière [F.] A protective metal covering for the knee, part of a suit of armor.

genre [F.] A species; a kind; style; manner; especially used to describe certain branches of the creative arts. (*This work belongs to the French nineteenth-century genre.*)

gens [F.] People; folks; servants.

gens d'armes [F.] Men of arms; soldiers; warriors.

gens de guerre [F.] Men of war; soldiers.

gens de lettres [F.] People of letters; literary people.

gens de loi [F.] Men of the law; lawyers.

gens de même famille [F.] People

of the same family; similar types; birds of a feather.

gens de mer [F.] Men of the sea; sailors.

gens de peu [F.] People of little; the lower classes; those who amount to nothing.

gens de robe [F.] Men of the robe, i.e., professional men.

gens du monde [F.] People of the world; men or women of society and high fashion.

gente de medio pelo [Sp.] Shabby genteel people; poor aristocrats.

gentil [F.] Well-mannered; trained in the arts of graceful behavior.

(un) gentil enfant [F.] A sweet child.

gentilhomme [F.] Gentleman; man of good breeding.

genus est mortis male vivere [L.] To live an evil life is a sort of death.

genus irritabile vatum [L.] The irritable tribe of poets.

Geopolitik [G.] Geopolitics.

germanice [L.] In the German style or way.

gérontisme [F.] Senility.

geschäftiger Müssiggang [G.] Busy idleness.

geste [F.] Act; gesture.

Gesundheit [G.] To your health; used as a salutation after a person has sneezed.

gharri [Hindi] In India, a carriage used to transport passengers.

ghat [Hindi] In India, a level platform, usually along a river, where clothes are washed, prayers are said, and the dead are cremated.

ghazi [Ar.] In Moslem countries, a great warrior proficient at killing unbelievers.

ghee [Hindi] In India, clarified butter used in cooking.

giaour [Turkish] In Islamic countries, an unbeliever; a heathen.

gibier de potence [F.] Game for the gibbet; a bird fit for the gallows; a criminal ripe for hanging.

gigot [F.] The cooked leg portion of any meat, such as a leg of lamb.

ginseng [Chi.] An edible root popular for centuries in China as a stimulant and said to induce longevity.

giovine santo, diavolo vecchio [It.] Young saint, old devil.

gita [Skr.] A song; a hymn.

gitano [Sp.] Gypsy.

giuoco di mano, giuoco di villano [It.] Practical jokes are the jokes of the low.

giusto [It.] Fair; exact; just; proper.

glacé [F.] (1.) Smoothed over with a sugar frosting; iced. (2.) Having a glossy surface.

glaube dem Leben [G.] Believe in life.

gli assenti hanno torto [It.] The absent are always in the wrong.

gloire [F.] Glory; greatness.

gloria [L.] Glory.

gloriae incendium fax mentis [L.] A burning desire for glory is a torch to the mind.

Gloria in Excelsis Deo [L.] Glory be to God on high.

Gloria Patri [L.] Glory to the Father.

gloria vana florece, y no grana [Sp.] Vainglory produces flowers but no seeds.

gloria virtutis umbra [L.] Glory is the shadow of virtue.

gloseur [F.] A complaining person; a carper; one who constantly finds fault.

Glück auf den Weg [G.] Best of luck along the way; used as a phrase of farewell.

glückliche Reise [G.] A happy journey; used as a phrase of farewell.

Glück macht Mut [G.] Luck makes courage.

gnothi seauton [Gr.] Know thyself.

gobe-mouche [F.] A catcher of flies, i.e., a silly person; a fool; a simpleton.

gober le morceau [F.] To swallow the bait; to be fooled.

gondola [It.] A long, narrow boat used to transport passengers on the canals of Venice.

gondolier [F.] The oarsman of a gondola (q.v.).

gopis [Skr.] In Hindu mythology, a group of female cowherds with whom the god Krishna sported while a young man.

gorge-de-pigeon [F.] The neck of a pigeon, i.e., iridescent; many colored.

gorget [F.] A protective metal collar made of overlapping rings, part of a suit of armor.

Götterdämmerung [G.] The twilight of the gods, i.e., the complete catastrophic collapse of something; total destruction and annihilation.

(der) gottgetrunkene Mensch [G.] The God-intoxicated man.

Gott mit uns [G.] God with us.

gouache [F.] A type of opaque paint similar to water color but compounded of a more inert pigment and characterized by a reflective surface when dry; also, a picture painted in this medium.

goût [F.] Taste; preference.

goutte [F.] A drop; a tiny amount.

gouvernante [F.] A governess; a maid; someone who watches over the affairs of a household or another person.

gouverneur [F.] A governor; a chief magistrate.

goy [Heb.] A non-Jewish person; a gentile; sometimes used disparagingly.

goyim [Heb.] Plural of *goy* (q.v.).

gradatim vincimus [L.] We conquer by degrees.

gradu diverso via una [L.] Different strides, but all in one direction.

Graeculus esuriens [L.] The hungry Greekling, i.e., a desperate man; one who will go to any lengths; supposedly used of Juvenal, who was not overly discriminative in the ways he chose to make his living.

Graf [G.] A title of nobility equal to that of a count.

grain de poivre [F.] A peppercorn.

grammatici certant, et adhuc sub judice lis est [L.] The experts argue, and still the question is unsolved.

grande dame [F.] A great lady; an imposing woman of great authority or respect; a matriarch.

grandee [Sp.] In Spain and Portugal, a title of exalted station.

grande parure [F.] In full dress.

grande passion [F.] A great passion; a deep and intense romantic attachment.

(les) grandes pensées viennent du coeur [F.] Great thoughts come from the heart.

grandioso [It.] In music, a direction indicating that a passage be rendered with pomp and flourish.

grand mal [F.] In medicine, a type of epilepsy.

grand'mère [F.] Grandmother.

grand monde [F.] The great world, i.e., the world of the upper classes; the aristocracy; high fashion.

grand oeuvre [F.] The great work; the masterpiece.

(i) gran dolori sono muti [It.] Great sorrows have no tongue.

gran dote cama de rencillas [Sp.] A great dowry is a bed of thorns.

grand-père [F.] Grandfather.

grand seigneur [F.] Great lord.

granero [Sp.] A grain bin; a granary.

gratia gratiam parit [L.] Kindness causes kindness.

gratia placendi [L.] The art of pleasing.

gratias agere [L.] To give thanks.

gratin [F.] The browned layer of crust formed on foods cooked au gratin (q.v.).

gratis dictum [L.] A statement not supported by fact.

gratis paenitet esse probum [L.] One regrets his honesty when it was not necessary.

grave [It.] In music, a direction indicating that a piece be played slowly and with gravity.

gravior remediis quam delicta erant [L.] Certain remedies are more dangerous than the disease.

gravis ira regum est semper [L.] Always grave is the wrath of kings.

grazie [It.] Thank you.

grenouille [F.] A frog.

grex venalium [L.] A herd of hirelings.

grimacier [F.] A grinner; an obsequious hypocrite; a humbug.

gringo [Sp.] Colloquially, a scornful word for foreigners, especially Americans, originating in Mexico and Latin America.

(la) grippe [F.] Influenza; flu.

gris [F.] The color gray.

grisaille [F.] A technique of ornamental painting employing monochromatic gray colors.

grisette [F.] A young French girl of uninhibited behavior coming from the peasant class.

gros bon sens [F.] Plain common sense.

gros mots [F.] Profanities; obscene words.

grosse Seelen dulden still [G.] Great souls suffer in silence.

grosse tête, peu de sens [F.] Large head, few brains.

grossièreté [F.] Coarseness; foolishness; impolite behavior.

grosso [It.] In music, a direction calling for a grand, impressive rendering.

guano [Sp.] A manure made from the excrement of birds inhabiting the coastal regions of Mexico and South America.

guarda costa [It.] The coastguard.

guardati da chi non ha da perdere [It.] Beware of he who has nothing to lose.

guérite [F.] A wicker arm chair with a long back that is crowned with a rounded hood.

guerra a muerte [Sp.] A war to the finish.

guerre [F.] War.

guerre à mort [F.] A war to the death.

guerre à outrance [F.] A war to the end; a fight to the death; a battle carried to its ultimate extremes.

guerre de plume [F.] A war of the pen; a war of words.

guerre des bouffons [F.] The war of the buffoons; an argument between idiotic characters; also, in 1754, a dispute between partisans of the Italian opera and the

French opera over the relative merits of their national operatic forms.

guerre d'usure [F.] A war of attrition.

guerre froide [F.] A cold war.

guet-apens [F.] Ambush; a surprise attack; a trap.

guindé [F.] Stilted; bombastic; overly formal.

guitarra [Sp.] Guitar.

gul [Persian] Rose; also, any flower in general.

gulab [Persian] Rose water.

guru [Skr.] In Hinduism, a religious teacher; one who attempts to raise the spiritual level of others through active or silent teachings.

gusto picaresco [It.] A roguish taste.

Güte bricht einem kein Bein [G.] Kindness breaks no bones.

guten Abend [G.] Good evening.

gute Nacht [G.] Good night.

guten Morgen [G.] Good morning.

guten Tag [G.] Good day.

gutta cavat lapidem [L.] The drop hollows out the stone.

gymkhana [Hind.] In India, an athletic contest in the western style, usually held at schools or universities.

gynecaeum [Gr.] In ancient Greece, that part of the home exclusively set apart for the women, the western equivalent of the harem quarters.

H

---

habanera [Sp.] A slow, sometimes erotic dance, native to Africa but commonly found in the Caribbean islands; also, the music for this dance.

habeas corpus [L.] In law, a writ summoning a party to court.

habemus papam [L.] We have a Pope; used as a formal declaration delivered to the crowds in front of St. Peter's Church, announcing that the College of Cardinals has chosen a new pope.

habent sua fata libelli [L.] Each book has its own fate.

habere et dispertire [L.] To have and to distribute.

habet et musca splenem [L.] Even a fly has a spleen. Even the most insignificant beings have spirit.

habitations ouvrières [F.] Workmen's dwellings; the housing of the working class.

habit de cheval [F.] Riding clothes.

habit de soirée [F.] Evening dress; formal attire, such as tuxedos or tails.

(l') habit ne fait pas le moine [F.] It is not the cowl that makes the monk.

(l') habitude est une seconde nature [F.] Habit is a second nature.

habitué [F.] An individual who frequents a certain location or who is consistently found among a certain class of people. (*The suspect was a confirmed habitué of night clubs and dance halls.*)

hablar sin pensar es tirar sin encarar [Sp.] To speak without thinking, is to shoot without aiming.

hacer castillos en el aire [Sp.] To build castles in the air.

hacienda [Sp.] A mansion, usually surrounded by extensive grounds.

hadith [Ar.] The religious traditions attributed to Mohammed.

hadj [Ar.] In Islam, a pilgrimage, usually to the holy city of Mecca.

hadji [Turk.] In Islam, a title of honor accorded any man who has made a hadj (q.v.) to the holy Moslem city of Mecca.

haec olim meminisse juvabit [L.] To remember these things hereafter will be a pleasure.

hae nugae seria ducent in mala [L.] Trifles such as these lead to serious mischief.

hafiz [Persian] In the Moslem religion, a title accorded to a man who has learned the entire Koran by heart and can recite any part of it at will.

haggada. See *aggada.*

haggadah. See *aggada.*

haikwan [Chi.] A system of rules

followed by Chinese sailors on the open seas.

hakeem [Ar.] In Moslem nations, a physician; also, a king; a ruler.

Hakenkreuz [G.] Swastika, used as an emblem by the German Third Reich.

hakim. See hakeem.

halakah [Heb.] The body of unwritten laws and customs governing daily life in Judaism.

haleeb [Ar.] Milk.

Hannibal ad portas [L.] Hannibal is at the gates, i.e., the enemy waits without.

hapax legomenon [Gr.] Said only once; used to describe an unusual word or phrase that is likely to appear only one time in a text or as an inscription.

Harfe [G.] A harp.

haricot [F.] Kidney-bean; also, beans in general.

haricots verts [F.] Green string beans.

hari-kari [Jap.] Among the Japanese military clans and especially among the Samurai warriors, a method of suicide by self-evisceration practiced in the event of disgrace.

harmattan [Sp.] One of the hot, dusty winds that blows seasonally on the west coast of Africa.

hasard [F.] Luck; chance; fortune.

Hasenpfeffer [G.] A stew consisting of heavily seasoned pickled rabbit's meat, often served with sour cream.

hashish [Ar.] The resin collected from the cannabis plant, smoked or eaten as an intoxicant.

Hassgesang [G.] A song of hatred.

Hast [G.] Haste; hurry; great rush.

hasta la vista [Sp.] Until we meet again; good-bye.

hasta luego [Sp.] Until soon; until we meet again; good-bye.

haud passibus aequis [L.] Not with equal steps.

Haupt [G.] The chief; the leader.

Haus [G.] House; home.

Hausfrau [G.] Housewife.

haute couture [F.] High fashion.

(la) haute politique [F.] High politics, i.e., government at its highest levels; top-level diplomacy. (*The amnesty question was* haute politique.)

haut et bon [L.] Great and good.

hauteur [F.] Arrogance; condescension; an attitude of haughty scorn toward others.

haut goût [F.] High taste; strong seasoning or, conversely, the slight hint of a particular flavor.

haut monde [F.] The high world, i.e., high society; fashionable company; the domain of the rich and aristocratic. (*He was driven by a need for acceptance in the* haut monde.)

Heauton Timoroumenos [Gr.] A self-tormentor; title of a play written by Menander and adapted to the Latin by Terence.

hegira [Ar.] The flight of Mohammed from Mecca to Medina in A.D. 622, used as a date to mark the founding of the Moslem religion; also, any flight or sudden departure.

heil [G.] Hail; used as a salutation or salute.

heilig [G.] Blessed; sacred.

(die) heilige Jungfrau [G.] The Blessed Virgin.

heim [G.] Home.

Heimweh [G.] Homesickness; nostalgia; an intangible longing.

helluo librorum [L.] A book eater; an avid reader; a bookish person.

herbe [F.] Herb; grass.

Herr [G.] Lord, master; used as a title of respect for a gentleman.

Herrenvolk [G.] In the doctrine of the Third Reich, a race of supermen.

hesterni quirtes [L.] Citizens of yesterday, i.e., recently emancipated slaves.

heu, quam difficile est, crimen non prodere vultu! [L.] Alas, how difficult it is not to betray guilt by our countenance.

heu, quantum misero poena mens conscia donat [L.] Alas, how much punishment does the sense of guilt afford the transgressor.

heureux au jeu, malheureux en amour [F.] Lucky at games, unlucky at love; the gambler's luck runs amuck with love.

heureux hasard [F.] A lucky chance; a happy coincidence.

heu, vitam perdidi, operose nihil agendo [L.] Alas, I have wasted my life, industriously doing nothing.

Hexentanz [G.] A witch's dance.

hiatus maxime deflendus [L.] A deficiency much to be regretted.

hibachi [Jap.] A brazier made of metal or wood.

hic est mucro defensionis meae [L.] This is the point of my defense.

hic et nunc [L.] Here and now.

hic et ubique [L.] Here and everywhere.

hic jacet [L.] Here lies; used as a common gravestone inscription preceding the name of the interred.

hic jacet lepus [L.] Here lies the hare, i.e., here is the trouble in the matter; this is the fly in the ointment.

hic requiescit in pace [L.] Here lies in peace; used as a common gravestone inscription preceding the name of the interred.

hic spe celer, illa timore [L.] One is quick from hope, the other from fear.

hidalgo [Sp.] A nobleman of the lower ranks.

hidalguia [Sp.] Nobility.

hiems [L.] The season of winter.

hier stehe ich; ich kann nicht anders; Gott helfe mir! amen! [G.] "Here I stand; I cannot do otherwise; God help me! Amen!": Martin Luther's famous words delivered before Emperor Charles V, in Worms, proclaiming his stand against the Roman Catholic Church.

himmel [G.] Heavens; used as an exclamation.

hinc illae lacrimae [L.] Hence these tears.

histoire [F.] History; tale; story; recitation.

(l') histoire n'est que le tableau des crimes et des malheurs [F.] "History is nothing but the picture of crime and misfortune": *Voltaire.*

hoc anno [L.] In this year.

hoc erat in more majorum [L.] This was in the custom of the fathers.

hoc genus omen [L.] All of this type or classification. (*All must be brought to justice: thieves, murderers, gangsters, prostitutes, and* hoc genus omen.)

hoch [G.] Good health; hail; used as a salutation.

Hochzeitsmarsch [G.] A wedding march.

hoc monumentum posuit [L.] This person erected this monument;

used as an inscription noting the builder of a statue or monument.

hoc sustinete, majus ne veniat malum [L.] Sustain this hardship lest a worse one take its place.

hodie mihi, cras tibi [L.] Today it's mine (i.e., the grave), tomorrow it's yours; used as a tomb inscription.

Hof [G.] A courtyard.

Hoffnung [G.] Hope.

hoi polioi [Gr.] The masses; the multitudes; the common people. (*She considered those without rank hoi poloi.*)

homard [F.] Lobster.

hombre [Sp.] A man; a fellow.

hombre de barba [Sp.] A smart fellow; a man of able mind and keen wit.

hombre de pecho [Sp.] A firm, spirited man.

hombre pobre todo estrazas [Sp.] A poor man is all schemes.

homem morto não falla [Port.] Dead men tell no tales.

homines, dum docent, discunt [L.] Men while they teach, learn.

hominibus plenum, amicis vacuum [L.] Full of men, empty of friends.

homini ne fidas nisi cum quo modium salis absumpseris [L.] Trust no man unless you have eaten a peck of salt with him.

hominis est errate, insipientis perseverare [L.] It is man who errs, it is the fool who persists.

hommage de reconnaissance [F.] A token of recognition.

homme [F.] Man; a person.

homme de cour [F.] A man of the heart; a knight; a courtier; also, a professional man; one involved in religious, military, or legal pursuits.

homme de lettres [F.] A man of letters; a writer; a literary type.

homme de loi [F.] A man of law; an attorney.

homme de plume [F.] A man of the pen; a writer, a critic.

homme d'esprit [F.] A man of wit; an individual of high intellect and clever humor.

homme d'importance [F.] A man of importance.

homme du monde [F.] A man of the world; a sophisticated individual; an aristocrat.

(l') homme incompris [F.] The unappreciated man.

homme propose et Dieu dispose [F.] Man proposes and God disposes.

homo antiqua virtute ac fide [L.] A gentleman of ancient virtue and loyalty.

homo homini aut deus aut lupus [L.] Man acts toward man either as a god or as a wolf.

homo multarum literarum [L.] A man of many letters; hence, a learned man; a scholar; an intellectual.

homo sapiens [L.] Reasoning man, i.e., the biological species of human beings; the race of man; the human tribe.

homo sine religione sicut equus sine freno [L.] A man who lacks religion is like a horse without a bridle.

homo sum: humani nihil a me alienum puto [L.] I am a human being: I consider nothing that is human to be foreign to me.

homo vitae commodatus non donatus [L.] To this life is man lent, not given.

homunculus [L.] A little man; a mannikin; also, in magic, a tiny living replica of a human being, created and controlled by a magician.

honesta mors turpi vita potior [L.] An honorable death is preferable to a dishonorable life.

honi soit qui mal y pense [F.] Shamed be he who thinks evil of it; used as the motto of the Order of the Garter, reputedly spoken by Edward III (1344) when he unashamedly wore the garter of the Countess of Salisbury.

honorarium [L.] A gratuitous payment, usually given as a gesture of gratitude. (*For his work entertaining the troops the government gave him an honorarium of ten dollars.*)

honores mutant mores [L.] Honors change the customs.

honor habet onus [L.] Honor is onerous; honor has its burdens.

honoris causa [L.] For the sake or cause of honor.

hopak [Russ.] A spirited Ukranian dance done in duple meter.

hôpital [F.] A hospital.

hora fugit [L.] The time flies.

horas non numero nisi serenas [L.] I number none but the sunny hours; used as a motto commonly found on sundials.

horresco referens [L.] I shudder to relate.

horror ubique [L.] Terror everywhere; used as the motto of the Scots Guards.

horror vacui [L.] Horror of emptiness; the abhorrence of a vacuum; also, a feeling of personal hopelessness.

hors concours [F.] Out of competition; not entered in the contest; used to describe an object in a competitive exhibition not to be judged with the rest of the entrees.

hors d'affaire [F.] Out of danger; safe.

hors de combat [F.] Out of combat; not able to function; incapacitated. (*Their key player was hors de combat.*)

hors de la loi [F.] Outside of the law; criminal.

hors de ligne [F.] Out of line; not common; extraordinary.

hors de propos [F.] Out of purpose; uncalled for; irrelevant. (*The flippant remark was hors de propos.*)

hors de saison [F.] Out of season; not appropriate; out of place. (*Everyone agreed that such a loud tie was* hors de saison *at the party.*)

hors de service [F.] Out of service; irreparable; not functioning.

hors d'oeuvre [F.] An appetizer served before the main meal.

ho sophos en auto peripherei ten ousian [Gr.] The man who is wise has his possessions within himself.

hostis humani generis [L.] An enemy of the human race.

hôte [F.] A guest; lodger; visitor.

hôtel des postes [F.] Town post office.

hôtel de ville [F.] City hall.

(l') hôtel-Dieu [F.] The central hospital of a town.

hôtelier [F.] An innkeeper; the host of a lodging establishment.

hôte payant [F.] A paying guest.

houppelande [F.] A great coat; a cloak.

houri [Persian] In Islam, female attendants believed to abide in paradise.

howdah [Hindi] A cushioned and

often highly ornate platform for passengers carried atop an elephant.

huissier [F.] A doorkeeper; an usher.

huîtres [F.] Oyster.

huit [F.] The number eight.

humano capiti cervicem jungere equinam [L.] To join a horse's neck to a human head.

humanum est errare [L.] To err is human.

hunc tu caveto [L.] Of him thou should beware.

Hund [G.] A dog.

hurler avec les loups [F.] To howl with the wolves. To do the same thing that everyone else does.

hurtig [G.] In music, a direction meaning quick, fast.

Hut ab [G.] Hats off; used as an exclamation.

(l') hyprocrisie est un hommage que le vice rend a la vertu [F.] Hypocrisy is the homage that vice renders to virtue.

I

ibidem [L.] In the same place; in same reference; used to avoid reference to a work previously cited; usually abbreviated as "ibid."

ibit eo quo vis qui zonam perdidit [L.] The man who has lost his money belt will follow wherever you wish.

ich [G.] I; myself.

ich bin der Geist, der stets verneint [G.] "I am the spirit that always denies"; said by Mephistopheles in Goethe's *Faust*.

Ich bin es müde über Sklaven zu herrschen [G.] "I am wary of ruling over slaves": *Frederick I.*

ich danke Ihnen [G.] I thank you.

ich dien [G.] I serve; used as the motto of the Prince of Wales.

ich habe genossen das irdische Glück, ich habe gelebt und geliebet [G.] "I have tasted the good of the earth, I have lived and loved": *Schiller.*

ich habe keine Zeit, müde zu sein [G.] "I have no time to be tired": *William I.*

ici [F.] Here; in this place.

ici-bas [F.] Here below.

ici on parle français [F.] French is spoken here.

iconographie [F.] Iconography.

idéal [F.] An ideal; a beautiful vision.

idée fixe [F.] A fixed idea; an obsession; a monomania. (*Revenge became for him an* idée fixe.)

idée mère [F.] The mother idea, i.e., an original concept responsible for the creation of a doctrine or body of ideas.

idées reçues [F.] Accepted ideas; standard concepts; doctrines that are agreed upon by everyone.

idem [L.] The same; used to avoid the repetition of a reference or a previously cited name.

idem quod [L.] The same as.

idem velle atque idem nolle [L.] To have the same likes and dislikes.

identique [F.] Identical; the same; matching.

id est [L.] That is to say; usually abbreviated as "i.e."

id genus omne [L.] All of that class; all of that type. (*Poets, writers, and* id genus omne.)

idoneus homo [L.] A fit man; a healthy specimen.

id usitatissimum [L.] That most trite of sayings.

Iesus Hominum Salvator [L.] Jesus Savior of Men.

Iesus Nazarenus, Rex Iudaeorum [L.] Jesus of Nazareth King of the Jews.

77

i frutti proibiti sono i più dolci [It.] Forbidden fruits are the sweetest.

ignaro [It.] A stupid person; a fool.

ignem gladio scrutare [L.] To stir the fire with the sword, i.e., to make a bad situation worse.

ignis fatuus [L.] A foolish fire, i.e., an illusion; a will-o'-the-wisp; an impossible fantasy.

ignobile vulgus [L.] The vulgar crowd.

ignorance crasse [L.] Crass ignorance.

ignorantia legis neminem excusat [L.] Ignorance of the law excuses no one.

ignoratio elenchi [L.] To ignore the argument, i.e., to refute an argument which is slightly different from that which one pretends to refute; hence, to reason fallaciously.

ignosce saepe alteri, nunquam tibi [L.] Pardon another often, yourself never.

ignoti nulla cupido [L.] For a thing unknown there is no desire; what the eye does not see the heart does not yearn for.

ignotum per ignotius [L.] Unknown by less known, i.e., to explain an obscure question by means of something even more obscure; cf. *obscurum per obscurius.*

ihram [Ar.] In Islam, a white cotton garment worn by a pilgrim on his journey to the holy city of Mecca.

il [F.] He; it.

il a changé tout cela [F.] He has changed all that.

il a inventé l'histoire [F.] He has invented history; said by Mme. Deffand of Voltaire.

il a la mer à boire [F.] He has the sea to drink, i.e., he has an impossible task.

il a le diable au corps [F.] He has the devil in him.

il connait l'univers et ne se connait pas [F.] He knows the universe and does not know himself.

île [F.] An island; an isle.

il est plus nécessaire d'étudier les hommes que les livres [F.] "It is more necessary to study men than books": *La Rouchefoucauld.*

il faut [F.] It is necessary.

il faut cultiver notre jardin [F.] "It is necessary to cultivate your own garden"; last words of Voltaire's *Candide.*

il faut de l'argent [F.] Money is necessary.

il faut laver son linge sale en famille [F.] "One should wash his dirty linen in private": *Napoleon.*

Ilias malorum [L.] An Iliad of woes; an endless string of problems or disasters.

ilka [Sc.] Each; every.

ille terrarum mihi praeter omnes angulus ridet [L.] That corner of the earth to me smiles sweetest of all.

illotis manibus [L.] With unwashed hands, i.e., without the proper preparation.

illud [L.] That.

illud jucundum nil agere [L.] That delightful doing of nothing.

illuminato [It.] A spiritually illuminated person; an enlightened man; a saint.

illustré [F.] Illustrated.

il n'est d'homme nécessaire [F.] There is no such thing as a necessary man; everyone is expendable.

il n'est pas nécessaire de tenir les choses pour en raisonner [F.] "It's not necessary to understand things in order to speak of them with confidence": *Beaumarchais.*

il n'y a de nouveau que ce qui est oublié [F.] There is nothing new except that which is forgotten.

il n'y a pas de petit ennemi [F.] There is no little enemy.

il n'y a point de héros pour son valet de chambre [F.] No man is a hero to his valet.

Il Penseroso [It.] The melancholy man; title of a poem by Milton.

ils [F.] They.

ils n'ont rien appris, rien oublié [F.] "They have learned nothing and forgotten nothing": said by Tallyrand of the émigrés (q.v.) who returned to France after the French Revolution.

il trouverait à tondre sur un oeuf [F.] He would find something to shave on an egg.

il vaut mieux tâcher d'oublier ses malheurs que d'en parler [F.] It's better to forget one's worries than to talk about them.

il y a des héros en mal comme en bien [F.] There are heroes of evil as there are of good.

imago [L.] An image.

im allgemeinen [G.] In general; generally speaking.

imam [Ar.] In Islam, one who leads the faithful in prayer.

imaret [Turkish] In Turkey, an inn; a small hotel.

im Auftrage [G.] For or by order; under instruction.

imbroglio [It.] A confused and perplexing situation; a complicated combination of factors.

Im härtesten Winter [G.] In the depth of winter.

imitatores, servum pecus [L.] Imitators, a servile herd.

im Jahre [G.] In the year.

immedicabile vulnus [L.] An incurable wound.

immensum quiddam et infinitum [L.] Something immeasurable and unbounded.

immonde [F.] Dirty; unclean; impure.

immunité [F.] Immunity; exemption.

impar congressus Achilli [L.] Unevenly matched against Achilles, i.e., unequally pitted against one of superior strength or ability.

imparfait [F.] Imperfect; having obvious defects.

impasto [It.] In art, a type of painting where thick layers of opaque pigment are built up on the surface of the canvas.

impayable [F.] Invaluable; priceless; inestimable.

impedimenta [L.] Those objects which impede mobility, especially heavy transportables such as baggage, carts, packages, etc.

impératrice [F.] An empress; a queen.

imperium [L.] (1.) Sovereignty; absolute power and control; dominion. (2.) In law, the right of the state to apply force in order to enact legislation.

imperium in imperio [L.] An empire within an empire; thus, one body of rule within a larger body of rule; used as the motto of the State of Ohio.

impie [F.] Impious; irreligious; without respect for sacred things.

impoli [F.] Rude; unmannered; impolite.

impolitica [Sp.] Discourtesy; rudeness; incivility.

impos animi [L.] Weak minded; like a moron.

imposer des peines [F.] To impose or inflict a punishment; to chastise.

impossibilité [F.] An impossibility.

impossible n'est pas un mot Français
[F.] Impossible is not a French
word.

imposteur [F.] An impostor; a
cheat.

impotentia generandi [L.] Sexual
impotence; inability to perform
copulation.

impresor [Sp.] A printer.

impressif [F.] Impressive; striking.

imprevisto [Sp.] Unexpected; un-
foreseen.

imprimatur [L.] Let it be printed;
used as a license to publish a
book; thus, official sanction; approval.

imprimé [F.] Printed matter, such
as a book, newspaper, document,
etc.

imprimerie [F.] A printing house.

imprimeur [F.] A printer; a press-
man.

imprimis [L.] In the first place.

improperia [L.] Reproaches; in the
Roman Catholic Church, chants
sung on the morning of Good
Friday.

impropre [F.] Wrong; improper;
indecent.

improvvisatore [It.] An improviser
of songs, stories, poems, etc.

impunitas peccandi illecebra [L.]
Impunity is an enticement to sin-
ning.

im Ruhestand [G.] In retirement;
retired.

imshi [Ar.] Go away; get out; used
as an exclamation.

imum coeli [L.] The undersky; the
meridian point opposite the *medium coeli* (q.v.).

in absentia [L.] In absence; during absence. (*He was given the
award in absentia.*)

in aëre piscari, in mare venari [L.]
To fish in the air, to hunt in the
sea.

in aeternum [L.] Forever; eternally.

inamorata [It.] A woman in love.

inamorato [It.] The beloved; the
lover.

inaperçu F.] Unperceived; unno-
ticed; unseen.

in aqua scribis [L.] You are writing
in water.

in arena aedificas [L.] You are
building on sand.

in articulo mortis [L.] At the point
of death. (*His last words were
delivered* in articulo mortis.)

in aula regis [L.] In the king's hall.

*in bello parvis momentis magni casus
intercedunt* [L.] In war great
events result from small causes.

in bianco [It.] In white; also,
blank; in blank.

in bona partem [L.] In an auspicious manner; favorably.

in caducum parietem inclinare [L.]
To lean against a falling wall.

in camera [L.] In secret; in cham-
bers; behind closed doors. (*The
committee met* in camera.)

incapaz [Sp.] Unfit; incapable.

in casa [It.] At home; in one's
house.

incendium [L.] A great fire; a conflagration.

in Christi nomine [L.] In the name
of Christ.

incipit [L.] Here begins; used to in-
troduce a story, narrative, poem,
etc.

incognito [It.] With one's identity
concealed by a disguise, change of
name, or both.

incommunicado [Sp.] Detained; kept
prisoner without access to outside communication.

inconnu [F.] Unknown.

inconquistable [Sp.] Unconquer-
able; invincible; impregnable.

inconstance [F.] Changeableness;
inconstancy; fickleness.

in contumaciam [L.] In law, held in contempt of court.

incrédule [F.] Incredulous; doubting; not trusting the available information.

incroyable [F.] Incredible; amazing; unbelievable.

in cruce spero [L.] I hope in the cross.

incunabula [L.] (1.) Early printed material, especially all books printed before 1500. (2.) In the cradle; in the state of infancy.

indaba [Zulu] In South Africa, a meeting; a conference.

indélicat [F.] Indelicate.

in Deo speramus [L.] In God we hope; used as the motto of Brown University.

in deposito [L.] For a deposit; pledged; placed in trust.

Index Expurgatorius [L.] The Expurgatory Index, a list of printed material prohibited to members of the Roman Catholic Church.

index nominum [L.] An index of proper names.

index rerum [L.] A subject index.

index verborum [L.] An index of words.

indigène [F.] Indigenous; native.

in divinis [L.] In divine things.

in dubiis [L.] In things doubtful; in questionable matters.

industrie F.] (1.) Skill; ability; dexterity. (2.) An industry; a business.

industrie clef [F.] A key or essential industry.

inédit [F.] Unpublished; not yet released.

in equilibrio [L.] In equilibrium.

in esse [L.] In actuality; in real existence. (*His reputed fortune did not exist* in esse.) Cf. *in posse*.

inest clementia forti [L.] Clemency is natural to a brave man.

in excelsis [L.] In the highest.

in extenso [L.] In full extension; at full length.

in extremis [L.] In an extreme situation; in great danger, especially of dying.

infâme [F.] Infamous; having an odious name and reputation.

infanta [Sp. and Port.] In Spain and Portugal, any daughter of a king.

infante [Sp. and Port.] In Spain and Portugal, any son of a king.

infanterie [F.] The infantry.

inférieur [F.] Under; below; lower.

in ferrum pro libertate ruebant [L.] They rushed upon the sword in pursuit of their liberty.

in fieri [L.] In the state of becoming; in creation.

infima species [L.] The lowest species.

in fine [L.] In the end; at the conclusion.

infine [F.] Infinite; endless.

in flagrante delicto [L.] While the crime blazes; in the act. (*The robber was caught* in flagrante delicto.)

in flamman flammas, in mare fundis aquas [L.] You pour fire into fire, water into the sea; you bring coals to Newcastle.

in forma pauperis [L.] In the form of a pauper; as a poor man.

in foro conscientiae [L.] In the court of conscience.

in foro divino [L.] In the divine court; before God.

in foro humano [L.] In a human court; in a court of law.

infra [L.] Beneath; lower; inferior; also, further down on the page or in the book; on a following page.

in fumo [L.] In smoke.

in futuro [L.] In the future.

in genere [L.] In kind; in similar things.

ingénieur civil [F.] A civil engineer.

ingénieur des mines [F.] A mining engineer.

ingénieur du son [F.] A sound engineer.

ingens telum necessitas [L.] A powerful weapon is necessity.

ingénue [F.] A naïve young girl; also, in the theatre, an actress who specializes in playing innocent maidens.

in globo [L.] In its entirety; in the full extent of its size.

ingratum si dixeris, omnia dixeris [L.] If you say ungrateful, you have said all, i.e., all vices are related to ingratitude.

in gremio legis [L.] In the bosom of the law; under judicial custody.

Inhaber [G.] Proprietor.

inhabile [F.] Unskilled; unfit for a particular job or occupation; inexpert.

in hoc signo vinces [L.] In this sign thou shalt conquer; words written on the cross, seen in a vision by Constantine the Great on the eve of his conversion to Christianity.

in horas [L.] Each hour.

iniquissimam pacem justissimo bello antefero [L.] I prefer the most unfair peace to the most righteous war.

initiatus [L.] An initiate.

initium sapientiae timor Domini [L.] Fear of the Lord is the beginning of wisdom.

in jure [L.] In law; in a court of justice.

injuriarum remedium est oblivio [L.] The best remedies for injuries are to forget them.

inklusive [G.] Inclusive.

Inländer [G.] A native.

in limine [L.] At the start; in the very beginning; on the threshhold.

in loco [L.] In place; in its proper location.

in loco parentis [L.] In the position or place of a parent; serving as a parental authority. (*He acted toward his niece* in loco parentis.)

in lumine tuo videbimus lumen [L.] In the light shall we see light; used as the motto of Columbia University.

in malam partem [L.] Toward the bad side; in an unfavorable way.

in mari aquam quaerit [L.] He searches water in the sea.

in medias res [L.] In the middle of things, especially in the middle of the plot of a story or play. (*The narrative began* in medias res.)

in memoriam [L.] In memory of.

innig [G.] Sincere; earnest; well-meaning.

in nomine [L.] In the name of.

innovamiento [Sp.] An innovation.

in nubibus [L.] In the clouds; hence, vague; uncertain; incapable of concrete actions.

in nuce [L.] In a nutshell.

innuendo [L.] An oblique hint or suggestion of something; an inference rather than a positive assertion. (*I resent your slanderous innuendos.*)

in oculis civium [L.] In the eyes of the citizens; publicly.

in omnia paratus [L.] In all things prepared.

inopem me copia fecit [L.] Plenty has made me poor.

in ovo [L.] In the egg, i.e., in the beginning.

in pace [L.] In peace.

in perpetuum [L.] In perpetuity; forever.

in petto. [It.] In the breast; hence, hidden; secret; clandestine.

in pios usus [L.] For pious purposes.

in posse [L.] Potentially; as a possibility of occurring or existing. (*The money existed* in posse.) Cf. *in esse.*

in posterum [L.] In or for the future.

in potentia [L.] In potentiality; possibly.

in potestate parentis [L.] In the power of a parent; within parental jurisdiction.

in praesenti [L.] At the present; now.

in principio [L.] In the beginning; at the start.

in propria causa nemo judex [L.] No one can serve as a judge in his own cause.

in propria persona [L.] In his own person; in his native and essential character. (*Stripped of all disguise, the devil appeared* in propria persona.)

in puris naturalibus [L.] Purely natural, i.e., in a state of nudity; naked.

in re [L.] In the thing; in the matter of; concerning.

in rebus agendis [L.] In the management of business affairs.

in rerum natura [L.] In the nature of things; occurring naturally; indigenous to the proper order of affairs.

inro [Jap.] In Japanese art, a small lacquer box used to hold medicine.

in saecula saeculorum [L.] For ages and ages; for eternity.

insalutato hospite [L.] Without saluting one's host; without saying good-bye.

insanus omnis furere credit caeteros [L.] Every madman thinks all other men mad.

inshallah [Ar.] God willing; if God so desires.

insidiator [L.] One who waits in ambush; a hidden assassin.

in situ [L.] In its original location; unmoved. (*The archaeologist showed a photograph of the cave with the pottery* in situ.)

insouciance [F.] Indifference towards everything; careless unconcern; heedlessness.

in spe [L.] In hope.

inspice cautus eris [L.] Look in the mirror and you will be wise, i.e., know yourself.

in spiritualibus [L.] In spiritual things.

instantia crucis [L.] The crucial instant.

instar omnium [L.] Worth all the rest.

in statu pupillari [L.] In the state of being a pupil.

in statu quo ante bellum [L.] As it was before the war.

in status quo [L.] In the state in which it was; in the former condition.

instituteur [F.] Teacher; instructor, especially one who instructs in a classroom.

in summo periculo timor misericordiam non recipit [L.] In great danger, fear turns a deaf ear to pity.

intaglio [It.] In art, a figure or pattern incised into a surface like metal or stone; also, the process of incising itself.

in te Domine speravi [L.] In thee, O Lord, have I trusted.

integer vitae scelerisque purus [L.] Blameless of life and free from guilt.

intellige ut credas [L.] Understand in order that you may believe.

in temporalibus [L.] In temporal things.

inter alia [L.] Among other things.

inter alios [L.] Among others; among other people.

inter arma silent leges [L.] Amid the clash of arms the law is silent, i.e., there is no justice during times of war.

interdum vulgus rectum videt [L.] Occasionally even the vulgar crowd sees things clearly.

interesado [Sp.] Partner; cohort.

intéressant [F.] Interesting; attractive.

Interessengemeinschaft [G.] A community of interests; a cartel.

intérieur [F.] The interior; the home; domestic life.

intermède [F.] A one-act play; an interlude.

intermezzo [It.] (1.) A short song or ballet given between the acts of a play or opera. (2.) In music, a brief passage connecting two different parts of a composition.

inter nos [L.] Between us; among ourselves.

internuncio. See *internunzio*.

internunzio [It.] A representative of the pope, of less rank than a *nunzio* (q.v.).

inter se [L.] Among ourselves.

inter spem et metum [L.] Between hope and fear.

intervallum [Sp.] An interval.

inter vivos [L.] Among the living; in law, pertains to a gift changing title from one living person to another.

in thesi [L.] As a thesis; as a proposition. (*The plan sounded good* in thesi.)

intimado [Sp.] An intimate associate; a bosom friend.

intime [F.] Intimate; close; cozy.

in totidem verbis [L.] In so many words.

in toto [L.] In total; as a whole.

intrada [It.] In music, an introductory composition; a prelude.

intrado [Sp.] Arrival; entrance.

intra muros [L.] Within the walls, especially of a city.

intransigeance [F.] Uncompromising; unrelenting; unmoving.

intransigeant [F.] An uncompromising person; one who will not alter his position.

in transitu [L.] In transit; while in the process of going.

introuvable [F.] Lost; missing.

in un batter d'occhio [It.] In the twinkling of an eye; in a second.

in usu [L.] In use.

in usum vulgi [L.] For the use of the crowd; for public use.

in utero [L.] In the womb; not yet born or created.

inutile [F.] Useless; of no profit or value.

in vacuo [L.] In a vacuum; hence, not pertaining to anything solid or concrete.

invenit [L.] He or she invented it.

inverso ordine [L.] The order reversed.

in Vertretung [G.] On behalf of; by order.

in vino veritas [L.] In wine, truth, i.e., the drunkard speaks honestly.

in virtute sunt multi adscensus [L.] In the approach to virtue there are many steps.

invita Minerva [L.] Against Minerva, i.e., without the blessings, such as natural ability and talent, which the goddess Minerva bestows.

ipsa quidem virtus pretium sibi [L.] Virtue is indeed its own reward.

ipsa sibi obstat magnitudo [L.] His very greatness stands in the way.

ipse dixit [L.] He himself said it; said of one who has delivered an authoritative statement on a subject; also, said ironically of one who pretends to such knowledge.

ipsissima verba [L.] The same words.

ira de irmãos, ira de diabos [Port.] The wrath of brothers, the wrath of devils.

ira furor brevis est [L.] Anger is a brief form of insanity.

(das) irdische Glück [G.] Earthly happiness; worldly fortune.

irrepit in hominum mentes dissimulatio [L.] Dissimulation creeps gradually into the minds of men.

irridens cuspide figo [L.] Through ridicule I wound with pricks.

isba [Russ.] In Russia, a small log cabin.

(l')istesso tempo [It.] In music, an indication that while the meter changes the beat stays the same.

ita dis placuit [L.] Thus it has pleased the gods.

ita est [L.] Thus it is; and so it is.

ita lex scripta est [L.] Thus is the law written.

ite missa est [L.] Go, the congregation is dismissed; words spoken by a priest at the termination of Communion services in the Roman Catholic Church.

iterum [L.] Again.

ivan [Persian] In Islamic architecture, a large vaulted hall bounded by walls on three sides and open on the fourth.

ivoire [F.] Ivory.

ivresse [F.] Inebriation; drunkenness.

izba. See isba.

izquierda [Sp.] On the left.

J

ja [G.] Yes; certainly.

jaboteur [F.] A gossip; one who chatters incessantly; a jabberer.

j'accuse [F.] I accuse; first lines of Emile Zola's famous open letter denouncing the persecutors of Dreyfus.

Jacquerie [F.] An insurrection of northeastern French peasantry in 1358 against the land-holding aristocracy; the name derives from the contemptuous title, Jacques Bonhomme, given members of the third estate by the nobility.

jacta est alea [L.] The die is cast; words reputedly said by Julius Caesar as he crossed the Rubicon River.

jäger [G.] A hunter; also, a rifleman.

Jahr [G.] Year.

Jahre lehren mehr als Bücher [G.] Years teach more than books.

jai alai [Sp.] A Spanish form of handball played on a walled concrete court with a hard rubber ball and long, ribbed wicker gloves.

j'ai doube [F.] I adjust; in chess, used to indicate that a player is adjusting a piece rather than moving it.

jalousie de métier [F.] Jealousy of the trade; professional jealousy.

jaloux d'acquérir de la gloire [F.] Desirous of acquiring glory.

jambeau [F.] A plate of armor designed to protect the shins and upper ankles.

jambiya [Ar.] A double-edged dagger with a rib running down the center of the blade.

jamma [Hindi] A cotton cloth worn by Indian men.

jam satis [L.] Enough by this time.

jangada [Port. and Sp.] A raft; a kind of catamaran used in parts of South America.

janitrix [L.] A female doorkeeper; a woman janitor.

januae mentis [L.] The doors of the mind.

januis clausis [L.] With closed doors; in private.

Janvier [F.] The month of January.

jao [Hindi] Go; get out of here.

japa [Skr.] In Hinduism, the repetition of a sacred name or phrase carried out as a religious exercise.

japa yoga [Skr.] In Hinduism, a form of yoga in which the devotee seeks union with higher forces through the audible and subvocal repetition of prayers.

jardin [F.] A garden; a park.

jardin des plants [F.] A botanical garden.

jardin fruitier [F.] A fruit garden.

jardinière [F.] A decorated flower pot or plant holder.

jardin potager [F.] A kitchen garden.

Ja und Nein ist ein langer Streit [G.] Yes and no is an old argument.

ja wohl [G.] Yes, indeed; but yes; certainly.

jeder Tag ist ein kleines Leben [G.] Every day is a small lifetime.

jeder Vogel hat sein Nest lieb [G.] Every bird loves its own nest.

jeder Weib will lieber schön als fromm sein [G.] Every woman prefers prettiness to saintliness.

jeel [Hindi] In India, a large body of water such as a lake, pool, bay, etc.

jefe [Sp.] The leader; the head; the commander.

jejunus raro stomachus vulgaris temnit [L.] A hungry man rarely spurns the common food.

jeloodar [Persian] In Persia, the head groom of a stable; one charged with the care and feeding of horses.

je maintiendrai [F.] I will maintain; used as the motto of the Netherlands.

je me fie en Dieu [F.] I trust in God.

je m'en vais chercher un grand peut-être [F.] I go to search a great perhaps; the dying words of Rabelais.

je ne cherche qu'un [F.] I seek but one; I seek only God.

je ne sais pas [F.] I do not know.

je ne sais quoi [F.] I know not what, i.e., an indefinable quality which makes something strangely alluring. (*She possesses a* je ne sais quoi *which makes her appealing.*)

je prends mon bien où je le trouve [F.] I take my property wherever I find it; words spoken by Molière in answer to a charge of plagiarism.

je suis prêt [F.] I am ready.

jet d'eau [F.] A stream of water; a fountain jet.

jet de gaz [F.] A jet of gas; a gas flame.

jet de lumière [F.] A ray of light.

jeter le manche après la cognée [F.] To throw the handle after the hatchet, i.e., to lose heart; to give up; to throw in the towel.

jeu [F.] Game; sport; pastime.

jeu de main [F.] Hand-play, i.e., play accompanied by blows; physical tomfoolery; roughhousing.

jeu de mots [F.] A play on words; a pun; a double-entendre (q.v.).

jeu d'esprit [F.] A witty comment; a smart saying; a joke.

jeu de théâtre [F.] A stage trick; a showy device to gain applause.

Jeudi [F.] Thursday.

jeune fille [F.] A young lady; an unmarried girl.

jeune premier [F.] In theater, the leading man in a play; the hero; the lover.

jeune première [F.] In theater, the actress playing a leading part.

jeunesse dorée [F.] Flaming youths; rich and slightly debauched young men of good family.

(le) jeu ne vaut pas la chandelle [F.] The game is not worth the candle.

jeune veuve [F.] In theater, the role of a young widow.

jeux de prince [F.] Games of princes; royal sports; also, amusements of nobility carried on at the expense of the humble.

je vis en espoir [F.] I live in hope.

jezail [Afghani] In Afghanistan, a long, heavy rifle.

jhil. See jeel

jhula [Hindi] In India, a swinging bridge made of rope or vines commonly found spanning river gorges in the Himalayas.

jihad [Ar.] In Islam, a holy war; also, any crusade carried out for a rightful and holy purpose.

jimigaki [Jap.] In Japanese metal work, a term applied to highly polished surfaces.

jinn [Ar.] In Islamic myths, a supernatural being, capable of magic transformations and endowed with great force for good or evil.

jinriksha [Jap.] In Japan, a two-wheeled carrier pulled by one or two bearers and used primarily for the transportation of paying passengers.

jnana [Skr.] In Hinduism, knowledge of the true self attained through self-investigation; also, in yogic philosophy, detachment of the senses from all external objects.

Joannes est nomen ejus [L.] His name is John; used as the motto of Puerto Rico, originally named after St. John the Baptist.

joci causa [L.] For the sake of a joke.

joculator [L.] A joker; a clown; a professional jester or comedian.

Johannistag [G.] St. John's Day; a midsummer's day.

joie de vivre [F.] The joy of living; a fun-loving attitude toward life; an exhilaration in the day-to-day events of ordinary existence.

joies de mariage [F.] The joys of marriage; used facetiously to characterize pleasures of a transient nature.

joindre les mains, c'est bien; les ouvrir, c'est mieux [F.] To clasp the hands in prayer is fine, to open them in giving is better.

jongleur [F.] Itinerant musicians in medieval France and England.

jornada [Sp.] A day's journey; also, in Mexico and the Southwest United States, a continuous stretch of wasteland.

jour [F.] Day; daytime.

jour de fête [F.] A day of feast; a festival day.

jour gras [F.] A fat day, i.e., a day on which meat may be eaten; a day of feasting; cf. *jour maigre.*

jour maigre [F.] A meager day, i.e., a day of fasting; also, in the Roman Catholic Church, a day on which meat is not eaten; cf. *jour gras.*

journal intime [F.] An intimate journal; a diary.

journal pour rire [F.] A journal for laughter; a comic newspaper or periodical.

(le) jour viendra [F.] The day will come.

joyeux Noël [F.] Joyous Noel; merry Christmas.

jubbah [Ar.] A long robe worn in Moslem countries as daily dress for both men and women.

jubilate Deo [L.] Rejoice in God.

jucunda rerum vicissitudo [L.] A pleasant change of circumstances.

jucundi acti labores [L.] Past labor is sweet.

Judaïque [F.] Jewish.

Judendeutsch [G.] A dialect of German spoken by Jews.

Judenhetze [G.] Agitation against Jews.

judex damnatur cum nocens absolvitur [L.] The judge is condemned when a guilty person goes free.

judex est lex loquens [L.] The judge is the law speaking.

judicieusement [F.] Judiciously; with discretion.

judicium capitale [L.] Capital judgment, i.e., a sentence of death.

judicium Dei [L.] The judgment of God.

judicium parium aut leges terrae [L.] The judgment of one's peers or the law of the land; a principle of the British legal system, dating from the signing of the Magna Carta, guaranteeing that a man can be judged only in the two ways mentioned above.

jugement [F.] Judgment; discretion; also, in law, the judgment in a lawcase.

jugement définitif [F.] A definitive judgment; also, in law, an absolute decree.

(Le) Jugement Dernier [F.] The Last Judgment.

juge sacrificium [L.] A perpetual sacrifice.

Juggernath [Hindi] A colossal statue of the Hindu god, Vishnu, carried on a wheeled chariot through the streets of South Indian villages, especially in the village of Puri in Orissa, during religious holidays. Worshippers have been said to throw themselves beneath its wheels; a juggernaut; any irresistible force that crushes all resistance in its path.

jugulare mortuos [L.] To butcher the dead; to kill the already slain.

Juillet [F.] The month of July.

Juin [F.] The month of June.

julienne [F.] A clear broth containing strips of vegetables; also, any meat or vegetable cut in strips.

Jungfrau [G.] A maiden; a virgin.

Junker [G.] A youthful German aristocrat, especially one native to Prussia.

juntate á los buenos y serás uno de ellos [Sp.] Seek the company of the good and you will be one of them.

junto [Sp.] United; joined together.

Jupiter ne quidem omnibus placet [L.] Not even Jupiter himself pleases everyone.

Jupiter pluvius [L.] Jupiter the Rain-giver.

Jupiter tonans [L.] Jupiter the Thunderer.

juramentado [Sp.] A member of the Moro tribe, a Philippine community embracing Islam, who has taken an oath to die fighting Christians.

jura regalia [L.] The privileges accorded a king or his family; the special allowances made for royalty.

jurare in verba magistri [L.] To swear by the words of the master, i.e., to accept without discrimination all dogma preached by a teacher; to take things on blind faith.

juravi lingua, mentem injuratam gero [L.] I have sworn with my tongue, but I have a mind unsworn.

jure belli [L.] By the rights of war.

jure divino [L.] By divine right.

jure humano [L.] Human right; by the right of being a man.

jure mariti [L.] In law, by the right of the husband.

jure matrimonii [L.] In law, by right of marriage.

jure non dono [L.] In law, by right, not by gift.

jure sanguinis [L.] In law, by the right of blood.

jure uxoris [L.] In law, by right of the wife.

juribasso [Malay] A master of language, i.e., an interpreter.

juris peritus [L.] Versed in the law.

jus [F.] Juice; gravy.

jus [L.] Law.

jus canonicum [L.] Canon law.

jus civile [L.] The civil law.

jus commercii [L.] The right of commerce.

jus et norma loquendi [L.] The law and rule of speaking; the common usage of a language.

jus gentium [L.] The law of nations.

jus gladii [L.] The right of the sword.

jus hereditatis [L.] The right of heredity.

jus inter gentes [L.] The law between nations.

jus jurandum [L.] An oath.

jus mariti [L.] In law, the right of a husband to inherit the property of his wife.

jus naturae [L.] Natural law.

jus nocendi [L.] The law of retaliation.

jus possessionis [L.] The law of possession.

jus post liminii [L.] The law whereby the rights and property, usurped during time of war, are returned to their proper owners.

jus primae noctis [L.] The right of the first night; the right of a feudal lord to deflower the brides of his vassals; cf. *droit du seigneur.*

jus privatum [L.] Private law.

jus proprietatis [L.] The right of property.

jus regium [L.] Right of the crown.

jus relictae [L.] In law, the right of a widow to inherit the property of her husband.

jus scriptum [L.] Written law.

jus suffragii [L.] The right of suffrage.

justa bella quibus necessaria [L.] Wars are just for those that find them necessary.

justa causa [L.] A just cause.

juste-milieu [F.] The just average; the golden mean; the middle course between extremes.

justitae tenax [L.] Tenacious of justice.

justitia omnibus [L.] Justice for all; used as the motto of the District of Columbia.

justitia soror incorrupta fides [L.] Uncorruptible faith, the sister of justice.

justitia suum cuique distribuit [L.] Justice renders to everyone his due.

justitia virtutum regina [L.] Justice is the queen of the virtues.

juvenilia [L.] Literature produced by children; also, the efforts of novice writers or artists; immature creations.

juventus [L.] Youth.

juxta fluvium puteum fodit [L.] He digs a well near a river; he is bringing coals to Newcastle.

j'y suis, j'y reste [F.] Here I am, here I stay; a statement made by Marie Maurice de MacMahon in 1855 during the Crimean War when advised to quit the Malakhov Tower.

K

Kaaba [Ar.] The most holy building in the Moslem city of Mecca, containing the sacred black stone, the main object of Moslem pilgrimage.

kabab [Hindi] Meat that has been turned and cooked on a skewer; cf. cabob.

kago [Jap.] In Japan, a palanquin.

kai ta loipa [Gr.] And so on; et cetera; and so forth.

kakemono [Jap.] A Japanese scroll painting mounted on fine brocade and hung in an alcove built exclusively for the purpose.

kalpa [Hindi] In Hinduism, an epochal measurement of time representing approximately four billion years and based on a day and night in the life of the god Brahma.

kalpa [Sk.] In Hinduism, an age of the world; a period of four billion years said to represent but one day and night in the life of the god Brahma.

kam [Hindi] Work: labor; one's occupation.

Kamerad [G.] Comrade; friend.

kamikaze [Jap.] During World War II, a Japanese aviator who has taken an oath to pilot his craft directly into an enemy ship, destroying himself along with the enemy.

Kampf ums Dasein [G.] The struggle for existence.

Kanaka [Polynesian] A Hawaiian; also, anyone from the Polynesian or Melanesian islands.

Kanonenfutter [G.] Cannon fodder.

Kapellmeister [G.] The conductor of an orchestra.

kaput [G.] Ruined; destroyed; all finished. (*Because of his stupidity in handling the money our whole business was soon kaput.*)

karate [Jap.] A form of self-defense originated on the Japanese island of Okinawa, characterized by open-handed attack aimed at certain vulnerable nerve centers throughout the body.

Karikatur [G.] Caricature; cartoon; a satirical drawing.

karma [Skr.] In Hinduism, the belief that all acts have consequences inexorably dependent on the quality of these acts; also, fate in general; destiny; the pattern of life.

Kasse [G.] A money box.

Katzenjammer [G.] The aftereffect of indulgence in intoxicating liquor; a hangover.

kaum gegrüsst, gemieden [G.] No sooner greeted than avoided.

kavass [Turkish] In Turkey, a guard attending an official dignitary or diplomat; also, a police officer.

kayak [Eskimo] A small one or two man lightweight canoe made of seal skin stretched over a wooden frame; also, a lightweight canvas canoe popular with sportsmen.

keddah [Hindi] In India, an area in which newly captured wild elephants are kept and trained.

kef [Ar.] Indian hemp; marijuana, especially that used in the Middle East; also, the torpid state resulting from the use of such narcotics.

keffieh [Ar.] In the Middle East, a bandana worn over the head as protection from the sun.

keine Rosen ohne Dornen [G.] No rose without a thorn.

kein Talent, doch ein Charakter [G.] No talent, but what a character.

Kellner [G.] A waiter; barman.

kepi [F.] In France, a round military cap.

kermis [Dutch] In the Netherlands, a popular country festival.

khamsin [Ar.] In the Near East, a hot wind originating in the desert.

khan [Ar.] In the Middle East, a stopping place on a road; an inn; a caravanserai.

khan [Turkish] Sir; lord; used originally as a title of nobility among the Tartars of Central Asia and today as a common title of respect in Moslem countries.

khana [Hindi] Food; a meal.

khedive [Turkish] Title accorded to Turkish governors in Egypt from the years 1867 to 1914.

khelwat [Ar.] Privacy; seclusion; also, a private conversation or interview.

khidmatgar [Hindi] In India and Persia, a waiter; a male servant assigned to service a particular task at an inn or resthouse.

kiaugh [Sc.] Pain; problems; worry; difficulty.

kibbutz [Heb.] A collectivist settlement in Israel.

kibei [Jap.] An American born to Japanese parents and educated in Japan; cf. nisei.

kibitz [Yidd.] Colloquially, to give unasked for advice; to intrude with one's own opinions when they are not solicited, especially during a card game, chess match, etc.

kibitzer [Yidd.] Colloquially, one who kibitzes (q.v.).

kimmer [Sc.] A young girl; a lass.

kimono [Jap.] A loose robe fastened with a sash, the traditional costume of the Japanese.

kinnikinnick [Algonquian] An herbal tobacco smoked by northeastern Indian tribes of the United States.

kinó [Russ.] The motion pictures; films; the cinema.

Kirche, Küche, und Kinder [G.] Church, kitchen, and children; said by William II to define a woman's responsibilities.

kismet [Turkish] Destiny; fate. (*Their meeting was not accident; it was kismet.*)

kittereen [Hindi] In West India, a wagon; a cart.

kiva [Southwest Indian] Among the Pueblo Indians, an underground chamber devoted to religious ceremonies and meeting of the tribal council.

kloof [Dutch] In South Africa, a deep-cut gorge; a gully; a precipitous ravine.

kohl [Ar.] A black salve, like mascara, used by women of the east to highlight and darken their eyes.

kolkhoz [Russ.] In Soviet Russia, a collective farm.

kolossal [G.] Colossal; enormous; gargantuan.

König [G.] King.

kop [Dutch] In South Africa, a hill; a mountain.

kopje [Dutch] In South Africa, a small hill or mountain.

korsh [Russ.] A vessel made of silver, wood or other materials, used as a ladle.

kowtow [Chi.] To knock the head, i.e., to bow and scrape the floor; to make an obsequious display before a superior.

(der) Krieg ist lustig den Unerfahrnen [G.] War is great fun for the greenhorn.

Kriegspiel or *Kriegespiel* [G.] War games in miniature, played with pins, models, flags, etc.; a game or exercise in strategy.

ktema es aei [Gr.] A possession forever.

kuchnia [Pol.] Kitchen.

kulak [Russ.] A peasant landlord; members of the land-owning lower class in Russia.

Kultur [G.] Culture; civilization.

Kulturgeschichte [G.] The history of art and society.

Kulturkampf der Menschheit [G.] The struggle of civilization.

kundalini [Skr.] In Hinduism, a force supposedly located at the base of the spine which when activated leads to a state of higher consciousness.

Kunst ist die rechte Hand der Natur [G.] Art is the right hand of nature.

kvas [Russ.] A bitter beer made of fermented rye or barley and popular in Russia.

Kyrie eleison [Gr.] Lord have mercy on us; a part of the traditional Mass.

L

---

labeur [F.] Work; labor.

labitur et labetur [L.] It flows and it will flow.

laborare est orare [L.] To labor is to pray.

labor callum obducit dolori [L.] Labor hardens one to suffering.

labor est etiam ipsa voluptas [L.] Labor even is pleasant.

labor ipse voluptas [L.] Labor itself is pleasure.

labor omnia vincit [L.] Labor conquers all; used as the motto of the State of Oklahoma.

labuntur et imputantur [L.] The hours fly away and are laid to our account.

lâcheté [F.] Cowardice; meanness.

lâcheur [F.] An unreliable man.

Lade nicht Alles in ein Schiff [G.] Do not put all the load on one ship; do not place all your hopes on one possibility.

Ladeplatz [G.] Loading place.

laesa majestas [L.] Lese majesty; a crime committed against a king; high treason; cf. *lèse-majesté.*

lagniappe [Creole F.] In Louisiana, a small gift given by a storekeeper to his customers in recognition of their patronage; hence, an inconsequential gift; a trifle.

laine [F.] Wool; also, a garment made of wool.

laisser-aller [F.] To let go; to relax all inhibitions; unlimited abandon.

laisser-passer [F.] Let pass, i.e., a card of admittance; a pass.

laissez-faire [F.] A policy of noninterference, especially a policy disallowing governmental regulation of economic affairs.

laitue [F.] Lettuce.

là, là [F.] So-so; middling; not too bad, not too good; *comme ci, comme ça* (q.v.).

lamé [F.] A fabric in which metallic threads, often gold or silver, are woven with threads of cotton, silk, or other fibers.

laminella [L.] A thin layer.

lampe à alcool [F.] A spirit lamp; a lamp that burns on alcohol.

(de)lana caprina [L.] Of the wool of a goat, i.e., concerning something that does not exist, such as goat's wool.

lanai [Hawaiian] In Hawaii, a porch or verandah.

Ländler [G.] An Austrian dance, done in slow triple-time and popular in the nineteenth century.

Landsting [Dan] The senatorial branch of the Danish legislature.

Landsturm [G.] A landstorm, i.e., a draft of male citizens during time of war.

Landtag [G.] A legislative assembly; formerly the name of the Prussian national lawmaking body.

Landwehr [G.] In Germany, an emergency militia; a national guard.

langage des dieux [F.] The language of the gods, i.e., poetry.

Langlauf [G.] In skiing, moving in a crosscountry direction.

Langläufer [G.] One who skis crosscountry.

langsyne [Sc.] Long ago.

langue [F.] Language; native tongue.

langue maternelle [F.] The mother tongue; the native language.

langue morte [F.] A dead language, i.e., a language no longer in common use, such as Latin; cf. *langue vivante*.

langue vivante [F.] A living language; one still in common use; cf. *langue morte*.

langueur [F.] Languor; lassitude; sluggishness; lack of interest in life.

lanx satura [L.] A dish filled with a variety of fruits; hence, a motley combination; a medley.

lapin [F.] A rabbit; also, the skin or fur of a rabbit.

lapis [L.] A stone.

lapis philosophorum [L.] The philosopher's stone; hence, a cure-all; a panacea; also, in alchemy, a magical stone which can transform base metals into gold.

lapsus [L.] An error; a slip; a lapse.

lapsus calami [L.] A slip of the pen.

lapsus linguae [L.] A slip of the tongue.

lapsus memoriae [L.] A slip of the memory.

lares [L.] In Roman religion, the gods that protect the home; household deities.

lares et penates [L.] Roman gods of the household.

larghetto [It.] In music, a direction calling for a medium-slow tempo.

largo [It.] In music, a direction calling for a slow, stately tempo.

larmes aux yeux [F.] Tears in the eyes.

larmes de crocodile [F.] Crocodile tears.

larmoyant [F.] Lachrymose; tearful; with tears in one's eyes. (*The drama was* larmoyant *for his unsentimental tastes.*)

lascar [Hindi] In India, a sailor; a seafarer.

lascia parlare a me [It.] "To me leave thou the task of speaking": *Dante.*

lasciate ogni speranza, voi ch'entrate [It.] "Abandon all hope, ye who enter here": the words written across the gateway of hell in Dante's *Inferno*.

latet anguis in herba [L.] A snake lurks in the grass.

lathe biosas [Gr.] Seek obscurity, i.e., live your life quietly; shun fame.

Latine [L.] Latin.

Latine dictum [L.] Spoken in Latin.

latrante uno, latrat statim et alter canis [L.] When one dog barks, another soon follows.

latte [It.] Milk.

lauda la moglie e tienti donzello [It.] Praise a wife and stay a bachelor.

laudari a laudato viro [L.] To be praised by a man who is praised.

laudator temporis acti [L.] A lauder of times gone by. One who is obsessed with the glories of the past.

laudum immensa cupido [L.] An unquenchable desire for praise.

laus Deo [L.] Praise God.

laus propria sordet [L.] Self-praise is degrading.

lavabo [F.] Wash-stand; wash-basin; sink; also, a washroom; a toilet.

lá vão leis onde querem cruzados [Port.] Laws go where dollars please.

Lawine [G.] An avalanche.

lebe wohl [G.] Farewell; good-bye.

leben [G.] To live; to be alive.

Lebensabend [G.] The evening of life.

leben sie wohl [G.] Good-bye; farewell.

lección [Sp.] Lesson; studies; lecture.

legalis homo [L.] A legal man, i.e., one who is in good standing with the laws of his community; a respectable citizen; also, in law, a man accorded all the rights and privileges of the existing legal system.

legato [It.] In music, a direction calling for a smooth rendering without any break in continuity or tempo.

léger [F.] Light; airy; nimble but lacking profundity.

légèreté [F.] Lightness; gaiety; frivolity.

legimus, ne legantur [L.] We read that others may be spared reading; used as an apology of the literary critic.

Légion étrangère [F.] The Foreign Legion.

légionnaire [F.] A member of any legion.

légume [F.] Vegetable.

légumes vert [F.] Green vegetables; greens.

Lehrer [G.] Teacher; master; instructor.

lei [Chi.] An ancient Chinese bronze vessel, sometimes cast in the shape of an animal.

lei [Hawaiian] A garland of flowers traditionally presented to visitors arriving or departing from the Hawaiian Islands.

leidenschaftlich [G.] In music, a direction calling for vehement and emotional rendering.

leitmotiv [G.] In opera and especially in Wagnerian opera, a musical passage that describes a particular character or situation and which recurs every time that character or situation appears.

lendemain [F.] Tomorrow; the next day.

lene tormentum [L.] Mild torment.

lentamente [It.] In music, a direction calling for a slow tempo.

lentando [It.] In music, a direction calling for a slowing of the tempo.

lentissimo [It.] In music, a direction calling for an extremely slow tempo.

leone fortior fides [L.] Faith is stronger than a lion.

leonem ex ungue [L.] From his claw we may know the lion.

leonine societas [L.] A lion's partnership, i.e., a relationship in which one partner is awarded all the profits while the other suffers all the disadvantages.

lèse-majesté [F.] Lese majesty; an act of crime or disrespect against a sovereign; high treason; cf. *laesa majestas.*

letras sin virtud son perlas en el muladar [Sp.] Learning without virtue is like pearls on a dunghill.

lettre chargée [F.] A registered letter.

lettre d'avis [F.] A letter of advice.

lettre de cachet [F.] A secret letter; a sealed letter, especially from one of great authority ordering the arrest of a citizen.

lettre de créance [F.] A letter of credentials.

lettre de crédit [F.] A letter of credit.

levada [Port.] An artificial watercourse built for purposes of agricultural irrigation.

leve fit, quod fertur, onus [L.] The well-shouldered burden is light.

levée en masse [F.] A large public gathering; an unruly mob; also, a public draft; a conscription.

lex [L.] Law.

lex appetit perfectum [L.] The law aims at perfection.

lex loci [L.] The law governing the place one inhabits.

lex mercatoria [L.] Mercantile law.

lex non cogit ad impossibilia [L.] The law does not force one to do impossible things.

lex non scripta [L.] The law that is not written; unwritten rules; common law.

lex scripta [L.] Written law; rules of law that are officially recorded in the books.

lex succurrit ignoranti [L.] The law helps the ignorant.

lex talionis [Lt.] The law of equivalent retaliation or recompense; an eye for an eye.

lex uno ore omnes alloquitur [L.] The law speaks with one mouth to everyone.

ley de fuga [Sp.] The law of flight; in Spanish America, the privilege of the police to kill any prisoner attempting to escape punishment.

libeccio [It.] In Italy, a southwest wind.

libertad y orden [Sp.] Liberty and order; used as the motto of Colombia.

libertas [L.] Liberty.

liberté, égalité, fraternité [F.] Liberty, equality, fraternity; a popular slogan during the French Revolution.

libraire [F.] A bookseller.

Libraire-éditeur [F.] Publisher and bookseller.

libre [F.] Free; independent; liberated.

libretto [It.] The text of an opera; also, a book containing such a text.

libro [Sp.] Book.

libros y amigos pocos y buenos [Sp.] Books and friends should be few and good.

licentia vatum [L.] Poetic license; the privilege of the creator to exaggerate for artistic effect.

Licht [G.] Light.

Liebe [G.] Love; affection.

Liebeslieder [G.] Love songs.

lied [G.] A song; a tune; also, the lyric of a song.

Lieder ohne Worte [G.] Songs without words.

Liedertafel [G.] An all-male singing society.

limae labor et mora [L.] The labor and delay of the file; the laborious hours spent polishing and refining a work of literature.

limbus [L.] Limbo.

linga [Skr.] In Hinduism, a stone phallus, representative of the god Siva and the animating energy he personifies.

lis litem generat [L.] Strife begets strife.

lis pendens [L.] A pending suit; in law, indicates that the court has control over all material evidence bearing on a case.

lis sub judice [L.] In law, a legal matter still before the judge; a lawsuit not yet concluded.

lit de justice [F.] The bed of justice; the throne occupied by the king of France during sessions of Parliament.

litem lite resolvere [L.] To clear up one problem by creating another.

literati [L.] The educated classes; the intelligentsia; men of letters.

literatim [L.] Literally; letter for letter.

littera scripta manet [L.] The written word remains.

litterae divinae [L.] Divine letters; the study of religion; theology.

litterae humaniores [L.] Humane letters; the study of humanities.

littérateur [F.] A man of letters; a literary man.

livre [F.] Book.

livre d'images [F.] A book of images; a picture book.

llano [Sp.] In the northern regions of South America, a broad, flat plain.

locanda [It.] A lodging house.

locataire [F.] A tenant; an occupant; lodger.

loco citato [L.] In the place cited; in the location stipulated; in the passage mentioned.

loco supra citato [L.] In the place cited above.

locum tenens [L.] A substitute; a deputy; one who takes the place of another, especially of a doctor, lawyer or clergyman.

locus classicus [L.] A passage from classical literature; also, a definitive text for the clarification of certain words or concepts.

locus criminis [L.] The place or scene of the crime.

locus paenitentiae [L.] Place for repentance.

locus poenitentiae [L.] Place for repentance, i.e., a jail; a prison.

locus sigilli [L.] The place of the seal.

locus standi [L.] A recognized position which carries with it the right to be heard or to exert authority. (*You have no* locus standi *in this argument.*)

logement garni [F.] Furnished lodgings.

lohan [Chi.] In China, a spiritually perfected man; a saint or sage.

loi [F.] Law; rule; statute.

loin des yeux, loin du coeur [F.] Far from the eyes, far from the heart.

(la) loi permet souvent ce que defend l'honneur [F.] The law often permits that which honor forbids.

l'on craint la vieillesse, que l'on n'est pas sûr de pouvoir atteindre [F.] We fear old age, which we are not even sure we will attain.

longe absit [L.] Far be it.

longéron [F.] A structural section of an airplane that runs from the front to the back of its fuselage.

longo intervallo [L.] With a long interval.

longueur [F.] A long-winded section of text; a dull passage from a book.

longum iter est per precepta, breve et efficax per exempla [L.] Long is the way of teaching through precepts, short and efficient through examples.

loquitur [L.] He or she speaks; used in stage directions.

lorette [F.] A woman of easy virtue; a *fille de joie* (q.v.); a courtesan. The name derives from a group of prostitutes who lived near the Church of Notre Dame de Lorette in Paris.

lorgnette [F.] An opera-glass.

lorgnon [F.] Eyeglasses; pince-nez.

lota [Hindi] In India, a round, metallic container for carrying water.

lotah. See lota.

loup-garou [F.] A werewolf; a man-beast; a monster.

loyal en tout [F.] Loyal in everything.

loyauté m'oblige [F.] Loyalty binds me.

lucidum intervallum [L.] An interval of temporary sanity. (*Between wars there was a brief* lucidum intervallum.)

lucifer [Dutch] A sulphur match.

lucri bonus est odor ex re qualibet [L.] Money smells good whatever be its origin.

lucri causa [L.] For the sake of gain.

ludere cum sacris [L.] To sport with things that are sacred.

lues commentatoria [L.] A plague of commentators; a reference to scholars who feel compelled to explain, analyze, and interpret the words of other authors.

lueur [F.] A glint; a gleam; a slight glimpse.

Luft [G.] Air.

Luftwaffe [G.] The air force of Nazi Germany.

lundi [F.] Monday.

lune [F.] The moon.

lunga pausa [It.] In music, a long pause.

lupus est homo homini [L.] Man is a wolf to man; men exploit each other.

lupus pilum mutat, non mentem [L.] The wolf changes his coat, not his ways.

lusingando [It.] In music, a direction calling for a soft, relaxing rendering.

Lustgarten [G.] A pleasure garden.

Lusthaus [G.] A lust house; a house of pleasure and hedonistic enjoyment.

Lustspiel [G.] A comedy.

lusus naturae [L.] A freak of nature; a monster.

luttuosamente [It.] In music, a direction calling for a melancholy rendering.

lux [L.] Light.

lux et veritas [L.] Light and truth; used as the motto of Yale University.

lux in tenebris [L.] Light in the darkness.

lux mundi [L.] Light of the world.

luxuria [L.] Debauchery; sexual indulgence.

lycée [F.] A French high school.

M

macchina [It.] Machine.

macédoine [F.] A mixture of chopped vegetables, served in a sauce or as a separate dish.

ma chère [F.] My dear.

machete [Sp.] A heavy knife used in the tropics for clearing brush or harvesting sugar cane.

machree [Anglo-Irish] My dear; used as a term of endearment.

macte animo [L.] Act in spirit; have strength.

macte nova virtute [L.] Go in renewed virtue.

macte virtute [L.] Proceed in virtue.

madame [F.] Lady; used as a title of respect for a married woman or a woman of position.

Mädchen [G.] A young girl; also, a servant girl; a maid.

mademoiselle [F.] Miss; used as a title of respect for an unmarried girl.

madre [Sp.] Mother.

maduro [Sp.] In cigar making, ripe; mellow, perfect.

maestosamente [It.] In music, a direction calling for a majestic rendering.

maestoso [It.] In music, a direction calling for a majestic, regal rendering.

maestro [It.] Master; Teacher; used especially in music or the arts.

ma foi [F.] My faith; indeed; I see; used as an exclamation.

magasin [F.] A small shop; a store.

maggiore fretta, minore atto [It.] The more haste, the less speed.

magia alba [L.] White, or benevolent, magic.

mágico [Port.] Magic; the supernatural.

magister [L.] Master; expert; teacher.

Magister Artium [L.] Master of the Arts.

magister caeremoniarum [L.] The master of ceremonies.

magister dixit [L.] The master has said it.

magister ludi [L.] Teacher of the school; also, master of the game.

magister populi [L.] Leader of the people; a dictator.

magna civitas, magna solitudo [L.] A great city, a great solitude.

magna cum laude [L.] With great praise; used as an honor bestowed upon worthy students at a graduation ceremony.

magnae fortunae pericula [L.] The perils involved in great fortune.

magna est veritas, et praevalet [L.] Great is truth, and it prevails.

magna est vis consuetudinis [L.]
Great is the power of habit.

magna inter molles concordia [L.]
There is great accord among the
dissolute.

magnalia [L.] Mighty words.

*magnam fortunam magnus animus
decet* [L.] A great mind becomes a great fortune.

magnas componere lites [L.] To
settle great disputes.

magna servitus est magna fortuna
[L.] A large fortune is a large
enslavement.

magnas inter opes inops [L.] Poor
amidst great riches.

magna vis est conscientiae [L.] The
power of conscience is great.

magni Dei datum [L.] A gift from
the great God.

magnifique [F.] Magnificent; splendid; wonderful; superb.

magnifique et pas cher [F.] Magnificent and not expensive.

magni nominis umbra [L.] The
shadow of a great name.

magno conatu magnas nugas [L.]
Great jokes with a great effort.

magno jam conatu magnas nugas [L.]
To produce insignificant sundries
with enormous labors.

magnum bonum [L.] A great good.

magnum in parvo [L.] Much in
little; a great amount in a small
space.

magnum opus [L.] A great work;
a masterpiece; one's finest accom-
plishment. (*Chartres is considered the magnum opus of Gothic
art.*)

magnum vectigal est parsimonia [L.]
Economy is a great revenue.

*magnus ab integro saeculorum nasci-
tur ordo* [L.] Once more the
great cycle of the ages begins.

*magnus Alexander corpore parvus
erat* [L.] Alexander the Great
was of small physique; good
things come in small packages.

mahal [Persian] Private apart-
ments; also, a palace; a royal
court.

maharaja [Skr.] In India, a king
of an Indian state or province.

maharani [Skr.] In India, the title
of a queen, the wife of a maharaja
(q.v.).

mahatman [Skr.] A great man; one
considered to be of the highest
wisdom and character; a saint.

Mahdi [Ar.] In Islam, the name of
the spiritual savior destined to
rule the world.

mahout [Hindi] In India and Persia, an elephant keeper.

Mai [F.] The month of May.

maidan [Ar.] In middle eastern
countries, a large open space used
as a market place and for pa-
rades, festivals, games, and public gatherings.

maillot [F.] A skin-tight garment
worn by dancers, athletes, gym-
nasts, etc.

main de justice [F.] The hand of
justice.

mains froides, coeur chaud [F.]
Warm hands, cold heart.

maintiens le droit [F.] Maintain
what is right.

mais [F.] But.

maison [F.] A house; building;
home; structure.

maison d'arrêt [F.] A house of arrest; a prison.

maison de campagne [F.] A house
of the country; a country house;
a summer place.

maison de jeu [F.] A house of
games; a gambling establishment;
a casino.

maison de repos [F.] A rest home.

maison de retraite [F.] A house of retreat, i.e., an old age home; a sanitarium.

maison de santé [F.] A house of health; a hospital; a rest home.

maison de tolérance [F.] A house of prostitution sanctioned by the government; a licensed bordello.

maison de ville [F.] A townhouse; also, a town hall; a central meeting place in a village.

maison garnie [F.] A furnished house.

maison meublée [F.] A furnished house.

mais où sont les neiges d'antan? [F.] "But where are the snows of yesteryear?" refrain from a poem by François Villon.

maître [F.] A master; a teacher; one who excels in his field.

maître d'armes [F.] A master in the art of fencing; also, a fencing instructor.

maître d'école [F.] A school master; a teacher.

maître de danse [F.] A dancing master.

maître des hautes oeuvres [F.] A master of high works, i.e., a hangman.

maître d'hôtel [F.] Hotel master; hotel manager; also, a butler; a male servant ranked high in the domestic hierarchy.

maître d'oeuvre [F.] A master of work; an overseer; a foreman.

maîtresse [F.] (1.) Mistress; lover. (2.) A female school teacher.

majolica [It.] A type of Italian pottery, dating from the Renaissance, in which a piece of pottery is covered with a thin enamel onto which a pattern is painted and fired.

majori cedo [L.] I yield to one greater.

mal [F.] Disease; sickness; pain; also, bad; wrong; evil.

malade [F.] A sick person; a convalescent.

malade imaginaire [F.] An imaginary illness; a hypochondriac's fantasy.

maladie du pays [F.] Sickness for one's country, i.e., homesickness.

maladresse [F.] Clumsiness; awkwardness; lack of skill; blundering.

mala fides [L.] Bad faith.

malaise [F.] An indefinable feeling of sickness or discontent; a condition of being out of sorts.

mala mens, malus animus [L.] Bad mind, bad heart.

malam rem cum velis honestare, improbes [L.] When you wish to give an evil thing dignity, criticize it.

malàpropos [F.] Out of place; inexpediently; unfittingly.

mal de dents [F.] A toothache.

mal de mer [F.] Seasickness.

mal de tête [F.] A headache.

mal di gola [It.] A sore throat.

mal du pays [F.] Homesickness.

male narrando fabula depravatur [L.] A good story is ruined by bad telling.

mal entendu [L.] Ill-heard; ill-advised; under an incorrect impression.

malentendu [F.] A mistake; misconception; misunderstanding.

male parta, male dilabuntur [L.] What is taken dishonestly disappears in profligacy.

male partum, male disperit [L.] What is ill-got is ill-spent.

male vincetis sed vincite [L.] Conquest will be difficult but conquer you must.

malevolo [It.] Malevolent; evil; hateful; also, a person who expresses such qualities.

malevolus animus abditos dentes habet [L.] The malevolent have secret teeth.

malgré [F.] In spite of; notwithstanding.

malgré lui [F.] In spite of himself.

malgré nous [F.] In spite of us.

malgré soi [F.] In spite of himself.

malheur [F.] Bad times; ill fortune; poor luck.

malheureusement [F.] Unfortunately.

malheur ne vient jamais seul [F.] Misfortunes never come alone.

mali principii malus finis [L.] From a bad beginning comes a bad ending.

malo modo [L.] In an evil mode; in a bad manner.

malum in se [L.] Evil in itself; an act or thing intrinsically wrong. (*Incest has forever been considered* malum in se.) Cf. *malum prohibitum.*

malum prohibitum [L.] An evil this is forbidden by law; an act or thing wrong by law rather than of itself; cf. *malum in se.*

malus animus [L.] Evil intent.

malus genius [L.] Evil genius.

mañana [Sp.] Tomorrow.

mandolino [It.] A mandolin.

manège [F.] Horsemanship; the art of riding; also, the place where it is taught; a riding academy.

manet cicatrix [L.] The scar still remains.

manger [F.] To eat; to take food.

manger son blé en herbe [F.] To eat one's corn in the blade; to count one's chickens before they are hatched.

mania a potu [L.] A drinking mania; insanity brought on by overindulgence in alcohol.

manière [F.] Manner; fashion; way; technique; style.

manièré [F.] Mannered; postured; abounding in insincere and affected mannerisms.

manqué [F.] Unsuccessful; lacking; falling short of the mark; failing to fulfill expectations.

man spricht Deutsch [G.] German is spoken.

mantapu [Hindi] The porch or vestibule of a Hindu temple.

manteca de puerco [Sp.] Fat of the pig; lard.

mantra [Skr.] In Hinduism, a word or sentence repeated over and over as an aid in meditation.

manu forti [L.] With a strong hand; with force.

manus e nubibus [L.] A hand from the clouds; divine intervention; cf. *deus ex machina.*

manzo [It.] Beef.

mappa [It.] A map.

marbré [F.] Mottled; marblized.

marchandise qui plaît est à demi vendue [F.] Merchandise which pleases is half-sold.

marche funèbre [F.] A funeral march; a dirge.

Märchen [G.] A story; a fairy tale; a myth; a folk tale.

marcher à pas de loup [F.] To walk with the steps of a wolf, i.e., to walk quietly; to go without being heard; to sneak.

marchesa [It.] In Italy, the wife of a marquis; a marchioness.

marchese [It.] In Italy, a nobleman one rank below a prince.

Mardi [F.] Tuesday.

Mardi Gras [F.] Fat Tuesday; the last day of Carnival.

mare [L.] The ocean; the seas.

mare altum [L.] The deep sea.

mare clausum [L.] A closed sea; an area of the high seas, usually close to the mainland, controlled by a particular country and held off-limits to strangers; cf. "mare liberum."

mare liberum [L.] The free seas; unrestricted areas of the ocean; cf. "mare clausum."

mare nostrum [L.] Our sea; used by the Romans for the Mediterranean.

margaritas ante porcos [L.] Pearls before swine.

mariage de convenance [F.] A marriage of convenience; a marriage or partnership formed for the sake of expediency rather than love.

mariage d'inclination [F.] A marriage of inclination; a marriage of love.

maristan [Persian] In Persia, a hospital; a sick ward.

markt [Dutch] The marketplace; the shopping area.

marquis [F.] In France and other European countries, a title of nobility signifying a rank above a count and below a duke.

marquise [F.] The wife of a marquis (q.v.).

marron [F.] Chestnut.

marron glacés [F.] Chestnuts preserved in sweet syrup or covered with frosted sugar.

Mars [F.] The month of March.

mars gravior sub pace latet [L.] Beneath the peace lurks a serious war.

marziale [It.] In music, a direction calling for a martial, military-like tempo.

mascabado [Sp.] Raw sugar; sugar that has not undergone the refining process.

masjid [Ar.] A mosque; the house of prayer for Mohammedans.

más vale saber que haber [Sp.] Better to know than to have.

maté [Sp.] A drink, popular in South America, made from the dried leaves of the Paraguay tea plant.

matelot [F.] A sailor.

mater [L.] Mother.

Mater dolorosa [L.] The sorrowing Mother; used as a name of the virgin; in religious literature and art, the image of the Virgin lamenting over the death of Christ.

materfamilias [L.] The mother of the family; a matriarch.

materia medica [L.] (1.) Medical materials; the supplies of medicine. (2.) The study of medicine.

materiem superabat opus [L.] The workmanship was superior to the materials.

mater timidi flere non solet [L.] The mother of a coward does not weep.

mauvais [F.] Bad; wrong; evil.

mauvaise honte [F.] False shame; unnecessary bashfulness.

mauvaise langue [F.] A wrong tongue, i.e., a slanderer; a gossip; one who tells lies or spreads malicious rumors.

mauvaise plaisanterie [F.] A bad joke; inappropriate jesting.

mauvais goût [F.] Bad taste.

mauvais sang [F.] Bad blood; mutual antagonism; enmity.

mauvais sujet [F.] A bad subject, i.e. a worthless person; a rake; a debaucher.

maxima bella ex levissimis causis

[L.] The biggest wars spring from the smallest causes.

maximum remedium irae mora est [L.] The most effective remedy for anger is delay.

maximus in minimis [L.] Very great in very small things.

maya [Skr.] In Hinduism, the forces of illusion which keep humanity bound to ignorance.

mazurka [Pol.] A Polish folk dance, resembling the Polka, danced in three-quarter or three-eighth time with the second beat heavily accentuated.

mea culpa [L.] By my fault; a prayer of self-accusation.

méchant [F.] Bad; wicked; spiteful; vicious.

(les) méchants sont toujours surpris de trouver de l'habileté dans les bons [F.] The wicked are always surprised to find ability in the good.

medano [Sp.] A sand dune.

médecine expectante [F.] In medicine, a treatment dependent on time rather than on medicine; a natural cure.

médecin, guéris-toi toi-même [F.] Doctor, heal thyself.

medice, cura teipsum [L.] Doctor, heal thyself.

medicus curat, natura sanat [L.] The doctor cures, nature makes well.

medio tutissimus ibis [L.] In the middle way you go with safety.

meditatio fugae [L.] In law, contemplation of flight from litigation.

meditatione unius [L.] By meditation on one alone.

meditullium [L.] The very center of a thing.

medium coeli [L.] Midheaven; the middle of the sky; the meridian; cf. *imum coeli*.

medium tenuere beati [L.] The happy people take the middle course.

mega biblion, mega kakon [Gr.] A large book, a large evil.

meglio cader dalle finestre che dal tetto [It.] It is better to tumble off the window than the roof.

meglio tardi che mai [It.] Better late than never.

mehr Licht [G.] More light; the last words of Goethe.

Mein Herr [G.] My lord; my master.

meisje [Dutch] A maid; a servant.

Meistersinger [G.] German musicians and poets formed into fraternities during the late Middle Ages for the purpose of promoting religious song and verse.

me judice [L.] In my judgment or opinion; with myself as judge. (*It was,* me judice, *an unforgivable deed.*)

melanzane [It.] Eggplant.

mêlée [F.] A free-for-all; a confused and disorganized fight or riot.

melitzanes papoutzakia [Gr.] Stuffed eggplant.

melius est parti semel, quem cavere semper [L.] It is better to suffer once than to forever be on one's guard.

melius inquirendum [L.] All the better for searching.

mélodrame. [F.] Melodrama.

memento mori [L.] (1.) Remember your death; used as a common tombstone inscription. (2.) A devotional object, such as a skull or cross, that reminds one of his mortality.

mémoire [F.] A memoir; a diary.

mémoire de lièvre [F.] The memory of a rabbit, i.e., a short-lived memory; a mind that tends to be forgetful.

memorabilia [L.] Things worthy of remembrance; nostalgic souvenirs.

memor et fidelis [L.] Mindful and faithful.

memoriae sacrum [L.] Sacred to the memory of.

memoria est thesaurus omnium rerum et custos [L.] Memory is the treasury and guardian of all things.

memoria in aeterna [L.] In eternal memory.

memoria technica [L.] An artificial memory, i.e., a method designed to aid or train the memory; a system of mneumonics.

memoriter [L]. By memory; by heart.

mem-sahib [Hindi] Madame; miss; used as a title of respect for Western women.

mendacem memorem esse oportet [L.] It is advisable for a liar to have a good memory.

mendacia linguae blandae [L.] The lies of a bland tongue.

menea la cola el can, nó por ti, sino por el pan [Sp.] The dog wags his tail not for you, but for the crust.

meno [It.] In music, a direction meaning less, as in meno mosso, less rapid.

mens [L.] Mind; intellect; judgment; thought.

mensa et toro [L.] From bed and board.

mens agitat molem [L.] Mind agitates the mass, i.e., it is thought which gives motion to matter.

Mensch [G.] A man; a human being.

Menschen Engel ist die Zeit [G.] "Time is man's good angel": *Schiller*.

(der) Mensch ist was er isst [G.] A man is what he eats.

Mensch werden ist eine Kunst [G.] To become a man is an art.

mens legis [L.] The mind or spirit of the law.

mens sana [L.] A sound mind.

mens sana in corpore sano [L.] A sound mind in a sound body.

menteur à triple étage [F.] A triple-degree liar.

(un) menteur est toujours prodigue de serments [F.] A liar is always lavish with vows.

mentiras de caçadores são as maiores [Port.] Sportsmen's lies are the greatest.

(la) mentira tiene las piernas cortas [Sp.] A lie has short legs, i.e., a lie is quickly caught up with.

mentis gratissimus error [L.] A most agreeable mental error.

meollo [Sp.] The marrow; the kernel.

meo voto [L.] By my desire.

mercado [Sp.] The marketplace.

mercante [It.] A merchant; a salesman.

merci [F.] Mercy; thank you; thanks.

Mercredi [F.] Wednesday.

mer de glace [F.] A sea of glass.

mère [F.] Mother.

mère de famille [F.] Mother of a family.

mésalliance [F.] A marriage consummated with one of inferior social standing.

mesdemoiselles [F.] Plural of *mademoiselle* (q.v.).

meshuga [Yidd.] Crazy; mad; insane.

meshugana [Yidd.] A crazy person; a madman.

meson [Sp.] A hostelry; a small inn.

messan [Gael.] A dog.

messeigneurs [F.] Plural of monseigneur (q.v.).

messieurs [F.] Plural of monsieur (q.v.).

mestizo [Sp.] In Spanish America, a person of blood.

meta incognita [L.] An unknown goal of a voyage.

métier [F.] A profession or calling to which one is particularly suited.

mettre de l'eau dans son vin [F.] To put water in his wine.

meum et tuum [L.] Mine and thine.

mezuzah [Heb.] In Judaism, a box containing scriptural verses and attached to a doorpost.

mezzo-rilievo [It.] In sculpture, a carving executed in relief, with the characters, ornaments, etc. projecting a moderate distance from the original surface, less than high relief but more than low.

mezzo tenore [It.] In music, a low tenor voice; also, one who sings in such a voice.

mezzo termine [It.] The middle term; midcourse.

Midi [F.] The south, especially of France.

miéntras que duermen todos son iguales [Sp.] All men are equal while they are asleep.

mignon [F.] Sweet; dainty; delicate, tiny.

mihi cura futuri [L.] My concern is for the future.

mijnheer [Dutch] Sir; used as a term of respect for a gentleman.

minauderie [F.] An affected expression; simpering manners.

minestrone [It.] A soup containing vegetables and vermicelli in a meat broth.

minima-de-malis [L.] Of evils, pick the least; choose the lesser of two evils.

minime [L.] Little; by no means.

mir [Russ.] In Russia, a town; a small village.

mirabile dictu [L.] Wonderful to tell.

mise en scène [F.] A stage set; hence, the setting in which a series of circumstances occur; the background before which events take place.

miserabile dictu [L.] Horrible to relate.

miserabile vulgus [L.] The miserable rabble; the wretched masses; the peasantry.

misericordia Domini inter pontem et fontem [L.] Between bridge and wave God may save.

missa cantata [L.] A hymn belonging to the Mass.

mit den Jahren steigen die Prüfungen [G.] "Trials increase with advancing years": *Goethe.*

Mittwoch [G.] Wednesday.

mitzvah [Heb.] (1.) A commandment. (2) An act of kindness performed; a good deed.

mobile vulgus [L.] The movable public, i.e., the suggestible masses; the easily manipulated throngs of common people.

moderado [Sp.] A conservative.

modo praescripto [L.] In the manner prescribed.

modus faciendi [L.] The mode or manner of doing something.

modus operandi [L.] Mode of operation; manner of doing something; a technique.

modus operandi in rebus [L.] Mode of operation in affairs.

modus vivendi [L.] A manner of living; a life style; also, a temporary living condition experienced while awaiting a settlement of arguments or litigation.

moiré [F.] Producing a watery or shimmering effect.

(le) mois prochain [F.] Next month.

mokshu [Skr.] In Hinduism, release from the bondage of life and consequently from transmigration; nirvana (q.v.).

mole ruit sua [L.] It falls by its own weight.

mollia tempora [L.] Favorable opportunities.

mollia tempora fandi [F.] Favorable opportunities for speaking.

molliter ossa cubent [L.] May his bones rest undisturbed.

molto [It.] A lot; very much.

molto bene [It.] Very good; excellent.

mon ami [F.] My friend.

Mond [G.] Moon.

monde [F.] The world; the general environment; also, society; the fashionable set.

mon metier et mon art, c'est vivre [F.] "My business and my art is to live": *Montaigne.*

mons [L.] Mountain; a great rock; a mass.

monseigneur [F.] My lord; sir; used as a title of respect.

monsieur [F.] Sir; commonly used as a title of respect.

monstrum horrendum, informe, ingens [L.] A monster, horrible, malformed, enormous.

Montag [G.] Monday.

montaña [Sp.] Mountain.

montani semper liberi [L.] Mountain men are always free; used as the motto of the State of West Virginia.

montero [Sp.] A cap worn by hunters.

monumentum aere perennius [L.] A monument more lasting than bronze.

(la) moquerie est souvent indigence d'esprit [F.] "Bantering is often poverty of wit": *La Bruyère.*

mora omnis odio est, sed facit sapientiam [L.] Every delay is hateful, but it gives wisdom.

morbidezza [It.] Softness; fineness; also, in the fine arts, extreme delicacy, as in the handling of flesh tones in a painting.

morceau [F.] A morsel; a tiny bite.

morceau honteux [F.] The shameful morsel, i.e., the last piece of food left on a plate, which manners forbid taking.

more majorum [L.] In the manner of one's ancestors.

morem fecerat usus [L.] Habit had produced the custom.

more probato [L.] In the manner approved.

more solito [L.] An unusual custom.

more suo [L.] In his own way.

Morgen [G.] Morning.

morro [Sp.] A round hill.

mors et vita [L.] Death and life.

mors janua vitae [L.] Death is the gateway to life.

mors omnia solvit [L.] Death dissolves everything.

mors peccati merces [L.] The wages of sin are death.

mors ultima ratio [L.] Death is the ultimate argument.

morsus [L.] A sting; bite.

mortalis nemo est, quem non attingat dolor morbusque [L.] There is no mortal whom pain and disease do not reach.

mort de ma vie [F.] Death of my life.

mortuo leoni et lepores insultant [L.] Even the rabbits insult a dead lion.

mosso [It.] In music, a direction calling for a rapid, lively rendering.

mot [F.] Word; saying; statement; slogan.

mot à double entendre [F.] A word with a double meaning; a pun.

mot à mot [F.] Word for word.

(le) mot de l'énigme [F.] The key to the enigma.

mot de passe [F.] A word of passage; a password.

mot d'ordre [F.] A word of order; a command.

mot juste [F.] The proper word; the exactly appropriate word or saying for the situation.

moto suo [L.] Of his own accord.

mot pour rire [F.] A word for laughter; a witticism; a humorous remark.

motu proprio [L.] By one's own motion; on one's own accord or volition; unaided.

mouchoir [F.] Handkerchief.

moue [F.] A grimace; a sour expression of distaste; a pout.

moulage [F.] The making of a mold in plastic, i.e., of a footprint, used especially for the purpose of criminal investigation.

moulin à paroles [F.] A chatterbox; a gossip; a wordy fellow.

mousquetaire [F.] A musketeer.

mousseline [F.] Muslin.

mousseline de laine [F.] Muslin made of wool.

mousseline de soie [F.] Chiffon.

mousseux [F.] Frothy; foaming; sparkling, as in wine.

moutonné [F.] Curled; ruffled; like lamb's fleece.

moyen âge [F.] The Middle Ages.

mozzetta [It.] A hooded cape, worn by ecclesiastics of the Roman Catholic Church.

muchacho [Sp.] A boy; a child.

mucho en el suelo, poco en el cielo [Sp.] If you get much on earth, you will get little in heaven.

mudra [Skr.] In Hinduism and Buddhism, a hand position signifying a religious concept or mode.

muezzin [Ar.] In Islam, one who calls the faithful to prayer from a minaret.

muito sabe o rato, mas mais sabe o gato [Port.] The mouse knows much but the cat knows more.

mullah [Turkish, Persian, and Hindi] In Islam, a venerable teacher of Islamic doctrine; also, a schoolteacher.

multa docet fames [L.] Hunger teaches one many things.

multi livissimam delectationem gravissimae utilitati anteponunt [L.] Many prefer the smallest pleasure to the most important benefit.

mündlich [G.] Verbally; by word of mouth.

mundus vult decipi [L.] The world desires to be fooled.

muscae volitantes [L.] Flying flies, i.e., strange floating spots and lines that play across the field of vision due to clusters of cellular material that collects in the vitreous humor of the eyes.

musée [F.] A museum.

mutatis mutandis [L.] The necessary changes being made.

mutato nomine [L.] The name
being changed.

mutato nomine de te fabula narratur
[L.] Change but the name and
the story might be told of you.

mutuus consensus [L.] Mutual consent

N

na [Sc.] No; not.

nabob [Hindi] (1.) In India, the representative of a monarch; the governor of a country or province. (2.) In India, a powerful man; an individual of great wealth and fame.

nacelle [F.] An enclosure on an aircraft used to hold the crew and passengers or to house an engine.

Nachbar [G.] Neighbor.

Nachbeterei [G.] Absolute loyalty to one leader or cause; blind obedience.

nachlässig [G.] Inattentive; heedless; uncaring of the consequences.

Nachricht [G.] News; information; a report on current events.

Nachspiel [G.] In music, a postlude; a closing piece.

Nacht [G.] Night; nighttime.

Nachtmusik [G.] Night music; a serenade.

nach und nach [G.] Little by little; slowly; gradually.

nación [Sp.] Nation; country; people.

Nacken [G.] The neck.

nacre [F.] Mother-of-pearl.

Naga [Skr.] In India, a snake; also, a species of snake deity believed to inhabit the interior regions of the earth.

nagana [Zulu] In South Africa, a cattle disease carried by the tsetse fly.

nager entre deux eaux [F.] To swim between two streams, i.e., to be indecisive.

naîf [F.] Naïve.

naissance [F.] Birth; beginning.

(la) naissance de la poésie [F.] The dawn of poetry.

naïveté [F.] Lack of sophistication; innocence; ingenuousness.

nam nihil egregious quam res discernere apertas [L.] For nothing is so praiseworthy as recognizing the facts.

não é honra acabar cousas pequenas [Port.] There is no honor in petty achievements.

nares [L.] The nostrils.

narghile [Persian] A water pipe; a hubble-bubble; an oriental smoking device designed to filter the smoke through water before it is inhaled.

Národni Výbor [Czec.] The National Governmental Council of Czechoslovakia.

narrateur [F.] A narrator; a storyteller.

nascentes morimur, finisque ab origine pendet [L.] We begin to die at the moment we are born, and the end is linked with the beginning.

nasci miserum, vivere poena, angus-

tia mori [L.] "To be born is misery, to live is suffering, to die is anguish": *St. Bernard.*

nascitur ars nova medendi [L.] A new art of healing has been born.

natale solum [L.] Native soil.

natio comoeda est [L.] It is a country of comic actors; a statement by Juvenal about Greece.

natura abhorret a vacuo [L.] Nature abhors a vacuum.

natura il fece e poi ruppe la stampa [It.] "Nature made him and then broke the mold": *Aristo.*

naturam expellas furca, tamen usque recurret [L.] You may drive nature out with a pitchfork, still she will ever return.

naturam mutare difficile est [L.] It is difficult to change nature.

natura non facit saltum [L.] Nature makes no leap; nature moves step-by-step.

natura semina scientiae nobis dedit, scientiam non dedit [L.] Nature has given us the seeds of knowledge not the knowledge itself.

naturel [F.] Natural; native; unspoiled; genuine.

nature morte [F.] Dead nature, i.e., a still life painting.

natureza [Port.] Nature; the outdoors.

naufragium sibi quisque facit [L.] Each man makes his own shipwreck.

naukar [Hindi] In India, a butler; a serving boy.

naumachia [Gr.] A spectacular naval maneuver, especially one staged for an audience; also, the place where such spectacles are held.

nausée [F.] Nausea; sickness; stomach problems.

nautilos [Gr.] A sailor; a seafarer.

nautique [F.] Nautical.

navarin [F.] Mutton stew, usually prepared with spring vegetables.

navet [F.] A turnip.

nazim [Hindi] In India, a general; a military executive.

nbeeth [Ar.] Wine.

nec amor nec tussis celatur [L.] One can disguise neither love nor a cough.

nec aspera terrent [L.] Not even difficulties will deter us.

nec bella nec puella [L.] Neither beautiful nor a girl.

nec cupias nec metuas [L.] Have neither desire nor fear.

ne cede malis [L.] Yield not to misfortunes.

necesse est ut multos timeat quem multi timent [L.] He who many fear must himself fear many.

necessitas non habet legem [L.] Necessity has no laws.

necessitas ultimum et maximum telum est [L.] Necessity is the last and strongest weapon.

nec habeo, nec careo, nec curo [L.] I have not, I want not, I care not.

nec placida contentus quiete est [L.] Nor is he made content with gentle rest.

nec prece nec pretio [L.] Neither by prayer nor by price.

nec quaerere nec spernere honorem [L.] Neither to seek honor nor to refuse it.

ne credas laudatoribus tuis [L.] Do not believe those who praise you.

nec scire fas est omnia [L.] Nor is it allowed to know all things.

nec tecum possum vivere nec sine te [L.] I can live neither with thee nor without thee.

nec temere, nec timide [L.] Neither with temerity nor with timidity, i.e., follow the middle path.

née [F.] Born; used to differentiate a maiden or given name from a married name. (*Warrants were issued for the arrest of Jane Rockwell, née Jane Hunt.*)

ne exeat [L.] Let him not leave; in law, a document disallowing a subject to depart from his designated area of confinement.

nefasti dies [L.] Days on which business is not conducted; thus, unfortunate days; unlucky parts of the month.

ne fronti crede [L.] Trust not appearances.

négligé [F.] (1.) A woman's loose-fitting dressing gown or sleeping garment, often made of sheer and delicate fabric. (2.) Any comfortable, loose-fitting and informal attire.

negro [Sp.] Black.

neiges éternelles [F.] Perpetual snow.

ne Jupiter quidem omnibus placet [L.] Not even Jupiter pleases everyone.

nemine contradicente [L.] Without a dissenting voice; unanimously.

nemine dissentiente [L.] With no one in argument; with complete accord; unanimously.

nemo bis punitur pro eodem delicto [L.] No man is punished twice for the same crime.

nemo dat quod non habet [L.] No one gives what he does not have.

nemo doctus unquam mutationem consilii inconstantiam dixit esse [L.] No wise man has ever said that change of plan is inconsistency.

nemo fit fato nocens [L.] Nobody becomes guilty by fate.

nemo laiditur nisi a se ipse [L.] No one is harmed except by himself.

nemo liber est, qui corpori servit [L.] No man is free who is a servant to the flesh.

nemo me impune lacessit [L.] No one attacks me with impunity; used as the motto of Scotland.

nemo mortalium omnibus horis sapit [L.] There is no one who is wise all the time.

nemo propheta acceptus est in patria sua [L.] No prophet is accepted in his own country.

nemo repente fuit turpissimus [L.] No one becomes corrupted all at once.

nemo solus satis sapit [L.] No one is wise enough alone.

ne nimium [L.] Not too much; never to the point of excess.

ne plus ultra [L.] Beyond which there is nothing better; the superior phenomena. (*Booth's Hamlet was considered the* ne plus ultra *of American Shakespearean theater.*)

ne prius antidotum quam venenum [L.] Take not the antidote before the poison.

ne puero gladium [L.] Give not a sword to a little boy.

neque semper arcum tendit Apollo [L.] Apollo does not always keep his bow bent; when it is not necessary to be tense, stay relaxed.

ne quid nimis [L.] Be moderate wisely.

nero-antico [L.] Black marble.

nervos belli pecuniam infinitam [L.] The sinews of war are unlimited money.

nervus probandi [L.] The sinew of proof, i.e., the key piece of evidence; the principal argument.

nescio quid [L.] I know not what.

nescis, mi fili, quantilla prudentia homines regantur [L.] You do not know, my son, with what a small amount of wisdom men are ruled.

nescit plebs jejuna timere [L.] A population that knows hunger knows no fear.

nescit vox missa reverti [L.] Once spoken a word cannot be retrieved.

nessun maggior dolore che ricordarsi del tempo felice nella miseria [It.] There is no greater pain than to remember happiness in times of anguish.

n'est-ce pas? [F.] Is it not so? Isn't it? (*You were thinking of me just a minute ago,* n'est-ce pas?)

net [F.] Clean; pure; without a spot.

netsuke [Jap.] A Japanese miniature carving in ivory, often of a humorous or bizarre subject.

neuf [F.] The number nine.

Neufchâtel [F.] A variety of creamy cheese made in France in the town of Neufchâtel.

Neujahr [G.] New Year.

névé [F.] The upper section of a glacier where the snow has granulated or turned to ice; also, a firn; a field of compacted or granulated snow.

nez [F.] Nose.

nez à nez [F.] Nose to nose; face to face.

nez retroussé [F.] An upturned nose.

niaiserie [F.] Foolishness; a silly thing; nonsense.

nichts [G.] Nothing; not anything.

nicht wahr [G.] Is it not true?; surely it is so.

Niersteiner [G.] A German white wine.

ni firmes carta que no leas, ni bebas agua que no veas [Sp.] Before you sign it, read it and think, look at the water before you drink.

nigaud [F.] A fool; a bumbling idiot; a silly person.

nihil [L.] Nothing; a worthless object; something of no account.

nihil ad rem [L.] Nothing to the thing; not to the point.

nihil dicit [L.] He says nothing; in law, said of a defendant who offers no explanation of his crime.

nihil est ab omni parte beatum [L.] Nothing is in all ways blessed.

nihil est quod ampliorem curam postulet quam cogitare quid gerendum sit de hinc incogitantos sors non consilium regit [L.] There is nothing that requires greater effort than to reflect on what must be done; hence, fate not counsel, rules those who do not reflect.

nihil obstat [L.] The Roman Catholic seal of approval, meaning nothing hinders, allowing that the work in question, i.e., a book, pamphlet, etc., has been reviewed and found fit for public distribution; also, any official seal of approval.

nihil sub sole novum [L.] Nothing new under the sun.

nil admirari [L.] To admire nothing; to be moved by nothing in the world; to be without awe.

nil conscire sibi, nulla pallescere culpa [L.] To be conscious of no fault, to grow pale before no crime, i.e., to be innocent of any wrongdoing; to have a clear conscience.

nil debet [L.] He owns nothing.

nil desperandum [L.] No reason for despair; do not despair.

nil dicit. See *nihil dicit.*

nil fuit unquam sic impar sibi [L.]

Nothing was ever so inconsistent in itself.

nil homine terra pejus ingrato creat [L.] The earth produces nothing worse than an ungrateful man.

nil nisi bonum [L.] Nothing but good.

nil nisi cruce [L.] Nothing except by the cross.

nil prodest, quod non laedere possit idem [L.] There is nothing advantageous that may not also be injurious.

nil sine numine [L.] Nothing without the divine command; used as the motto of the State of Colorado.

nil sole et sale utilius [L.] Nothing is more useful than sun and salt.

nil ultra [L.] Nothing beyond.

ni l'un ni l'autre [F.] Neither the one nor the other.

nimium altercando veritas amittitur [L.] In excessive altercation truth is lost.

nimium ne crede colori [L.] Trust not too much in looks.

n'importe [F.] It is of no matter; never mind.

los niños y los locos dicen las verdades [Sp.] Children and fools tell the truth.

nirvana [Skr.] In Buddhist philosophy, a state of complete desirelessness; thus, a condition of psychological and physiological freedom from the laws and restrictions of terrestrial existence; also, colloquially, ecstasy, great happiness; unbounded pleasure.

nisei [Jap.] An American born of Japanese immigrant parents; cf. "issei," "kibei."

nisus formativus [L.] Creative energy.

ni te malae mentis homines insat: auri

cupid: dux [L.] Let not evil-minded men lead you astray with an insatiable lust for gold.

nitor in adversum [L.] I strive against adversity.

Nizam [Hindi and Persian] In India, since 1713 the title of rulership adopted by the emperors of Hyderabad.

No [Jap.] A form of Japanese religious drama performed by costumed actors and accompanied by music and a chanting chorus.

nobilitas sola est atque unica virtus [L.] Virtue is the true and only nobility.

nobis judicibus [L.] Ourselves being the judges; in our own opinion.

noblesse [F.] Nobility; aristocracy; the upper classes of any society and especially of France.

noblesse de style [F.] A nobleness of style; perfection of bearing; a grand manner.

noblesse oblige [F.] Nobility obliges, i.e., those in positions of high rank or social standing are morally bound to aid their inferiors, as well as to deport themselves with a dignity appropriate to their station.

noche [Sp.] Night; nighttime.

(la) noche es capa de pecadores [Sp.] Night is the cloak of the sinners.

Noël [F.] Christmas.

no es cosa [Sp.] It makes no difference; it does not matter.

noesis [Gr.] Cognition; realization based on an empirical confrontation.

noeud d'amour [F.] A love knot.

no hay cerradura si es de oro la garzúa [Sp.] There is no effective lock if the pick is made of gold.

no hay mal que por bien no venga

[Sp.] There is no evil which may not turn out well.

noir [F.] Black.

noir d'ivoire [F.] Ivory black.

noix [F.] Nut; walnut; also, the meat of a nut.

noix d'acajou [F.] A cashew nut.

nolens volens [L.] Willing or unwilling; willy-nilly.

noli irritare leones [L.] Do not irritate lions; if you put your hand in the fire you will get burned.

noli me tangere [L.] Touch me not; the words spoken by Christ (John 20:17) to the Virgin immediately upon rising from his tomb.

nolle prosequi [L.] To be unwilling to prosecute; in law, a record stating that the prosecution will stop action in a given suit.

nolo contendere [L.] I do not wish to contend; in law, a plea from the defendant accepting the fact that he has been convicted but still maintaining his innocence.

nombre [F.] Number; quantity.

nombre d'or [F.] The golden number.

nom de demoiselle [F.] Maiden name.

nom de guerre [F.] A name of war, i.e., an assumed name in time of war; also, a traveling name.

nom de plume [F.] A pen name; a writer's pseudonym.

nom de théâtre [F.] A name of theater, i.e., a stage name.

nomen [L.] The middle or second name of a Roman citizen, i.e., Julius in the name Gnaeus Julius Agricola.

nominatim [L.] By name; specifically; this or that particular one.

nominis umbra [L.] The shadow of a name.

non [F.] No; not.

non assumpsit [L.] He did not undertake; in law, the refusal of a plea of *assumpsit* (q.v.).

non bene olet, qui bene semper olet [L.] He smells not well, whose smell is all perfume.

non capisco [It.] I do not understand.

non compos. See "non compos mentis."

non compos mentis [L.] Not of sound mind; incapable of rational thinking; deranged.

non constat [L.] It is not clear; it is not plain.

non cuivis homini contingit adire Corinthum [L.] It is not every man's destiny to visit Corinth (a city famed for its beauty and luxurious life-style).

non culpabilis [L.] Not guilty.

non decet [L.] It is not fitting; it is not right.

non deficiente crumena [L.] As long as the purse does not fail; as long as the funds hold out.

non deficit alter [L.] Nothing is wanting.

nondum omnium dierum sol occidit [L.] My sun has not yet set.

non ens [L.] Nonbeing; nothing; the nonexistent.

non equidem invideo; miror magis [L.] In truth, I do not envy; I only wonder.

non est ab homine nunquam sobrio postulanda prudentia [L.] Prudence is not to be expected from a man who is never sober.

non est fumus absque igne [L.] No smoke without fire.

non est inventus [L.] He has not been found.

non est vivere sed valere vita est [L.] Not to live but to be well, that is life.

non fa caso [It.] It is of no importance.

non intelligunt homines, quam magnum vectigal sit parsimonia [L.] Men know not how great a revenue is economy.

non libet [L.] It does not please.

non licit [L.] It is not permitted.

non liquet [L.] It is not clear.

non mi ricordo [It.] I do not remember.

non multa sed multum [L.] Not many but much; little quantity, much quality.

non nella pena, nel delitto è la infamia [It.] Disgrace does not consist in the punishment but in the crime.

non nisi grandia canto [L.] Only of the great things do I sing.

non nobis solum [L.] Not for ourselves alone.

non nostrum inter vos tantas componere lites [L.] It is not our duty to settle such grave debates; said facetiously of any trifling argument.

non obstante [L.] Notwithstanding.

non ogni giorno è festa [It.] Every day is not a holiday.

non omne licitum honestum [L.] Not everything legal is honest.

non omnia possumus omnes [L.] We cannot all do everything.

non omnis moriar [L.] I shall not wholly die.

non opus est verbis, credite rebus, ait [L.] There is no use of words, believe what is before your eyes.

nonpareil [F.] Unequaled; supreme; unparalleled.

non passibus aequis [L.] With steps that are not equal.

non placet [L.] It does not please; a vote of opposition.

non possumus [L.] We are not able.

non progredi est regredi [L.] Not to go forward is to go backward.

non prosequitur [L.] He does not prosecute; in law, the judgment brought against a plaintiff who fails to appear in court for a trial.

non quam multis placeas, sed qualibus, stude [L.] Do not care how many but whom you please.

non quo, sed quo modo [L.] Not by whom, but in what manner.

non sans droict [O.F.] Not without right; used as the motto on William Shakespeare's coat of arms.

non semper erit aestas [L.] It will not always be summer; if there are good times there are sure to be bad.

non sequitur [L.] It does not follow; an irrationally connected sequence of words or concepts; the derivation of a particular result which could not logically spring from a particular cause.

non sibi sed omnibus [L.] Not for oneself but for everybody.

non sum qualis eram [L.] I am not what I was.

non troppo [It.] In music, a direction meaning not excessively, with moderation.

non troppo presto [It.] In music, a direction meaning not too fast.

nonum prematur in annum [L.] Let it be kept for nine years; words said by Horace in reference to poetic writings which by their subjective nature should be kept, studied, refined, and considered for a long period of time before they are made public.

non vacat exiguis rebus adesse Jovi

[L.] Jupiter has no time to attend to trivial matters.

no pensando se pierden todos los necios [Sp.] All foolish people fail because they fail to think.

no perdona el vulgo tacha de ninguno [Sp.] The vulgar never forgive the fault of anyone.

nord [F.] North; in a northern direction.

norma loquendi [L.] A standard of speaking; a rule of language.

nos aper auditu, linx visu, simia gustu, vultur odoratu, superat aranea tactu [L.] The boar excels us in hearing, the lynx in sight, the ape in taste, the vulture in smell, and the spider in touch.

noscere volunt omnes, mercedem solvere nemo [L.] Everyone wants to know, nobody wants to pay.

nosce te. See *nosce te ipsum.*

nosce te ipsum [L.] Know thyself.

nosce tempus [L.] Know thy time.

noscitur ex sociis [L.] He is known by his companions.

nostalgico [It.] A nostalgic type; someone with a constant sentimental attachment to the past.

nostro periculo [L.] At your own risk.

nota bene [L.] Note well; mark this; take heed.

notabilia [L.] Things that are worthy of being noted.

notatu dignum [L.] Worthy of note.

Not kennt kein Gebot [G.] Want knows no law.

Notre-Dame [F.] Our Lady; used as a name of the Virgin.

Notre-Seigneur [F.] Our Lord; used as a name of Jesus Christ.

notturno [It.] A nocturne; a musical work referring to the evening or set in a nighttime atmosphere.

n'oubliez pas [F.] Do not forget.

nous avons changé tout cela [F.] "We have changed all that": *Molière.*

nous avons tous assez de force pour supporter les maux d'autrui [F.] "We all have the strength to bear the misfortunes of others": *La Rochefoucauld.*

nous dansons sur un volcan [F.] We are dancing on a volcano.

nous verrons [F.] We shall see.

nouveau [F.] New; fresh; recent.

nouveau riche [F.] The new rich, i.e., those who have recently earned their money, as opposed to those who were born to it; a term of opprobrium indicating parvenu status.

nouveauté [F.] Newness; change; novelty.

nouvelle [F.] News; the latest information; also, a story.

nouvellement [F.] Recently; lately; just now.

novella [It.] A short tale characterized by a compact plot and a tight, fast-moving story structure, a form introduced in Boccaccio's *Decameron*; also, a short novel.

Novembre [F.] The month of November.

novena [It.] In the Roman Catholic Church, a devotional prayer of nine days performed to derive a specific benefit.

novissima verba [L.] The last words.

novo [Port.] New; recent; unused.

novum [L.] An ancient game of dice, the aim of which was to throw either a nine or a five.

novum homo [L.] A new man, i.e., a newcomer; the latest arrival; a parvenu.

novus ordo seclorum [L.] A new order of the ages; used as the motto on the Great Seal of the United States of America.

novus rex, nova lex [L.] New king, new laws.

nox [L.] Night.

noyade [F.] A drowning; also, a mass drowning; a drowning pogrom.

nu [F.] Nude; naked; bare.

nuance [F.] A subtle difference, especially in tone or color; thus, a slight degree of change or gradation in anything perceptible by the senses.

nuda veritas [L.] The naked truth.

nudis oculis [L.] With the naked eye.

nudum pactum [L.] A nude pact, i.e., an agreement or contract drawn up without proper legal procedure; an informal pact.

nuevo [Sp.] New; modern; fresh.

nugae canorae [L.] Tuneful trifles; pleasant nonsense.

nugas magno conatu magnas [L.] Much nonsense at great effort.

nuit [F.] Night.

nulla calamitas sola [L.] No calamity comes alone.

nulla dies moerore caret [L.] No day without sorrow.

nulla dies sine linea [L.] Not a day without a line being drawn or written.

nulla regula sine exceptione [L.] There is no law that does not have an exception.

nulli sapere casu obtigit [L.] No man ever became wise by accident.

nulli secundus [L.] Second to none;

the best in the field; the finest available.

nullo fata loco possis excludere [L.] From nowhere can you exclude the fates.

nullum est jam dictum quod non dictum est prius [L.] Nothing is said today that was not said yesterday.

nul n'est content de sa fortune, ni mécontent de son esprit [F.] No one is satisfied with his fortune nor dissatisfied with his understanding.

numero deus impare gaudet [L.] The gods delight in odd numbers.

nummi boni [L.] Genuine coin; real money.

nunc [L.] Never.

nunc aut nunquam [L.] Now or never.

nunc est bibendum [L.] Now it is the time for drinking.

nuncio. See *nunzio.*

nunc vino pellite curas [L.] Now drive away all cares with wine.

nunquam aliud natura, aliud sapientia dicit [L.] Nature and wisdom are never at strife.

nunquam non paratus [L.] Never not prepared.

nunzio [It.] The representative of the pope at a foreign court or government.

nuptiae [L.] Nuptials; the marriage ceremony.

nutri canes, ut te edant [L.] Feed the dogs until they start to eat you.

nux [L.] Nut; also, a nut tree.

nyet [Russ.] No; not; negative.

nymphe du pavé [F.] A nymph of the pavement, i.e., a streetwalker; a young prostitute.

O

obbligato [It.] (1.) In music, an accompaniment or passage which cannot be dispensed with; an obligatory part. (2.) In music, an accessory accompaniment written for a voice or instrument; also, an accompaniment in general.

ober [G.] Upper; higher; above.

obeso [It.] Obese; fat; rotund.

obiit [L.] He or she died; used as a death notice.

obiter dictum [L.] (1.) Something said in passing; a casual remark. (2.) In law, an offhand remark made by a judge; an incidental opinion as opposed to a formal legal statement.

obiter scriptum [L.] Something written in an offhand manner; incidental writings.

objet d'art [F.] An art object; any worthy article, usually small, created by an artist.

obligato. See "obbligato."

obra de común, obra de ningún [Sp.] Everybody's business is nobody's business.

obrar bien, que Dios es Dios [Sp.] Do right, for God is God.

obrigado [Port.] Thank you.

obscurum per obscurius [L.] The obscure by the obscure, i.e., to explain one obscurity by another; to attempt to solve a mystery with an even greater mystery; cf. ignotum per ignotius.

obsequium amicos, veritas odium parit [L.] Submission breeds friends, truth breeds hatred.

observanda [L.] Those things which are to be observed; the observed objects.

obsta principiis [L.] Resist the beginning, i.e., take care of all troubles at the beginning; check all difficulties while they are still small.

obstupui steteruntque comae et vox faucibus haesit [L.] I was astonished, my hair stood on end, and my voice stuck in my throat.

ob turpem causeam [L.] For a base cause; for an immoral reason.

ob vitae solatium [L.] For the pleasures of life.

ocasión [Sp.] Occasion; chance; opportunity.

occasio furem facit [L.] Opportunity makes the thief; cf. (l')occasion fait le larron.

occasionem cognosce [L.] Know the occasion; seize your opportunity.

(l')occasion fait le larron [F.] Opportunity makes the thief; cf. occasio furem facit.

occupato [It.] Occupied; busy; in the process of being used.

occurrent nubes [L.] Clouds will intervene.

octavo [L.] In printing, denotes a particular size of printer's sheet, usually 6 x 9½ inches, to be bound into a section of eight leaves; also, any book of this size.

Octobre [F.] The month of October.

oculis subjecta fidelibus [L.] Under one's faithful eyes.

oculi, tanquam speculatores, altissimum locum obtinent [L.] The eyes, like sentinels, occupy the highest location in the body.

o curas hominum! o quantum est in rebus inane [L.] O the cares of men, how much emptiness is in his affairs.

odalisque [F. from Turkish] A concubine; a female slave or serving girl who spends her life exclusively confined to a harem.

Odelsting [Norw.] Lower part of the Norwegian house of legislature.

oderint dum metuant [L.] Let them hate as long as they fear.

o dii immortales! ubinam gentium sumus? [L.] O ye immortal gods; where in the world are we?

odi memorem compotorem [L.] I hate a drinking companion who has a memory.

odi profanum vulgus [L.] I hate the common crowd.

odium in longum jacens [L.] A grudge that has long been kept.

odium medicum [L.] Medical hatred, i.e., hatred among doctors; professional jealousy in the medical profession.

odium theologicum [L.] Theological hatred, i.e., hatred among men of religion; jealousy among theologians.

odi, vedi, e taci, se vuoi vivere in pace [L.] Listen, see, and keep your tongue between your teeth, if you want to live in peace.

oeil [F.] Eye.

oeil-de-boeuf [F.] A bull's eye, i.e., a round or oval window popular for three hundred years in European architecture.

oeil de maître [F.] The eye of the master.

oeillade [F.] A glance; a quick look, often of a flirtatious nature.

oenomel [L. from Gr.] A drink composed of honey and wine and popular in ancient Greece.

oeuf [F.] An egg.

oeuf brouillés [F.] Scrambled eggs.

oeuf dur [F.] A hard-boiled egg.

oeufs pochés [F.] Poached eggs.

oeuvre [F.] Work; creation, especially a work of literature.

oeuvre de chair [F.] Work of the flesh, i.e., sexual intercourse; adultery; promiscuity.

oeuvres inédites [F.] Unpublished works; unpublished books.

officina [L.] Workshop; factory; place of production.

officina gentium [L.] The workshop of nations.

ofrecer mucho especie es de negar [Sp.] To offer many things is a form of denial.

oggi [It.] Today; this day.

ogni cane è leone a casa sua [It.] Every dog is a lion at home; every dog barks in his own yard.

ogni medaglia ha il suo rovescio [It.] Each medal has its reverse side.

ogni promesso è debito [It.] Promises are debts.

ognuno per se, e Dio per tutti [Sp.]

Everyone for himself, and God for everyone.

ohe! jam satis est [L.] Stop, it is already enough.

ohne Hast, ohne Rast [G.] Without haste, without rest; used as the motto of Goethe.

ohne Kaiser kein Reich [G.] "Without an emperor, no state": *Bismarck.*

oignon [F.] An onion.

ojalá [Sp.] Would to God; used as an oath.

ole [Sp.] Bravo; hooray.

oleo [L.] Oil.

óleo [Port.] Oil.

oleo tranquillior [L.] Smoother than oil.

oleum addere camino [L.] To add oil to the fire; to exacerbate an already troublesome situation.

olla male fervet [L.] The pot boils badly, i.e., things are not running smoothly; affairs are not going well.

ollapodrida [Sp.] A Spanish dish consisting of a number of different kinds of meats and vegetables chopped up and mixed together; hence, a motley mixture.

Om [Skr.] In Hinduism, a word believed to contain within itself all the sounds of the universe, commonly used as a mantra (q.v.), as a prayer, and in the performances of magic rituals.

o matre pulchra filia pulchrior [L.] Oh daughter more beautiful than a beautiful mother.

omen faustum [L.] A favorable omen.

omne bonum desuper [L.] Everything of benefit is from above.

omne ignotum pro magnifico est [L.] Everything that is a mystery is believed to be magnificent.

omne majus continet in se minus [L.] Everything great contains within itself the lesser.

omnem movere lapidem [L.] To leave no stone unturned.

omne scibile [L.] Everything knowable.

omnes eodem cogimur [L.] We are all driven to the same quarter, i.e., to death.

omnes honores bonis [L.] All honors to the good.

omne trinum perfectum [L.] Every perfect thing is three-fold.

omne tulit punctum [L.] He has gained universal approval.

omne tulit punctum qui miscuit utile dulci [L.] The man who has combined the useful with the agreeable has gained universal approval.

omne vivum ex ovo [L.] Everything alive has come from the egg.

omnia ad Dei gloriam [L.] All things to the glory of God.

omnie bona bonis [L.] To the good everything is good.

omnia mea mecum porto [L.] Everything that is mine I carry with me.

omnia mors aequat. [L.] Death levels all.

omnia non pariter sunt omnibus apta [L.] All things are not equally suited for all men.

omnia vanitas [L.] All is vanity.

omnia vincit amor [L.] Love conquers all.

omnia vincit amor, et nos cedamus amori [L.] Love conquers all, and let us too yield to love.

omnia vincit labor [L.] Labor conquers all.

omnibus hoc vitium est [L.] This fault exists in everyone.

omnibus invideas, livide, nemo tibi

[L.] You may envy everyone, Oh, envious one, but no one envies you.

omnis Gallia in partes tres divisa est [L.] "All of Gaul is divided into three parts": opening lines of Caesar's *Gallic War*.

on aime sans raison, et sans raison l'on hait [F.] We love without reason, and without reason we hate.

on commence par être dupe, on finit par être fripon [F.] One starts by being a dupe, one ends by being a cheat.

on connait le véritable ami dans le besoin [F.] One knows the true friend in times of need; a friend in need is a friend indeed.

onde não entra o sol entra o medico [Port.] Where the sun does not come, the doctor does.

on dit [F.] One says; it is said; they say.

on-dit [F.] A rumor; an unsubstantiated report; hearsay.

on ne fait rien pour rien [F.] One does nothing for nothing.

on ne peut pas sonner et aller à procession [F.] One cannot ring the bells and walk in the procession as well; you cannot have your cake and eat it too.

on n'est jamais si heureux ni si malheureux qu'on s'imagine [F.] One is never so happy nor so unhappy as he imagines.

on ne tromps point en bien [F.] One never deceives for a good purpose.

on parle français [F.] French is spoken.

on revient toujours à ses premières amours [F.] One always returns to his first loves.

onus [L.] A burden; weight.

onus probandi [L.] The burden of proof.

onza [Sp.] An ounce.

onza de oro [Sp.] A Spanish doubloon.

ope et consilio [L.] With aid and council.

opéra bouffe [F.] Humorous opera; an operatic genre which began as a series of comic interludes between the acts of serious opera and evolved into its own separate form.

opéra comique [F.] Comic opera; a form of opera originated in the early part of the eighteenth century, in which for the first time spoken dialogue was mixed with a musical accompaniment.

operae pretium est [L.] This is payment for work, i.e., it is worthwhile.

opera omnia [L.] All the works; the total of all the labors.

opere citato [L.] In the work cited; in the passage mentioned.

opes regum corda subditorum [L.] The wealth of kings is the hearts of their people.

opinionâtre [F.] Opinionated; selfwilled; obstinate.

opprobrium medicorum [L.] The disgrace of doctors, i.e., a disease or malady which medical science is not capable of curing.

Optik [G.] Optics; the study of optics.

optima interpres legum consuetudo [L.] Custom is the best translator of the law.

optime [F.] Very well; excellent.

optimismo [Sp.] Optimism.

optimus est portus poenitenti, mutatio consilii [L.] Change of behavior is the best refuge for a sinner.

optimus interpres rerum usus [L.] Experience is the best interpreter of things.

opum furiosa cupido [L.] An all consuming madness for money.

opus [L.] A work; a labor; a composition.

opus opificem probat [L.] The work proves the workman.

or [F.] Gold; the color gold.

ora e sempre [It.] Now and always.

ora et labora [L.] Pray and labor.

ora pro nobis [L.] Pray for us; in the Roman Catholic Church, the refrain of a litany.

orator fit, poeta nascitur [L.] The orator is made, the poet is born.

orbis scientiarum [L.] The circle of science; hence, the circle of scientific knowledge; the extent of scientific understanding.

orchestre [F.] Orchestra; band.

ordem e progresso [Port.] Order and progress; used as the motto of Brazil.

ordinaire [F.] Ordinary; common; vulgar; average.

ordo [L.] Order; series of events; in the Roman Catholic Church, a schedule of yearly religious festivals and holidays.

ore tenus [L.] As far as the mouth, i.e., spoken and not yet proven or accomplished.

organismo [Sp.] An organization; social arrangement.

origo mali [L.] The origin of evil.

orizzonte [It.] The horizon.

orné [F.] Decorated; ornamented; adorned.

oro [Sp.] Gold; the color gold.

oro y plata [Sp.] Gold and silver; used as the motto of the State of Montana.

orra [Sc.] Odd; not evenly grouped.

os [L.] In anatomy, a bone; a section of a bone; also, an oral cavity; an orifice.

os à ronger [F.] A bone to pick, i.e., a problem to talk out; a difficulty to clear up.

osculum [L.] A kiss.

osculum pacis [L.] A kiss of peace.

o si sic omnia [L.] Oh, if everything were but like this.

ospitale [It.] A hospital; sickhouse.

Ostern [G.] Easter.

o tempora! o mores! [L.] Oh the times; oh the manners.

otia dant vitia [L.] Leisure makes vices.

otium cum dignitate [L.] Leisure with dignity; a refined laziness.

otium sine dignitate [L.] Leisure without dignity.

otium sine litteris mors est [L.] Leisure without books is death.

otium umbratile [L.] Ease in retirement.

ottava [It.] In music, an octave.

ottava rima [It.] In poetry, a stanza of eight iambic lines with the first six lines rhyming alternately and the last two forming a rhyming couplet.

ottocento [It.] The nineteenth century.

où [F.] Where; whither.

oubli [F.] Forgetfulness; inability to remember; inadvertence.

oublier je ne puis [F.] I cannot forget.

oubliette [F.] A medieval underground dungeon with a trap door on the top.

oui [F.] Yes; but certainly.

ouï-dire [F.] Hearsay; rumor; word of mouth.

ourie [Sc.] Dark; clouded over; dreary; damp.

ouro é o que ouro vale [Port.] Gold is that which is worth gold.

ousia [Gr.] Substance; stuff; materials of existence.

où sont les neiges d'antan? [F.] "Where are the snows of yesterday?": *François Villon.*

outrance [F.] The final limit; the last extreme; the utmost.

outrance à toute [F.] To the uttermost; to the last degree.

outré [F.] Beyond the limits of propriety; extravagant; nonconventional; bizarre.

outre mer [F.] Beyond the sea.

ouvrage de longue haleine [F.] A long-winded work; an inflated performance.

ouvrier [F.] A worker; a laborer; a mechanic.

ouvrière [F.] A working girl; a female laborer.

oveja que mucho bala, bocado pierde [Sp.] The sheep that bleats too much, loses a mouthful.

oy [Sc.] A grandchild.

oye. See "oy."

oyer et terminer [F.] To hear and to determine; in law, a hearing.

oyez!! oyez! [F.] Hear ye; hear ye.

P

Paar [G.] A pair; a couple.

pabulum [L.] Food; sustenance; a basic nourishment.

pace [L.] With leave of; with respect to.

pace tua [L.] With your consent; by your permission.

pacte de famille [F.] Pact of the family; a family agreement.

pactum illicitum [L.] An unlawful agreement; an illegal pact or partnership.

padrone [It.] (1.) The chief; the master; the leader. (2.) A patron; employer. (3.) In Italy, an innkeeper; a hotel master.

pagano [It.] Heathen; pagan; unholy.

paga o justo pelo peccador [Port.] The just man pays for the sinner.

pahar [Hindi] Mountain.

pailasse [F.] A mattress stuffed with hay or straw.

paillard [F.] A lecherous person; a wanton individual; one dedicated to perverse pleasures.

paille [F.] Straw; hay.

paillon [F.] A fine sheet of metal used in gilding; also, any thin wrapper or covering.

pain [F.] Bread.

pain bénit [F.] Consecrated bread.

pain grillé [F.] Toast.

paix et peu [F.] Peace and little, i.e., a peaceful existence with a little money.

palabra [Sp.] A word, i.e., a spirited conversation; giddy talk; gossip.

palais [F.] A palace; court.

palais de justice [F.] The palace of justice, i.e., the courts of law.

palais de vérité [F.] The palace of truth.

pâle de colère [F.] Pale with rage; livid.

paletot [F.] A woman's overcoat or woolen jacket.

pallida Mors [L.] Pale death.

palma [Sp.] A palm tree.

palman qui meruit ferat [L.] Let him who has won it bear the palm; used as the motto of Lord Nelson.

palma non sine pulvere [L.] The palm is not without dust.

pan [Hindi] In India, a mixture of areca nut and spices, folded into a green leaf and chewed as a refreshment.

panache [F.] A plume or grouping of feathers, especially those on top of a helmet.

panada [Sp.] A dish made of boiled bread that has been sweetened and mixed with wine.

panatela [Sp.] A long, tapered cigar.

panne [F.] A soft, shiny fabric having a smooth, velvety nap.

pannier [F.] A large basket, often made out of wicker and designed for transporting baggage.

panocha [Sp.] A coarse, unrefined Mexican sugar.

pantaloni [It.] Pants; trousers.

pantun [Malay] An extemporaneous poem, popular among the Malays, consisting of four lines, each ending in an alternating rhyme.

panzer [G.] Covered by armor; protected by shields of armor; also, furnished with armored units; accompanied by major protective forces; also, a tank.

papier collé [F.] Pasted paper, i.e., a collection of sundry scraps of paper and "found" objects, randomly pasted on a background.

papier-mâché [F.] A durable decorative material made from a mixture of paper pulp and paste, molded while wet into different shapes and usually painted when dry.

papillon [F.] A butterfly.

papillons noirs [F.] Black butterflies, i.e., black or gloomy thoughts; morose ideas.

papillote [F.] Paper that has been oiled for cooking.

päpstlich [G.] Pertaining to the pope; papal.

par accès [F.] By fits and starts.

par accident [F.] By accident; without reason.

par accord [F.] By accord; by agreement.

parang [Malay] A straight-edged knife used in Indonesia and Malaysia.

para todo hay remedia sino para la

muerte [Sp.] There is a remedy for everything except death.

par avance [F.] In advance; by anticipation; coming up.

par avion [F.] By airplane; used as a direction written on a letter indicating it should go airmail.

par bene comparatum [L.] A perfect pair.

parbleu [F.] A polite oath, similar to "heavens."

par boutades [F.] By whim; by fits and starts.

par-ci par-là [F.] Here and there; a little bit; once in a while occasionally.

par conséquent [F.] In consequence; consequently; as a result.

par contrecoup [F.] As a result; consequently.

par dépit [F.] For spite; done out of spite.

pardonnez-moi [F.] Pardon me.

parem non fert [L.] He cannot endure an equal.

pareu [Tahitian] A decorative cotton fabric worn as a skirt in Polynesia.

par excellence [F.] Pre-eminently; beyond all others.

par hasard [F.] By chance; by accident; at random.

pari passu [L.] With equal speed; with the same progress; with equal pace; side by side. (*Tell the riders they must proceed* pari passu.)

pari ratione [L.] For a similar reason; by like reasoning.

paritur pax bello [L.] Peace is produced by war.

Parkplatz [G.] A parking place; a parking lot.

par le droit du plus fort [F.] By the right of the strongest.

parlementaire [F.] Parliamentary.

parler [F.] To speak; to talk; converse.

parler à tort et à travers [F.] To speak wrong and across, i.e., to speak nonsense; to talk gibberish; to indulge in meaningless conversation.

parlez-vous français? [F.] Do you speak French?

par nobile fratrum [L.] A noble pair of brothers; birds of the same feather; two individuals of similar type.

parole d'honneur [F.] Word of honor; promise; oath.

paroles aigres [F.] Sharp words; a caustic exchange; biting comments.

par oneri [L.] Equal to the burden; prepared for the task.

par parenthèse [F.] By parenthesis; parenthetically; as an afterthought.

par pari refero [L.] I return like for like; I give tit for tat.

par précaution [F.] By way of precaution.

par privilège [F.] By privilege.

pars adversa [L.] The adverse party.

pars pro toto [L.] A part for the whole.

parsque est meminisse doloris [L.] The power of recollection is part of our pain.

parterre [F.] A bed of flowers, usually planted in a symmetrical design.

Parthis mendacior [L.] More deceptive than the Parthians (who were known for their treachery).

parti [F.] A cause; a political party; a side.

particeps criminis [L.] A sharer in a crime; a criminal participant.

(le) parti conservateur [F.] The conservative party.

partie [F.] (1.) An amusement; a game; a diversion. (2.) A line of business; a specific profession; an occupation.

partie carée [F.] A square party; i.e., a gathering of four people, usually two men and two women.

partim [L.] Partly; in part.

parti pris [F.] Prejudgment; prejudice.

(le) parti travailliste [F.] The labor party.

partizione [It.] Division; partition.

partout [F.] Everywhere; all over.

parturiunt montes, nascetur ridiculus mus [L.] The mountains are in labor, a ridiculous mouse will be born of them; much work for little result.

parva componere magnis [L.] To compare small things with great.

parvum parva decent [L.] Little people become their little fate.

pas [L.] Step; pace; walk; stride.

pas à pas [F.] Step by step.

pas à pas on va bien loin [F.] Step by step one goes a long way.

pas de ballet [F.] A ballet step; a maneuver in dance.

pas de bourrée [F.] An even-paced walking step in ballet.

pas d'action [F.] The narrative parts of a ballet; a story ballet.

pas de deux [F.] A dance or ballet figure performed by two people.

pas de trois [F.] A dance or ballet performed by three people.

pasha [Turkish] In Turkey, a title of respect.

pas mal [F.] Not bad; pretty good; good enough.

paso [Sp.] Step; pace; gait; walk.

paso á paso [Sp.] Step by step; by degrees.

paso á paso van lejos [Sp.] Step by step goes far.

passade [F.] In fencing, a motion forward followed by a thrust.

passage d'armes [F.] Passage of arms.

passato il pericolo gabbato il santo [It.] The danger passed, the saint is mocked.

passé [F.] Old; outdated; out of style.

passe-parole [F.] A password; also, in the military, an order passed from the head of a troop to the end by word of mouth.

passe-partout [F.] (1.) Pass anywhere, i.e., a master key; a pass key; a pass. (2.) A light picture frame made up of a piece of picture glass fastened by strips to a pasteboard mat. (3.) A thick gummed mat used to frame pictures.

passetemps [F.] A pastime; an amusement; an entertainment.

pas seul [F.] A dance or ballet figure for one person; a solo performance.

pas si bête [F.] Not such a fool; not so stupid.

passim [L.] Here and there; far and wide; indiscriminately placed.

pasticcio [It.] A work of fragments; a mess; a hodgepodge; a motley collection.

pastiche [F.] A dramatic literary, or artistic presentation that imitates other works; a hodgepodge.

pastorum carmina ludo [L.] I play the songs of the shepherds.

pâté [F.] (1.) A finely ground meat paste. (2.) A small pie, sometimes filled with meat or vegetables.

pâte [F.] Paste; glue.

pâté de foie gras [F.] A paste made from ground goose liver.

pater [L.] Father.

paterfamilias [L.] Father of the family; a patriarch; the male head of a home, not necessarily the father.

paternoster [L.] Our Father; the Lord's Prayer.

pater patriae [L.] Father of his country; a founder of a nation.

pathétique [F.] Pathetic; sad; moving.

pâtisserie [F.] A shop that sells pastries; a bakery; also, a pastry; a fancy cake.

patres conscripti [L.] The conscript fathers; hence, the senators of ancient Rome.

patria cara, carior libertes [L.] A nation is dear, but dearer is liberty.

(la) patrie de la pensée [F.] The fatherland of thought; used as a nickname of Germany.

patriis virtutibus [L.] By ancestral virtues; by the virtues of one's descendants.

patris est filius [L.] The son of his father; like father, like son.

pattes de mouches [F.] Feet of flies, i.e., bad writing; a scrawl; a scribble.

pauca sed bona [L.] Few but good.

pauca verba [L.] Few words; quiet; reticent.

paupertas omnium artium repertrix [L.] Poverty is the inventor of all the arts.

pauvre diable [F.] Poor devil; unfortunate fellow; unlucky man.

pavé [F.] The pavement; the street.

pax [L.] Peace.

pax Britannica [L.] The British peace, i.e., the period when fear of Britain's power kept the peace.

pax in bello [L.] Peace in war.

pax regis [L.] The king's peace.

pax Romana [L.] The Roman

peace, i.e., the period when fear of Roman power kept the peace.

pax tamen interdum, pacis fiducia nunquam est [L.] Sometimes there is peace, but there is never a certainty of its continuance.

pax vobiscum [L.] Peace be with you; in the Roman Catholic Church, a blessing.

pays [F.] Country; rural territory; region; land.

paysage [F.] Landscape; rural scenery; also, landscape painting.

paysagiste [F.] A landscape painter; one who specializes in painting rural scenes.

paysan [F.] A rustic; one with peasantlike manners; a country bumpkin.

paysanne [F.] A countrywoman; a peasant girl.

paysannerie [F.] The peasantry; the lower classes, especially those who dwell in the country; rustics.

paz [Sp.] Peace.

paz y justicia [Sp.] Peace and justice; used as the motto of Paraguay.

peccadillo [Sp.] A slight sin; a petty wrong.

peccatum [L.] Sin; wrongdoing; evil.

peccavi [L.] I have sinned; a prayer of self-accusation.

pêche [F.] A peach.

péché mignon [F.] A sweet transgression; a pretty little sin; a pet vice.

pedibus timor addidit alas [L.] Fear added wings to his feet.

pedir peras al olmo [Sp.] To look for pears on the elm tree.

peignoir [F.] A loose robe worn by women; a bathrobe.

peine forte et dure [F.] Punishment strong and severe.

peintre [F.] A painter.

pejor est bello timor ipse belli [L.] The fear of war is worse than the war itself.

pelote [F.] A ball; a pellet; also, a pin cushion; a ball of thread.

pena de azote [Sp.] A public whipping; a flogging.

pendente lite [L.] Pending the suit.

penetralia mentis [L.] The interior parts of the mind; the inner workings of thought.

pensée [F.] Thought; idea; reflection.

penseroso [It.] Sadness; melancholy; a saturnine condition.

pensez à moi [F.] Think of me.

pension [F.] A boarding school; a boarding house; also, the fee for staying in such establishments; payment for room and board.

per accidens [L.] By accident; haphazardly; by chance.

per amusare la bocca [It.] To please the palate.

per angusta ad augusta [L.] Through the narrow path to majestic ends.

per annum [L.] By the year; yearly.

per aspera ad astra [L.] Through trammels to the stars.

per capita [L.] By head, i.e., for each person; by the individual.

per conto [It.] Upon account.

per contra [L.] To the contrary; to the reverse; on the other hand.

per curiam [L.] By the court.

per diem [L.] By the day; each day; also, an amount of money paid each day; a daily allowance. (*He collected his per diem.*)

perdu [F.] Lost; gone; ruined; wasted.

père [F.] Father.

père de famille [F.] The father of a family; the paterfamilias (q.v.).

peregrinatio [L.] A pilgrimage; a

journey to faroff places, usually for religious purposes.

pereunt discrimine nullo amissae leges [L.] Abandoned laws disappear without making any difference at all.

per fas et nefas [L.] Through right and wrong.

perfervidum ingenium Scotorum [L.] The rash character of the Scots.

perfide Albion [L.] Perfidious Albion; said by Napoleon of England.

per gradus [L.] Step by step; by degrees.

pericula veritati saepe contigua [L.] Truth is often attended with danger.

periculum [L.] Danger.

periculum fortitudine evasi [L.] By courage I have evaded the danger.

periculum in mora [L.] Danger in delay.

périlleux [F.] Perilous; dangerous.

per incuriam [L.] By carelessness; through lack of attention; by neglect.

per interim [L.] In the interim; meanwhile; while waiting.

perjuria ridet amantum Juppiter [L.] Jupiter laughs at the perjuries of lovers.

per legem terrae [L.] By the law of the land.

per mare, per terram [L.] By sea, by land; used as the motto of the British Marines.

per mensem [L.] By the month; monthly. (*He is paid* per mensem.)

per minas [L.] By threats; by warnings. (*When promises failed, he succeeded* per minas.)

permitte divis cetera [L.] Leave the rest to the gods.

pernicibus alis [L.] With swift wings.

perpetuum mobile [L.] Perpetual motion; a constant state of movement.

perpetuum silentium [L.] Perpetual silence.

perruquier [F.] A wig maker; one who sells wigs.

per saltum [L.] By a leap; in one bound; jumping over the intermediary phases.

per se [L.] Of itself; through itself; intrinsically. (*Matinees per se were no longer given.*)

persona ficta [L.] A fictitious person; a nonexistent man.

persona grata [L.] An acceptable person; a person who is welcome; an individual allowed entry to an establishment, social situation, country, etc.

persona muta [L.] A mute person; one who is seen but does not speak; in the theater, a silent actor; an extra.

persona non grata [L.] A nonacceptable person; one who is not welcome; a social or political outcast; a pariah.

per stirpes [L.] By stocks or families; in law, a case in which the relatives of a deceased heir receive property originally intended for that heir.

per totam curiam [L.] By the whole court; unanimous.

per viam [L.] By the way of.

pervigilum [L.] A vigil; a watching all night.

pessimi exempli [L.] Of the worst example.

pessoribus orti [L.] A nobody; one of common birth.

petit [F.] Small; tiny; insignificant; little.

petit à petit [F.] Little by little; bit by bit; by degrees.

petit bleu [F.] A little blue, i.e.,

a telegram that is printed on blue paper.

petit caporal [F.] The Little Corporal; used as a nickname of Napoleon.

petite dame [F.] A lover; a mistress.

petits fours [F.] Little pastries; delicate cakes.

petit-maître [F.] Little master; a young person well-versed in the latest fashions; a swell; a fop.

petite-maîtresse [F.] Young mistress; a young lady of good breeding, well-versed in the fashions of the day; a woman about town.

petit mal [F.] A mild form of epilepsy.

petit monde [F.] The small world, i.e., the world of the small people; the ordinary masses; the common crowd.

petit souper [F.] A little supper; a small, intimate dinner party given for one or two couples.

petits pois [F.] Little peas; fresh green peas.

pétroleur [F.] An arsonist, especially one who uses gasoline to set fires.

petto [It.] The breast; cf. *in petto*.

peu à peu [F.] Little by little; a little at a time; *petit à petit* (q.v.).

peu de bien, peu de soin [F.] Little wealth, little worry.

peu de chose [F.] A little thing; a trifling concern; a matter of small importance.

peu de gens savent être vieux [F.] Few people know how to be old.

peu d'hommes ont été admirés par leurs domestiques [F.] "Few men have been admired by their servants": *Montaigne*.

peu important [F.] Of little importance; immaterial; trifling.

peur [F.] Fear; dread; apprehension.

peut-être [F.] Perhaps; maybe, perchance.

pezzo [It.] Piece; bit; also, a piece of money; a coin.

Pfeffer [G.] Pepper.

phantasia, non homo [L.] A phantom, not a real man.

philosophe [F.] One of the school of eighteenth-century trend philosophy; a philosophical person.

philosophia [L.] Philosophy.

phonanta sunetoisi [Gr.] A word to the wise.

pia desideria [L.] Pious regrets.

pia fraus [L.] A pious fraud.

pianissimo [It.] In music, a direction calling for a soft, muted rendering.

pianoforte [It.] A piano.

piazza [It.] (1.) A large open square found in many Italian towns; a town square. (2.) A porch; a veranda; an arcade.

picador [Sp.] In bullfighting, a horseman whose job is to agitate the bull with a long spear.

picaro [Sp.] A vagabond; a rascal.

picarón [Sp.] A scoundrel; a rogue.

piccolo [It.] Small; little; tiny.

piccolo monde [It.] A small world.

pictura pascit inana animum [L.] He feeds his mind with an empty picture.

pictura poema mutum est [L.] A picture is a silent poem.

pièce de résistance [F.] The finest dish of a meal; the high point of a meal; also, the high point of any event. (*The concerto was the* pièce de résistance *of the evening.*)

pièce d'occasion [F.] A piece for the occasion; a thing prepared especially for the situation; something special.

pièce justificative [F.] Proof; official evidence; a documented illustration of legality, such as a passport or state paper.

pied-à-terre [F.] A foot on the earth, i.e., a second home; a temporary house.

pierre [F.] Stone.

Pietà [It.] In the fine arts, the motif of the Virgin holding the crucified body of Christ.

pietas est fundamentum virtutum omnium [L.] Piety is the basis of all virtue.

pietra dura [It.] Hard stone, i.e., the technique of mosaic work; stone inlay.

pietra mossa non fa muschis [It.] A rolling stone gathers no moss.

pignus [L.] In Roman law, a pledge; security; pawn; token.

pilau [Persian and Turkish] An Eastern dish made of boiled rice, raisins, spice, and meat.

piña [Sp.] Pineapple.

pince-nez [F.] Spectacles that clamp onto the bridge of the nose.

pinxit [L.] He or she painted it; used after the signature of the artist on a painting.

pirouette [F.] In dance, a pivoting or whirling movement.

pis aller [F.] The worst going; the worst possible choice; a last resort; the least desirable possibility.

piscem natare doces [L.] You are trying to teach a fish how to swim, i.e., you are trying to advise an expert.

piton [F.] (1.) In mountain climbing, a metal peg or bar hammered into rock to hold a rope. (2.) A steep and pointed mountain peak.

più [It.] In music, a direction meaning more.

pizzicato [It.] In music, played by plucking; plucked.

place aux dames [F.] Give place to the women; make way for the ladies.

placebo [L.] In medicine, a substance given to placate rather than cure; a sugar pill.

place d'armes [F.] A parade ground.

placet [L.] It pleases; an affirmative vote.

plafond [F.] A ceiling.

plage [F.] The beach; the seashore.

plaidoyer [F.] In law, the speech for the defense; the counsel's address.

plaisanterie [F.] Humor; jesting; facetiousness.

(le) plaisir de la critique nous ôte celui d'être vivement touché de très-belles choses [F.] The pleasure of criticism takes from us that pleasure of being deeply moved by beautiful things.

plaît-il [F.] What is your pleasure?

planté là [F.] Planted there; left on the spot; abandoned; left in the lurch.

Plattdeutsch [G.] A dialect of North Germany.

Platz [G.] Place; splot; area.

plaudite, cives [L.] Applaud, citizens.

plein pouvoir [F.] Full power.

pleno jure [L.] With total authority; with unquestioned power.

(les) plus courtes folies sont les meilleures [F.] The shortest follies are the best.

plus in posse quam in actu [L.] More in the possibility than the actuality.

plus ou moins [F.] More or less.

plus sage que les sages [F.] More wise than the wise.

plus salis quam sumptus [L.] More good taste than expense.

plus scire satius est, quam loqui [L.] It's better for one to know more than he utters.

poca roba, poco pensiero [It.] Little money, little worry.

pocas palabras [Sp.] Few words.

poco a poco [It.] Little by little; a little bit at a time; slowly.

pococurante [It.] Easy going; careless; indifferent; also, a person who displays such characteristics.

poco fiele fa amaro molto miele [It.] One drop of gall spoils a pot of honey.

podestà [It.] Authority; power; also, a legal officer; one who possesses power.

poesis est vinum daemonum [L.] Poetry is the wine of the devil.

poeta nascitur, non fit [L.] The poet is born, not made.

poignard [F.] A dagger; a poniard.

poilu [F.] A soldier stationed in the front line trenches during World War I; thus, any French soldier; a French fighting man.

point d'appui [F.] A point of support; a prop; a fulcrum; a base of operations.

point de nouvelles, bonnes nouvelles [F.] No news, good news.

poisson [F.] Fish; seafood.

poisson de mer [F.] Fish from the sea; salt-water fish.

poisson de rivière [F.] Fresh-water fish.

poivre [F.] Pepper.

poivre de Cayenne [F.] Cayenne pepper.

polisson [F.] A scamp; a troublesome child; a brat; a rascal.

politikon zoon [Gr.] A political animal; Aristotle's definition of man.

politique [F.] Politics; governmental affairs; policy.

pollice verso [L.] Thumbs down; with thumbs turned to the ground, i.e., with the hand signal in ancient Rome indicating a negative decision.

pomme de terre [F.] Potato.

pompa paupertatis [L.] False splendor.

pompon [F.] A tuft or ball, made of feathers, silk, ribbon, etc., used decoratively on hats and helmets.

pondere, non numero [L.] By weight, not by number.

ponte [It.] Bridge.

popolo [It.] Nation; people.

popularis aura [L.] A popular wind, i.e., popular regard; public appreciation; acceptance by the masses.

portamento [It.] In music, an uninterrupted glide from one tone to another, especially with voice or stringed instrument.

porte-chaise [F.] A sedan; a sedan chair.

porte-cochère [F.] A grand entrance gate for carriages, usually attached to a large estate or institution.

porte-monnaie [F.] A purse for carrying money; a pocketbook.

portière [F.] A door curtain; a curtain strung across an entranceway.

portmanteau [F.] A leather suitcase fastened with leather straps, originally designed to fit behind a saddle; also, a small satchel or trunk.

portolano [It.] A medieval map on which harbors and ports are indicated.

posada [Sp.] A lodging house; a tavern; hotel.

posse comitatas [L.] In law, a group of private citizens on call to aid a sheriff or marshal in his law-enforcement duties; a posse.

possunt quia posse videntur [L.] They can because they think they can.

post bellum [L.] After the war.

post bellum auxilium [L.] Aid after the war; hence, help offered when the trouble has passed.

post coitum tristis [L.] A certain sadness or melancholy sometimes experienced after the act of sexual intercourse.

post diluvium [L.] After the flood; usually refers to the Biblical floods.

poste [F.] In France, the postal service; a post office; the mail.

post equitem sedet atra cura [L.] Behind the man on the horse sits black care, i.e., behind the man of wealth care and anxiety still lurk.

poste restante [F.] To be kept at the post office until called for; used in addressing letters.

post hoc [L.] After this, following this case or situation.

postiche [F.] False; artificial; a substitute; a sham.

post litem motam [L.] After the argument began.

post meridian [L.] After midday; in the afternoon; commonly abbreviated P.M.

post mortem [L.] After death; taking place following a death.

post nubila, jubila [L.] After sadness, gladness.

post obitum [L.] Following death.

post partum [L.] After birth.

post prandium [L.] After the feast; following the dinner.

post proelia praemia [L.] After the battles, the loot.

post tenebras lux [L.] After the darkness, light.

post tot naufragia, portum [L.] After so many shipwrecks, a port.

potage [F.] Soup.

potage purée de pois cassés [F.] Split pea soup.

potage queue de boeuf [F.] Oxtail soup.

pot-au-feu [F.] Pot of fire, i.e., a meat broth mixed with vegetables.

(le) pot au lait [F.] The pot of milk; the milk jug.

potiche [F.] A Chinese or Japanese vase, of round or polygonal shape, and usually made of porcelain.

poudre aux yeux [F.] Dust in the eyes, ie., having the wool pulled over the eyes; something that hides the truth in a situation.

poule [F.] A hen; fowl; chicken.

poulet rôti [F.] Roast chicken.

poulet sauté [F.] Sauteed chicken.

pour ainsi dire [F.] So to speak; one might say.

pourboire [F.] For drinking, i.e., money for drinking; also, a tip to one who serves liquor; a gratuity.

pourparler [F.] For to speak, i.e., light talk; casual conversation, often as a preliminary to executive meetings or treaty talks.

pour passer le temps [F.] In order to pass the time.

pour prendre congé [F.] In order to take leave; to take leave.

pour toujours [F.] For always; forever.

pousette [F.] In dance, a movement in which partners join hands and swing in a circle.

pou sto [Gr.] A spot where I may stand, i.e., Archimedes' claim that if he had a place to stand and a lever he could move the world.

praedictio boni [L.] Prediction of happy events.

praemia virtutis [L.] The rewards of virtue; the prize of righteousness.

praemonitus, praemunitus [L.] Forewarned, forearmed.

praestat cautela quam medela [L.] Prevention is better than cure.

praestat injuriam accipere quam facere [L.] It is better to suffer an injury than to inflict one.

précieux [F.] Precious; valuable; fine.

précis [F.] A brief outline; a summary.

préfet [F.] The chief administrator; the prefect.

(les) préjugés, ami, sont les rois du vulgaire [F.] "Prejudice, friend, rules the vulgar multitude": *Voltaire.*

premier danseur [F.] The leading male dancer of a ballet corps.

première [F.] The leading lady in a play; a famous actress; also, a leader; one who commands.

première danseuse [F.] The leading female dancer of a ballet corps.

premier pas [F.] The first step.

(le) premier soupir de l'amour est le dernier de la sagesse [F.] The first sigh of love is the last of wisdom.

prendre courage [F.] Take courage.

prendre la balle au bond [F.] To take the ball on the rebound.

prendre la lune avec les dents [F.] To grip the moon with the teeth; to do that which is deemed impossible.

près [F.] Near; by; on hand; almost; about.

près de [F.] Near; near to; in the proximity of.

(le) présent est gros de l'avenir [F.] "The present is big with the future": *Leibnitz.*

presidio [Sp.] A military fort; a walled garrison; also, in Spain, a prison; a jail.

prestissimo [It.] In music, a direction calling for a rapid tempo.

presto maturo, presto marcio [It.] Soon ripe, soon rotten.

pretas [Skr.] In Buddhism, souls damned to a term in hell; a suffering soul.

prêt pour mon pays [F.] Ready for my country.

preux [F.] Brave; gallant; valiant.

preux chevalier [F.] A gallant knight.

prévenance [F.] Obligingness; kind intentions; good will.

prie Dieu [F.] A desk for kneeling; a prayer stool.

prima caritas incipit a se ipso [L.] Charity begins with one's self.

prima donna [It.) (1.) The featured female vocalist in an opera; a female opera star. (2.) A self-centered, difficult, demanding person.

prima facie [L.] On initial impression; at first view; apparent only at the beginning.

prima inter pares [L.] First among her equals.

primo [L.] At the beginning; in the start; initially.

(il) primo maggio [It.] The first of May.

primo mihi [L.] First for myself.

primo nomo [L.] The principal performer; the star.

primo uomo [It.] The best man in a play or opera; the male star.

primum mobile [L.] The prime mover; the first cause, i.e., God.

principiis obsta [L.] Struggle against the beginnings, i.e., be prepared for difficulty at the start of any venture or circumstance.

principium [L.] A principle.

prior tempore, prior jure [L.] First in time, first in right; first come, first served.

pris [F.] Taken; taken from; caught.

Privatdocent [G.] A lecturer or teacher at a university whose salary is paid by student donations.

Privatdozent. See *Privatdocent.*

privatum commodum publico cedit [L.] Private advantage yields to public advantage.

prix fixe [F.] Fixed prices, especially in a restaurant where all meals on the menu have one price.

probatum est [L.] It has been proven.

probitas laudatur el alget [L.] Uprightness is praised and freezes; if virtue is praised it becomes static.

pro bono publico [L.] For the public good; for the welfare of the people.

procès-verbal [F.] (1.) In law, a detailed report of legal proceedings; a court record. (2.) The minutes of any meeting; a report on a conference.

prochain [F.] Near; nearby; immediate.

pro Christo et patria [L.] For Christ and country.

procul a Jove, procul a fulmine [L.] Far from Jove, far from his thunderbolt; distant from power, distant from trouble.

pro delictum [L.] Because of crime; in law, to question the right of an individual with a criminal record to sit on a jury.

pro Deo et ecclesia [L.] For God and church.

pro Deo et rege [L.] For God and the king.

prodesse quam, conspici [L.] To be useful rather than to be looked at.

prodromos [Gr.] A forerunner.

pro ecclesia et pontifice [L.] For church and pope.

pro et contra [L.] For and against.

profanum vulgus [L.] The vulgar multitude; the profane crowds; the common masses.

pro forma [L.] For form; as a matter of the proper etiquette; for propriety.

pro hac vice [L.] For this turn.

projet [F.] Project; scheme; concept; plan.

projet en l'air [F.] A project in the air, i.e., an impossible scheme; a fantasy; a castle in the air.

pro libertate patriae [L.] For the liberty of one's nation.

pro memoria [L.] For memoriam; in remembrance; for a memorial.

prôner [F.] To lecture; to sermonize; to boast.

prôneur [F.] A lecturer; a long-winded speaker; an inflated talker.

pro nunc [L.] For now; for the meantime.

pronunciamento [Sp.] A proclamation; announcement; a statement of authority, usually of a political nature.

pro patria [L.] For one's country; for the nation to which one belongs.

propos de table [F.] Words of the table; table-talk; dinner conversation.

proprio jure [L.] In one's own right.

proprio motu [L.] Of one's own

motion; of one's own accord; through one's own incentive.

proprio vigore [L.] By one's own vigor; through one's own strength.

propter hoc [L.] On account of this; due to this case, state, or situation.

pro rata [L.] In proportion; according to one's share.

pro rege et patria [L.] For king and country.

pro re nata [L.] For an emergency; for the occasion as it occurs; for a special case.

pro salute animae [L.] For the well-being of the soul.

prosciutto [It.] A ham that has been preserved by smoking.

prosit [L.] May it do good; used as toast.

prosphoron [Gr.] Bread, especially that which is leavened from clean wheat, baked into a flat, round loaf, stamped with a sacred seal, and used in Holy Communion in the services of the Greek Orthodox Church.

protégé [F.] A person kept in the care or tutelage of another.

pro tempore [L.] For the time being; temporarily.

proverbe [F.] A saying; a proverb; a tale with a moral.

providentia divina [L.] Divine providence.

pro virtute felix temeritas [L.] Instead of virtue a lucky audacity.

prudens quaestio dimidium scientiae [L.] Half of wisdom is knowing how to ask the proper questions.

prudentia est rerum expetendarum fugiendarumque scientia [L.] Prudence is the knowledge of things to be sought and avoided.

prud'homme [F.] A proud man;

hence, an honest man; a skillful and diligent worker.

pucelage [F.] Maidenhood; virginity.

pucka [Hindi] Good; authentic; genuine.

pugnis et calcibus [L.] With fists and heels; with all one's might; *à corps pendu* (q.v.).

pukka. See pucka.

pulchrum est digito monstrari et dicier hic est [L.] It is an elevating experience to be pointed out and have people say "it is he"; it is gratifying to be recognized as a famous person.

pulvis et umbra sumus [L.] We are all dust and shadow.

punctatim [L.] Point for point.

punctum comparationis [L.] A point of comparison.

punkah [Hindi] A large fan suspended from the ceiling and kept in motion by a rope and pulley.

purdah [Hindi and Persian] In Moslem countries, a veil; a screen behind which women are kept; also, in Moslem countries, a law which states that all women must be veiled in public.

purée de pois [F.] Puree of pea soup.

pur et simple [F.] Pure and simple.

pur sang [F.] A pure blood; an aristocrat; one of high birth and breeding.

pur troppo [It.] It is but too true.

Putsch [G.] A sudden attempt to overthrown an existing government.

putti [It.] Angel children; cherubs; cupidlike winged children, commonly found in the paintings and sculpture of Renaissance and Baroque Europe.

Q

qahwah [Ar.] Coffee.

qibla [Ar.] In Islam, that direction which faces the holy city of Mecca; also, that wall in a mosque which faces in this direction.

qua [L.] As; as such; in the capacity of. (*The banker qua banker cares little about the character of his customers as long as their money is good.*)

quadrille [F.] A French dance, done by two or more couples moving in squares, popular in the nineteenth century; also, the music for that dance.

quadrimum [L.] Wine that has been aged for four years; hence, the best wine in the house.

quadrivium [L.] The four ways; the four mathematical disciplines, part of the medieval system of the seven liberal arts, comprising arithmetic, astronomy, music, and geometry; cf. trivium.

qua ducitis adsum [L.] Wherever you lead I am with you.

quae amissa salva [L.] Objects that are lost are safe.

quaecumque sunt vera [L.] Whatsoever things are true; used as the motto of Northwestern University.

quae e longinquo magis placent [L.] Things from a distance please that much more.

quae fuerunt vitia, mores sunt [L.] What were once vices now are all the fashion.

quae nocent docent [L.] That which harms teaches.

quae peccamus juvenes, luimus senes [L.] In old age we pay for the excuses of our youth.

quaere [L.] Seek; question; inquire; in law, an annotation inserted in legal records calling for further investigation of a matter.

quae regio in terris nostri non plena laboris? [L.] What region in any land is not filled with our labors?

quaere verum [L.] Seek the truth.

quaeritur [L.] It is asked; the question is brought up.

quaesitum [L.] The outcome of an investigation or inquest; the final result; the conclusion of an argument.

quaestio fit de legibus, non de personis [L.] The question is confined to the laws, not to persons.

quaestio vexata [L.] The vexed question, i.e., a problem which cannot be resolved. (*The* quaestio vexata *of prejudice was once again raised.*)

quae supra nos nihil ad nos [L.]

The things above us or beyond our comprehension we do not trouble over.

quae sursum volo videre [L.] I desire to see the things which are above.

quae te dementia cepit? [L.] What madness has seized you?

quae vide [L.] Which see; plural of *quod vide* (q.v.).

quai [F.] A wharf; a dock; a long pier where cargos are transferred from land to ship and vice versa.

quaich [Gael.] A shallow drinking vessel.

quaigh. See quaich.

qualis ab incepto [L.] As from the beginning; as if starting from scratch.

qualis artifex pereo! [L.] What an artist dies with me; the last words of the Roman Emperor Nero.

qualis rex, talis grex [L.] As the king, so the people; as the shepherd, so the flock.

qualis vita, finis ita [L.] The way you live determines the way you will die.

qualité [F.] Quality; excellence; talent.

quamdiu se bene gesserit [L.] As long as he behaves himself.

quam multa injusta ac prava fiunt moribus [L.] How many injustices and wrongs are enacted through custom.

quam prope ad crimen sine crimine [L.] How close one can get to guilt without being guilty.

quam proxime [L.] As nearly as possible.

quam Romae fueris, Romano vivite more [L.] When in Rome do as the Romans do.

quand il n'y a point de vent chacun sait naviguer [F.] When there is no wind every man is a navigator.

quand la porte est basse il faut se baisser [F.] When the door is low it is necessary to stoop.

quand même [F.] Nonetheless; whatever the circumstances may be; notwithstanding.

quando Dio non vuole, il santo non puole [It.] When God will not, the saint cannot.

quand on emprunte, on ne choisit pas [F.] When one borrows, one does not choose.

quand on voit la chose, on la croit [F.] When one see it, one believes it.

quandoque bonus dormitat Homerus [L.] Even good Homer sometimes nods, i.e., even the greatest masters occasionally wax dull.

quand tout le monde a tort, tout le monde a raison [F.] When all the world is in the wrong, all the world is in the right.

quand un chien se noie, chacun lui offre à boire [F.] When a dog is drowning, everyone offers him a drink.

quanti est sapere! [L.] What a fine thing it is to be clever.

quantum libet [L.] As much as you please.

quantum meruit [L.] As much as has been deserved; in law, a recompense judged fair when no prior rate of payment has been arranged.

quantum mutatus ab illo! [L.] How changed from him; how different he is from before.

quantum placet [L.] As much as pleases you.

quantum sufficit [L.] As much as suffices.

quantum valeat [L.] As much as

it is worth; as far as it goes. (*The argument is sound,* quantum valeat.)

quantum valebat [L.] As much as it was worth.

quantum vis [L.] As much as you wish.

quarta luna nati [L.] Born in the fourth moon, i.e., ill-starred; unlucky.

quartetto [It.] A quartet.

quartier [F.] An area; a district; a part of a town or city.

quartier latin [F.] The Latin Quarter; in Paris, a bohemian section of the city located on the left bank of the Seine.

quarto [L.] Having four leaves, hence eight pages, to the sheet; also, a book or magazine with pages of this size.

qua se [L.] In itself; by its own nature.

quasi agnum committere lupo [L.] As it were to entrust a lamb to a wolf.

quasi dicat [L.] As if one should say.

quasi dictum [L.] As if said.

quatre [F.] (1.) The number four. (2.) A card or die marked with four pips.

Quatsch [G.] Ridiculousness; rot; twaddle.

quattrocentisto [It.] An artist of the fifteenth century, especially one in Italy; cf. "quattrocento."

quattrocento [It.] The fifteenth century, especially the art and literature in Italy at that time.

quatuor [F.] A quartet.

que besa su mano [Sp.] Who kisses your hand; used as a formal closing of a letter to a woman, abbreviated Q.B.S.M.

que dit-on de nouveau? [F.] What news do you have?

que faire? [F.] What to do? What should I do?

que ha? [Port.] What is the trouble?

qué hay? [Sp.] What is the matter?

qué hora es? [Sp.] What time is it?

que la terre est petite à qui la voit des cieux [F.] How small is earth to one who sees it from heaven.

quella guerra è giusta, che è necessaria [It.] "A just war is one which is undertaken through necessity": *Machiavelli.*

quelle bêtise [F.] What a stupidity.

quelque [F.] Some; a few.

quelque chose [F.] Something; some small thing.

quelquefois [F.] Sometimes.

quem ama o perigo n'elle perecerá [Port.] He who loves danger will die by it.

quem canta, seus males espanta [Port.] He who sings drives away grief.

quem Deus vult perdere, prius dementat [L.] If God wishes to destroy, he first makes insane.

quem di diligunt adolescens moritur [L.] Whom the gods love die young.

quem poenitet peccasse, paene est innocens [L.] The one who repents is almost innocent.

quem pouco sabe, asinha o reza [Port.] The man who knows little soon displays it.

quem saepe transit casus aliquando invenit [L.] Who oft escapes mishaps is hit at last.

que n'ai-je le temps! [F.] Had I but the time.

quenelle [F.] A dumpling made with chopped fish or meat and bound with eggs.

que ne parlez-vous? [F.] Why do you not speak?

que sais-je? [F.] What do I know? Used as the motto of Montaigne.

queso [Sp.] Cheese.

qu'est-ce que c'est? [F.] What is it?

question extraordinaire [F.] The extraordinary question; a form of medieval torture in which prisoners were stretched on the rack while being questioned.

questo non mi calza [It.] That does not please me.

questo vento non cribra la biada [It.] This wind winnows no grain.

que ta chemise ne sache ta guise [F.] Do not let your cap know the thoughts it covers.

quête [F.] A search; a quest.

queue [F.] (1.) A braid at the back of the head; a pigtail. (2.) A file of people or vehicles; a waiting line.

queue-de-cheval [F.] The tail of a horse.

que voulez-vous? [F.] What do you wish?

que vous faut-il? [F.] What do you need?

qui aime bien, tard oublie [F.] He who has really loved forgets but slowly.

qui amicus est amat, qui amat non utique amicus est [L.] One who is a friend loves, but he who loves is not always a friend.

qui bene interrogat bene docet [L.] The one who questions well teaches well.

quiche au fromage [F.] A cheese tart served open-faced.

quicquid agunt homines [L.] Whatever men do; that which concerns humanity.

quicquid praecipies esto brevis [L.] Whatever be your advice, be brief.

quid caeco cum speculo [L.] What has a blind man to do with a mirror?

qui dedit beneficium taceat; narret; qui accepit [L.] The one who bestows a benefit should remain silent about it, the one who receives it should proclaim it.

qui derelinquunt legem, laudant improbos [L.] Those that forsake the law praise the wicked.

quid est dulcius otio litterato? [L.] What is sweeter than literary leisure?

quid faciendum? [L.] What is to be done?

quid leges sine moribus vanae proficiunt? [L.] What purpose laws without morals?

quidlibet ex quolibet [L.] Anything out of anything; one thing into another. (*The statesman can make* quidlibet ex quolibet, *a peasant into a king or a king into a peasant.*)

quid novi? [L.] What news?

quidnunc [L.] A busybody; a gossip; one who constantly interferes in other people's affairs.

qui docet discit [L.] He who teaches learns.

qui donne tôt, donne deux fois [F.] Who gives quickly gives twice.

quid pro quo [L.] This for that; one thing given in fair exchange for another; tit for tat.

quid rides [L.] Why do you laugh?

quid rides? mutato nomine de te fabula narratur [L.] Why laugh? With a change in the name the story might tell of you.

quid Romae faciam? Mentiri nescio [L.] What shall I do in Rome? I know not how to lie.

quid times [L.] What do you fear?

quid verum atque decens [L.] That which is true and honorable.

quien [Sp.] Who; whom; whoever.

quien busca el peligro perece en el [Sp.] The one who seeks danger, perishes therein.

quien calla otorga [Sp.] Silence gives consent.

quien mucho duerme, poco aprende [Sp.] Who sleeps much learns little.

quien no há visto á Sevilla no há visto maravilla [Sp.] He who has never been to Seville has never yet seen true wonders.

quien pregunta no yerra [Sp.] Who asks does not err.

quien quiere tomar, convienele dar [Sp.] He who would receive, must give.

quién sabe [Sp.] Who knows?

quieres hacer del ladron, fiate del [Sp.] If you would make a thief honest, trust him.

qui est maître de sa soif est maître de sa santé [F.] He who is master of his thirst, i.e., for alcohol, is master of his health.

quieta non movere [L.] Not to disturb things that are at rest, i.e., to let sleeping dogs lie.

quieto [It.] Quietly; tranquilly; without noise.

qui facit per alium facit per se [L.] The man who does something through another does it himself; thus, in law, the instigator of a crime is as culpable as the one who actually perpetrates it.

qui in communi societate vivere nequit aut deus est, aut bestia [L.] The man who cannot live in society is either a god or a beast.

qui invidet minor est [L.] He who envies is small.

qui male agit odit lucem [L.] Who does evil hates the light.

qu'importe? [F.] What does it matter?

qui n'a qu'un oeil, bien le garde [F.] He who has only one eye must guard it well.

qui n'a santé n'a rien [F.] Who has not health has not anything.

qui nescit dissimulare nescit regnare [F.] He who knows not how to dissemble knows not how to reign; a favorite epigram of Louis XI of France.

qui non proficit, deficit [L.] Who does not go forward goes backward.

quinquennium [L.] A period of five years.

qui parcit nocentibus innocentes punit [L.] Who spares the guilty punishes the innocent.

qui parle, sème; qui écoute, recueille [F.] He who speaks, sows; he who listens, reaps.

qui paye, a bien le droit de donner son avis [F.] He who pays has the right to give his advice.

qui pense? [F.] Who thinks?

qui plus sait, plus se tait [F.] The more one knows, the more silent he becomes.

qui prouve trop, ne prouve rien [F.] Who proves too much proves nothing.

quipu [Sp.] A system of knotting small colored cords onto a single main cord, used by the ancient Peruvians for mathematical calculations and for recording significant dates and events.

quis custodiet ipsos custodes [L.] Who will guard the guards themselves?

qui sentit commodum, sentire debet et onus [L.] The one who feels the advantage ought to feel the burden too.

qui s'excuse s'accuse [F.] He who excuses himself accuses himself.

quisque suae fortunae faber [L.] Each man forges his own fortune.

quis, quid, ubi, quibus, auxiliis, cur, quomodo, quando [L.] Who, what, where, by what aids, why, how, when; questions to ask in order to ascertain the facts in a case.

quis separabit? [L.] Who shall separate us? Used as the motto of the Order of St. Patrick.

qui tacet consentit [L.] He who remains silent gives his consent.

quitasol [Sp.] An umbrella; a parasol; a sunshade.

qui timide rogat, docet negare [L.] He who asks timidly makes denial easy.

qui transtulit sustinet [L.] He who is transplanted sustains; used as the motto of the State of Connecticut.

quitter [F.] To leave; to abandon; to quit.

quitter le monde [F.] To leave the world, i.e., to enter a monastery.

qui un punit, cent menace [F.] One is punished, a hundred menaced.

qui va là? [F.] Who goes there?

qui vit content de rien possède toute chose [F.] The one who lives contented owns everything.

qui vive [F.] On the alert; watchful; attentive.

qui vult decipi, decipiatur [L.] He who wishes to be fooled, let him be fooled.

quoad [L.] As far as; with respect to; concerning.

quoad minus [L.] So much the less.

quoad omnia [L.] As regards all things; as pertains to everything.

quoad sacra [L.] As regards sacred things.

quocunque modo [L.] In whatsoever way; by whatever means.

quod bonum, felix, faustumque sit [L.] May it be good, happy, and of good omen.

quod Deus avertat [L.] Which may God avert. (*In case of accident,* quod Deus avertat, *he becomes the heir.*)

quod Deus vult [L.] What God wishes.

quod erat demonstrandum [L.] Which was to be demonstrated.

quod erat faciendum [L.] Which was to be done.

quod est [L.] Which is; commonly abbreviated *q.e.*

quod facis, fac citius [L.] Whatever you do, do quickly.

quod hoc sibi vult? [L.] What does this mean?

quod nota [L.] Which mark; which take note of.

quod potui perfeci [L.] That what I could do, I did.

quod scripsi, scripsi [L.] What I have written, I have written.

quod vide [L.] Which see; commonly abbreviated q.v.

quo fas et gloria ducunt [L.] Where duty and glory lead; used as the motto of the British Royal Artillery.

quo jure? [L.] By what law? By what jurisdiction or legal authority?

quondam [L.] (1.) Formerly; as before; in past times; heretofore. (2.) A person deprived of his position; one who no longer occupies a certain post or occupation.

quo pacto   [L.]   How? By what
    means?
quot homines, tot sententiae   [L.]
    As many men, so many opinions.
quo vadis   [L.]   Whither goest thou?
quo warranto   [L.]   In law, a writ
demanding that a person produce
a warrant proving that he has
been legally authorized to hold
public office or to practice certain
privileges.

R

rabat [F.] A reduction of price; a discount.

rabbin [F.] A rabbi.

rabido ore [L.] With rabid mouth; raving.

racahout [F.] In North Africa, a concoction of crushed acorns, similar in taste to chocolate, used to feed invalids.

raccolta [It.] A gathering; a harvest.

Rache [G.] Revenge; vengeance.

raconteur [F.] A person who is expert at telling stories.

radeau [F.] A raft.

radunanza [It.] A gathering; an assembly.

rafale [F.] In the military, a swift and intense bombardment which is repeated at regular intervals.

rafraîchissements [F.] Refreshments.

raga [Skr.] A traditional form in Hindu religious music, composed of a theme made up of five or more notes upon which a musician improvises various melodies and rhythms.

raggee [Hindi] A cereal grass cultivated as a staple food throughout the far east.

ragione [It.] A commercial property; a business firm.

ragoût [F.] A highly seasoned dish of meat scraps and vegetables; a stew.

Rahmenerzählung [G.] A story within a story.

raia [Turkish] In Turkey, a non-Moslem.

railleur [F.] Bantering; joking; jeering.

raisin [F.] Grapes.

raison d'état [F.] A reason or purpose of state.

raison d'être [F.] A reason for being; a justification for the existence of someone or something. (*Revenge for the robbery became their raison d'être.*)

raison froide [F.] Cold or calculated reasoning.

raisonnable [F.] Reasonable; rational; logical.

raisonné [F.] Arranged in systematic order; classified.

raisonneur [F.] A reasoner, i.e., one who argues or reasons well; a logician.

raj [Hindi] Rule; domination by a government. (*He was descended from the Bengali raj.*)

raja [Hindi from Skr.] A Hindu king; an emperor.

rajah. See raja.

rakee. See raki.

raki [Turkish from Ar.] An intoxi-

153

cating drink distilled from grains and grapes.

râle [F.] A rattling in the throat; an abnormal sound accompanying regular breathing, often a sign of impending death.

rallentando [It.] In music, a direction to slowly decrease the tempo; also, any musical passage so decreased.

ramassage [F.] Gathering; collecting.

rambla [Sp.] A dry bed or ravine; a gully.

ramequin [F.] A cheese preparation made with bread crumbs or puff pastry and baked in a mold; also, a pottery mold used to hold such a dish.

ramoneur [F.] A chimney sweep; in England this word was used by sweeps in an attempt to improve the image of their profession.

ranchera [Sp.] In Spanish America, a woman rancher; the wife of a ranchero (q.v.).

ranchero [Sp.] In Spanish America, a wrangler employed on a ranch; also, the owner of a rancho (q.v.).

rancho [Sp.] In Spanish America, a small farm or ranch.

ranee. See rani.

rani [Hindi] Title of a Hindu queen; the wife of a raja (q.v.).

ranz des vaches [F.] A song of Swiss cowherds.

rapide [F.] Swift; rapid; fast.

rapidement [F.] Rapidly; quickly; swiftly.

rapporteur [F.] A reporter; one who tells a story; a talebearer.

raptim [L.] Quickly; with haste.

raptor, largitor [L.] Ravisher, lav-

isher, i.e., one who is both rapacious and prodigal.

rara avis. See *rara avis in terris.*

rara avis in terris [L.] A rare bird on the earth, i.e., a special kind of person; a prodigy.

raram facit misturam cum sapientia forma [L.] Wisdom and beauty are rarely united in one person.

rareté [F.] Rarity; scarcity.

rari nantes in gurgite vasto [L.] Here and there some swimming in a vast whirlpool.

rarus sermo illis et magna libido tacendi [L.] Rarely do they speak and much is their reverence for silence.

rasgado [Sp.] In guitar playing, a rapid sweeping of the strings with the thumb.

rastaquouère [F.] A showy and boastful adventurer; also, one who pretends to nobility despite a dubious ancestry.

rast' ich, so rost' ich [G.] If I rest, I rust.

ratero [Sp.] A pickpocket; a thief.

Rathaus [G.] In Germany, a town hall.

Ratskeller [G.] In Germany, the cellar of a town hall, used as a bar or tavern; any tavern.

ratio decidendi [L.] The reason for deciding; the rationale behind a choice.

ratio est radius divini luminis [L.] Reason is a ray of divine light.

ravioli [It.] Small pasta shells stuffed with spiced meat or cheese and usually covered with a meat sauce.

ravissant [F.] Ravishing; charming; adorable.

ravissement [F.] Rapture; delight; ecstasy.

rayah. See raia.

rayon [F.] A ray; a beam of light.

rayonnant [F.] Radiant; beaming; wreathed in smiles.

razón [Sp.] Reason; the rational faculty.

razzia [F.] In North Africa, a raid, especially against non-Moslems.

re [L.] Concerning; in the matter of.

réalité [F.] Reality.

realpolitik [G.] The politics of the realist, as opposed to those of the philosopher or idealist; hence, real or practical politics, usually the kind supported by force rather than reason.

reata [Sp.] A rope used to tie horses together and to keep them in a single file; also, a drove of horses and mules so tied.

reboisement [F.] Reforestation; the replanting of trees in a burned or logged-out area.

rebours [F.] Contrary; reverse; the wrong way.

rebus sic stantibus [L.] As things stand.

recamara [Sp.] A closet or wardrobe; a private room; also, in Mexico, a bedroom; a boudoir.

réchauffé [F.] A dish of food scraps that has been reheated; hence, stale stuff; old and trite news.

recherche [F.] Research; inquiry; investigation of a person or circumstance.

recherché [F.] Exquisite; uncommon; refined; out of the ordinary.

Recht [G.] Law; right; justice.

récidive [F.] A relapse into criminal behavior; the repetition of an offense.

récipé [F.] A recipe or prescription.

reciproque [F.] Reciprocal; mutual.

récitateur [F.] One who recites or repeats something.

recitativo [It.] In music, presented as a recitation or speechlike declamation of narrative passages in oratorios, operas, and cantatas.

reclus [F.] Closed up; secluded; hidden.

reconnaissant [F.] Thankful; grateful.

reconnoîter [F.] To make an examination or observation of; to survey an area of land, especially for military purposes.

recte et sauviter [L.] Justly and mildly.

rector chori [L.] Master of a choir.

rectus in curia [L.] Good standing in court.

reçu [F.] An indication of payment received; a receipt.

recueil [F.] A collection; a selection, especially of literary works.

recueillement [F.] Meditation; contemplation; quiet thought.

reculer pour mieux sauter [F.] To draw back in order to make a better leap, i.e., to retreat in order to best position oneself for an advance.

rédacteur [F.] An editor.

reddite quae sunt Caesaris Caesari; et quae sunt Dei Deo [L.] Render unto Caesar the things that are Caesar's, and unto God the things that are God's.

redintegratio amoris [L.] A renewal of love.

redolet lucerna [L.] It smells of the lamp, i.e., it reeks of the midnight oil; hence, it is labored and overdone.

redowa [F. and G.] A dance of Bohemian origin, resembling the waltz in one form, the polka in another.

reductio ad absurdum [L.] A reduction to absurdity; thus, to disprove an argument by showing how that argument, if carried to its logical conclusion, would become absurd.

reductio ad impossibile [L.] A reduction to an impossibility; the reduction of a premise to an impossible conclusion.

réel [F.] Real; genuine; in actual existence.

reflet [F.] A sheen or lustre, said especially of pottery.

reformado [Sp.] (1.) In the military, a soldier not on active duty; also, a disgraced or dishonorably discharged soldier. (2.) One dedicated to reforming himself or others.

regalado [Sp.] Delicate; dainty; suave.

re galantuomo [It.] The honest king; said of Victor Emmanuel II of Italy.

regalis [L.] Royal; regal; in the style of a king.

regard [F.] A look; a glance.

regard en coulisse [F.] A sideward glance; a look from the corner of the eye.

regarder [F.] To look at; to regard.

regardez [F.] Look; look here; used as an exclamation.

regard tendre [F.] A tender glance; a loving look.

regia via [L.] The royal way; the king's road.

regicida [Sp.] Regicide; the murder of a king.

regidor [Sp.] Ruling; governing; also, in Spain, an alderman or councilman.

régie [F.] A public administration; in France, the office of taxation and public works.

regina [L.] A queen; an empress.

région [F.] A region; a territory; a section of land.

regione del stato [It.] A region of state.

régisseur [F.] A manager; a director; also in theatre, a stage manager.

registre [F.] A register; an account book or notebook.

regium donum [L.] A royal gift.

regius [L.] Royal; used in reference to British professors whose chairs at a university have been founded by royal decree.

règle [F.] A rule; a model; a pattern of behavior; also, a basic principle; a law.

règlement [F.] A regulation; a law; a system of rules.

regnant populi [L.] The people rule; used as the motto of the State of Arkansas.

Reich [G.] An empire; a kingdom.

Reichsbank [G.] The state bank in Germany under the Third Reich.

Reichstag [G.] In Germany, the legislative assembly; the parliament.

reine [F.] A queen; an empress.

re infecta [L.] With the thing unfinished; with one's business or purpose unaccomplished. (*The meeting was broken up and disbanded* re infecta.)

Reiter [G.] A rider, especially a horseman or trooper.

reja [Sp.] An ornamental grating or railing made of iron.

rejectamenta [L.] Rejected parts; garbage; material to be disposed of, especially excrement.

relâche [F.] A rest; an intermission; a respite; also, in theater, a cancellation of a performance.

relata refero [L.] I tell the tale as it was told to me.

relevé [F.] (1.) In ballet, raised into point or half point. (2.) Pungent; heavily spiced.

relievo [It.] In sculpture, raised relief.

religieuse [F.] A pious woman; a nun.

religieusement [F.] Religiously; carefully; faithfully.

religieux [F.] A pious man, one who has dedicated himself to church work or taken monastic vows; a priest; a monk.

religio laici [L.] The religion of the layman; the commoner's creed.

religio loci [L.] The sanctity of a place; the holiness of a location.

Religio Medici [L.] Religion of a doctor; the title of a book by Sir Thomas Brown.

reliquiae [L.] The remains; the relics.

rem acu tetigisti [L.] You have touched the thing with a needle, i.e., you have found the essential problem or question; you have hit the nail on the head.

remarque [F.] In engraving, a distinguishing picture or mark made in the margin of a plate, used to indicate the state of development of that plate and removed before the printing process begins; also, any proof or print from a plate bearing this mark.

remblai [F.] An embankment; a bank.

remède [F.] A remedy for sickness; a medicine.

remerciement [F.] Thankings; phrases or exclamations of thanks.

remisso animo [L.] With mind remiss; listlessly.

remis velisque [L.] With oars and sails.

remis ventisque. See *remiss velisque.*

remittitur [L.] It is remitted, i.e., it is returned.

remuda [Sp.] A collection of horses from which the day's mount is chosen.

renard [F.] A fox.

rencontre [F.] A meeting; an encounter, often of an unfriendly nature such as a duel or altercation.

rendezvous [F.] A place appointed for a meeting; also, the meeting itself; also, to gather together at one spot; to come for an appointment.

renegado [Sp.] A renegade; a rebel; an outlaw.

renegador [Sp.] One who blasphemes sacred things.

renommée [F.] Renowned; famous; celebrated.

renovate animos [L.] Renew your courage.

rénovateur [F.] A renovator; one who restores a thing to its original condition.

renovato nomine [L.] By a revived name.

renseignement [F.] Information; reference; a collection of facts or pertinent data.

rentes [F.] Stocks; annuities; funds producing interest.

rentier [F.] A landlord; one who owns land or buildings and collects rent from them; a person of property.

repagula [L.] Bolts; bars.

repartimiento [Sp.] Distribution; apportionment; partition; also, in Spanish America, an allotment of territory made by the early Spanish conquerors.

repas [F.] A meal; a repast.

répertoire [F.] (1.) The list of plays which a theater company has rehearsed and is capable of performing; also, the individual parts each actor can play. (2.) An index; a catalogue.

replâtrage [F.] A plastering-up; hence, a shaky reconciliation; an uneasy truce.

réplique [F.] An answer; a quick retort; a rejoinder.

répondez s'il vous plaît [F.] Respond, please; commonly abbreviated as *R.S.V.P.*

répondre en Normand [F.] To answer like a Norman, i.e., to give an evasive reply.

repos [F.] Sleep; rest; peace.

reposoir [F.] A resting place; also, in France, a street altar for the monstrance.

repoussé [F.] Done in relief; a method of hammering relief patterns into metal; also, a decoration done in such a technique.

république [F.] A republic; a commonwealth.

repuesto [Sp.] (1.) Retired; secluded; out of touch. (2.) A sideboard; a cupboard or larder.

requiescat [L.] A prayer for the soul of a dead person.

requiescat in pace [L.] May he or she rest in peace.

rerum primordia [L.] The prime elements of things.

res [L.] A thing; a matter; a case.

res adjudicata [L.] In law, a case that has been decided upon and which cannot be revived in court.

res alienae [L.] Other people's belongings.

res angusta domi [L.] Scanty means at home; domestic poverty.

rescate [Sp.] Random-money; also, exchange; barter.

res cogitans [L.] That thing which thinks; the cerebral substance; the mind.

réseau [F.] (1.) In astronomy, a grid superimposed over photographs of stellar images to aid in measurement and calculation. (2.) In lace work, a net or mesh ground; a foundation.

res est sacra miser [L.] A person in distress is a sacred object.

res extra mentem [L.] A thing outside the mind; something which exists in reality rather than in thought or imagination.

res gestae [L.] Things accomplished; deeds; exploits; also, in law, the material facts or circumstances in a case.

res in cardine est [L.] The thing is at a crucial point; the affair has reached its crisis.

res inter alios [L.] A thing between others.

res ipsa loquitur [L.] The thing speaks for itself. (*No need to praise it,* res ipsa loquitur.)

résistance [F.] Resistance; opposition; also, during World War II, the French Resistance movement.

res judicata [L.] In law, a thing already legally decreed or decided upon in court.

res nihili [L.] A thing of no importance; a nonentity.

res nullius [L.] A thing of no value; a nullity.

résolu F.] Resolved; determined; finished.

respice finem [L.] Look to the end; have the final outcome in mind.

respice funem [L.] Beware of the hangman's rope; a pun on the phrase *respice finem* (q.v.).

respondeat superior [L.] Let the

superior, i.e., the teacher or he who knows most, respond.

respublica [L.] The commonwealth.

res secundae [L.] Things favorable.

restaurateur [F.] The owner of a restaurant.

resumé [F.] A summary; an abridgement.

resurgam [L.] I shall rise again.

retablo [Sp.] A retable; an altarpiece.

retenue [F.] Caution; self-control; reserve.

retourner [F.] To return; to go back.

retraite [F.] Seclusion; retirement; also, a hiding place; a shelter.

retroussé [F.] Turned up. (*He was born with a nose retroussé.*)

réunion [F.] A reunion; a reconciliation; a coming together.

revanche [F.] Revenge; requital; also, in sports, a return match.

rêve [F.] A dream; a fantasy; an illusion.

réveillon [F.] A meal eaten during the night; a midnight repast.

revenant [F.] Pleasing; attractive; prepossessing.

revenons à nous moutons [F.] Let us return to our sheep, i.e., let us get back to the subject; in the French farce, *Pierre Pathelin,* said by a judge to a witness whose testimony had strayed from the point.

re vera [L.] In truth; in actuality.

rêveur [F.] A dreamer; a muser; one prone to fantasies.

révolte [F.] A rebel; one who revolts; a renegade.

rex [L.] A king; an emperor; a ruler.

rex non potest peccare [L.] The king can do no wrong.

rex nunquam moritur [L.] The king never dies.

rex regnat, sed non gubernat [L.] The king reigns but does not govern.

rex regum [L.] King of kings.

rez-de-chaussée [F.] The ground floor; the ground level.

rhododaktylos eos [Gr.] The rosy-fingered dawn; a common phrase in Homer's *Odyssey.*

riata. See reata.

ribaldo [It.] A scoundrel; a rascal.

richesse [F.] Riches; treasure; opulence.

rideau [F.] A curtain; a screen.

ridentem dicere verum, quid vetat [L.] What prohibits one from speaking the truth gaily?

ridere in stomacho [L.] To laugh in secret.

ride si sapis [L.] Laugh, if you are wise.

ridotto [It.] A large public festival, often in the form of a masked ball, popular in eighteenth-century England.

rien [F.] Nothing; nought; a trifle.

rien de tout [F.] Nothing at all.

rien ne pèse tant qu'un secret [F.] "Nothing weighs so heavily as a secret": *La Fontaine.*

rien n'est beau que le vrai [F.] "Nothing is beautiful but the truth": *Boileau.*

rifacimento [It.] A reinstatement; a reestablishment, especially of a work of literature or musical composition.

rigor mortis [L.] An afterdeath condition in which the muscles of a corpse grow stiff and rigid.

rigueur [F.] Severe; harsh; cf. "de rigueur."

rime [F.] A rhyme; also, a poetic verse that rhymes; a line in a poem.

rinforzando [It.] In music, an abrupt stress on a single note; also, a sudden and unexpected crescendo.

riposte [F.] (1.) In fencing, a return thrust. (2.) A quick answer; a retort.

rira bien qui rira le dernier [F.] Who laughs last laughs best.

rire [F.] To laugh; to smile; to look happy.

rire dans sa barbe [F.] To laugh in his beard; to laugh up one's sleeve.

ris de veau [F.] The sweetbreads of a calf.

rissole [F.] A sausage-shaped roll filled with diced meat or fish.

risum teneatis, amici [L.] Could you prevent yourself from laughing, friends?

risus [L.] Laughter; a laugh.

ris [F.] Sweetbreads.

riso [It.] Rice.

risorgimento [It.] A rebirth; a revival, especially the revival of learning and the arts which took place in fourteenth-century Italy; also, the rebirth of political unity in Italy during the nineteenth century.

risotto [It.] Rice cooked with meat sauce and cheese.

risqué [F.] Bordering on the obscene; approaching the indelicate. (*He told a risqué story that made us blush.*)

rissolé [F.] Browned by frying in fat.

risu inepto res ineptior nulla est [L.] Nothing is so foolish as the laughter of fools.

ritardando [It.] In music, a direction indicating that the tempo should be gradually slowed.

Ritter [G.] A knight; a nobleman.

rive droite [F.] The right bank of a river.

rive gauche [F.] The left bank of a river, especially of the Seine in Paris.

rivière [F.] (1.) A river; a stream. (2.) A necklace of precious stones; a string of gems.

rixatur de lana caprina [L.] He quarrels over goat's wool, i.e., over something that does not exist.

robe de chambre [F.] A bathrobe; a dressing gown.

roche moutonée [F.] In geology, a rock that has been abraded by glacial movement.

roi [F.] A king.

roi fainéant [F.] An idle king; a king in name only; a do-nothing ruler.

(le) roi le veult [F.] The king wants it; used as the seal of royal consent on a bill in Parliament.

(le) roi le veut. See *le roi le veult.*

(le) roi s'avisera [F.] The king will please himself; used as an indication of a royal refusal to ratify a bill from Parliament.

Roi Soleil [F.] The Sun King; a title of Louis XIV of France.

rôle d'équipage [F.] The role of a ship's crew.

Rollmops [G.] A strip of pickled herring, rolled up with small onions and bits of pickle and secured with a toothpick.

Rollschweller [G.] In music, the pedal of an organ which controls crescendo.

Roma locuta, causa finita [L.] Rome has spoken, the cause is ended; said of any statement which is authoritative or final.

roman [F.] A novel; a work of fiction.

roman à clef [F.] A novel or romance in which certain real-life characters are introduced under fictitious names.

roman-feuilleton [F.] A serialized story in a newspaper.

roman-fleuve [F.] A river-novel; a long and rambling novel which covers many generations of the same family or society.

romantique [F.] Romantic.

rondeau [F.] A poem of French origin, composed of thirteen lines in which the first lines are repeated as a refrain after the eighth and thirteenth lines.

rondino [It.] A short rondo (q.v.).

rondo [It.] A musical composition in which the main theme is repeated after the completion of each subordinate theme.

rosarium [L.] A rose garden.

rosé [F.] Pink; rose-colored; also, a dry red wine popular in France; cf. *vin rosé*.

rôti [F.] A roast; roasted meat, usually beef or veal.

roturier [F.] A person of low birth; a commoner.

roué [F.] A rake; a debauched person; a licentious rascal.

rouge et noir [F.] Red and black; a gambling card game played on a table marked with red and black diamonds on which the bets are placed.

roulade [F.] In music, a vocal passage consisting of trills, arpeggios, rapid scales or similar figures, all sung as single syllables.

rouleau [F.] A small roll, especially a paper roll in which coins are kept.

roux [F.] A paste of butter and flour used to thicken soups or gravies.

royaume [F.] A kingdom; the realm of a king.

ruat coelum [L.] Let the heavens fall.

rubato [It.] In music, fluctuations of tempo; a tempo which is alternately accelerated and decelerated.

rudis indigestaque moles [L.] A rude and undigested mass.

rue [F.] Street.

Ruhm [G.] Fame; glory; renown.

Rührtrommel [G.] In music, a tenor drum.

ruin señor cria ruin servidor [Sp.] A bad master makes a bad servant.

ruit mole sua [L.] The proper form.

rusé [F.] Cunning; clever; deceitful.

ruse contre ruse [F.] Cunning against cunning; guile against guile.

ruse de guerre [F.] A trick of war; a military stratagem or ploy.

ruse in urbe [L.] The country in the city, i.e., a city dwelling with all the benefits of rural life.

rustique [F.] Rustic; quaint; simple.

ryot [Hindi] In India, a peasant farmer.

S

sabot [F.] A wooden shoe popular among the European peasantry.

sabretache [F.] A leather pouch worn on the sword belt by members of a cavalry corps.

sabreur [F.] A gallant and attractive soldier; a swashbuckler.

sac [F.] A sack; a bag; a pouch.

saccage [F.] Sacking; routing; plundering.

sac de nuit [F.] A night bag; a knapsack or small overnight carrying case.

sacellum [L.] A small shrine; an altar.

sacer vates [L.] An inspired bard.

sacramentum fidelitatis [L.] A vow of fidelity; a promise of faithfulness.

sacré [F.] Sacred; holy; consecrated.

Sacré-Coeur [F.] The Sacred Heart, i.e., the Sacred Heart of Jesus Christ.

sadhu [Skr.] In India, a holy man; one who has renounced society for a life of prayer and contemplation.

saepe est sub pallio sordido sapientia [L.] Wisdom is often found under a tattered cloak.

saeva indignatio [L.] Fierce indignation.

saevis inter se convenit ursis [L.] Bears that are savage to others are yet at peace among themselves.

saevis tranquillus in undis [L.] Calm amidst the waves.

sagace [It.] Sagacious; wise; shrewd.

(le) sage entend à demi mot [F.] The wise man understands at half a word.

sage-femme [F.] A midwife.

sage politique [F.] A wise policy; an intelligent plan or program.

sagesse [F.] Wisdom; prudence; sagacity.

saggio fanciullo é chi conosce il suo vero padre [It.] It is a wise son that knows his own father.

sahib [Hindi] Mister; sir; used as title of respect for Europeans by the natives of India.

sain et sauf [F.] Safe and sound.

saint de bois [F.] A saint made of wood, i.e., a false saint; a pretender to sanctity.

Saint-Esprit [F.] The Holy Ghost.

Saint-Père [F.] The Holy Father, i.e., the Pope.

saison [F.] A season of the year.

saison en enfer [F.] A season in hell; a period of anxiety, especially one of great spiritual sufferings.

sake [Jap.] In Japan, an intoxicating beverage made from rice.

sakhia [Ar.] In Middle Eastern countries, a water wheel driven by oxen.

sakka [Ar.] A water carrier.

sal [L.] Salt.

sala [It.] A hall; a room.

salaam [Ar.] In Moslem countries, a greeting or salutation; also, a deep bow to the ground; an obeisance.

salaam aleikum [Ar.] Peace be on you; used as a greeting.

sala da pranzo [It.] A dining room.

salade [F.] A salad.

salade de fruits [F.] A fruit salad.

salaire [F.] A salary; payment for an occupation; recompense.

sal Atticum. See *sal Atticus.*

sal Atticus [L.] Attic salt, i.e., great wit; wisdom.

salé [F.] Salted; preserved or seasoned with salt.

sale bête [F.] A dirty beast; a dirty dog.

salle à manger [F.] A dining room.

salle d'armes [F.] A room of arms; a chamber where fencing is taught and sporting combats are held.

salle d'attente [F.] A waiting room.

salle d'audience [F.] A court room.

salle de bains [F.] A bathroom.

salon [F.] (1.) A drawing room; a reception room, especially one belonging to a rich or fashionable person, where celebrities gather to discuss current literary or political topics. (2.) A gathering of distinguished people. (3.) In Paris, a yearly exhibition of well-known contemporary painters.

salon de coiffure [F.] A hairdresser's shop.

salon de thé [F.] A tea room.

salsicca [It.] Sausage.

saltarello [It.] In Italy, a lively dance characterized by skips and hops at the beginning of each measure; also, the music for such a dance.

saltimbanque [F.] A jester; a joker; a clown, especially one who performs for an audience.

saludador [Sp.] A quack, especially one who pretends to have magical healing powers.

salus mundi [L.] The welfare of the world.

salus populi suprema lex esto [L.] Let the welfare of the people be the supreme law; used as the motto of the State of Missouri.

salva conscientia [L.] With a healthy conscience; without moral reservations.

salva dignitate [L.] Without loss of dignity.

salvam fac reginam, O Domine [L.] God save the Queen.

salvator [L.] A spiritual savior.

salve [L.] Hail, hello; used as a greeting.

salvo honore [L.] Without loss of honor.

sal volatile [L.] A mixture of ammonium bicarbonate and ammonium carbonate, used in the production of smelling salts.

salvo pudore [L.] Without violation or loss of modesty; unstained.

salvo sensu [L.] The sense being preserved; the meaning being kept.

sambouse [Turkish] A pie-shaped pastry stuffed with spices and meats.

Samedi [F.] Saturday.

samisen [Jap.] In Japan, a three-stringed instrument plucked or strummed like a banjo.

samovar [Russ.] A large metal urn with a spigot at the bottom, used to hold tea.

sampan [Chi.] In China, a flat-bottomed riverboat with a single sail, used to haul passengers and small cargo.

samsarma [Skr.] In Buddhist and Hindu philosophy, the endless cycle of birth, suffering, and death common to all humanity; hence, the eternal flow of human life and activity on earth.

samshu [Chi.] In China, an intoxicating drink distilled from rice or millet.

samurai [Jap.] In ancient Japan, a caste of courtier-warriors, protectors of feudal landlords and followers of a strict ethical code based primarily on Zen Buddhism.

sanbenito [Sp.] A black garment painted with flames and devils, worn by prisoners sentenced to the auto-de-fé (q.v.) during the time of the Spanish Inquisition; also, during the time of the Inquisition, a yellow robe worn by converted heretics.

sancta majestas [L.] Sacred majesty.

sancta simplicitas [L.] Sacred simplicity.

sanctum [L.] A sacred place; a place for seclusion and meditation.

sanctum sanctorum [L.] (1.) The holiest of the holies; the most holy place. (2.) Colloquially, a hiding place; a room where one sequesters himself from the world.

Sanctus [L.] In the Roman Catholic Church, the last section of the Preface of the Mass.

sang [F.] Blood.

sang-de-boeuf [F.] Blood of beef; hence, a deep red glaze approaching a claret used to color certain Chinese porcelains.

Sängerfest [G.] A song fest; a festival of choral melodies.

sang-froid [F.] Tranquillity under trying circumstances; coolness during an emergency. (*His sang-froid during the fire amazed us all.*)

sangre azul [Sp.] Blue-blood, i.e., an aristocrat; one who is well-born.

sangria [Sp.] A sweetly flavored and partially diluted red wine, served chilled or with ice.

sannyasi [Skr.] In Hinduism, a homeless mendicant who has devoted his life to seeking spiritual liberation.

sans [F.] Without; free from.

sans amis [F.] Without friends; friendless; alone.

sans appel [F.] Without appeal; without second consideration; in law, a decision which cannot be appealed.

sans cérémonie [F.] Without ceremony.

sans changer [F.] Without changing.

sans-coeur [F.] Without heart, i.e., a heartless and unemotional person.

sans-culotte [F.] A man without britches; during the French Revolution, a Jacobin; thus, an anarchist; any person radical in his political views.

sans Dieu rien [F.] Without God, nothing.

sans doute [F.] Without doubt; unquestionably.

sansei [Jap.] An American citizen born of nisei (q.v.) parents; cf. "issei."

sans façon [F.] Without fashion; hence, informally; without ceremony.

sans faute [F.] Without fail. (*He leaves at eight o'clock* sans faute.)

sans gêne [F.] Without embarrassment; unconcernedly; also, any person who acts in such a way.

sans nombre [F.] Without number. (*People,* sans nombre, *poured into the arena.*)

san pareil [F.] Without parallel; unto itself; unique.

sans peur [F.] Without fear; unafraid.

sans peur et sans reproche [F.] Without fear and without reproach.

sans rien faire [F.] Without doing anything.

sans rime et sans raison [F.] Without rhyme or reason.

sans souci [F.] Without care; without worry or sadness.

sanes tache [F.] Without a spot; unblemished; pure.

santa cosa [It.] A sacred matter.

santé [F.] Health; physical well-being.

santé passe richesse [F.] Health before wealth.

sapere aude [L.] Dare to be wise.

sapientia [L.] Wisdom; supreme understanding.

saraband [F. and Sp.] A stately Spanish dance of Moorish origin; also, the music for that dance.

sari [Hindi] In India, a single piece of silk or cloth wrapped around the body and tucked in at the stomach, the native dress of Indian women.

sarong [Malay] In Malaysia, a colored silk or cloth garment worn by men and women.

sartor [L.] A tailor; usually used humorously.

sartor resartus [L.] The tailor retailored.

satanique [F.] Satanic; diabolical; like the devil.

sat habeo [L.] I have enough.

satis eloquentiae, sapientiae parum [L.] Much eloquence, little wisdom.

satis quod sufficit [L.] What suffices satisfies.

satis, superque [L.] Enough and more than enough.

satis verborum [L.] Enough of words.

sauce hollandaise [F.] Dutch sauce; a savory sauce made with egg yolks and lemon juice, usually served with vegetables.

sauce piquante [F.] A piquant-tasting sauce; a spicy gravy.

saucisson [F.] Sausage.

saucisson en croûte [F.] Sausage baked in pastry crust.

Saul! Saul! Quid me persequeris? [L.] Saul! Saul! Why does thou persecutest me?; words heard by Paul at the moment of his conversion.

sauna [Finnish] A type of steam bath, popular in the Scandinavian countries, in which steam is produced by pouring water over hot stones.

sauve qui peut [F.] Save (himself) who can; thus, an overwhelming defeat or rout from which one should take flight.

savane [F.] A savanna; a swamp.

savant [F.] A man of much learning; a wise man; a sage.

savoir [F.] To know; to have knowledge of; to understand.

savoir-faire [F.] To know how to do; thus, always knowing how to do the appropriate thing; knowledge of the proper behavior under any situation.

savoir-vivre [F.] Knowing how to live; thus, well-bred; having the proper manners for all occasions.

sayid [Ar.] A Moslem descended from Mohammed.

sayyid. See "sayid."

scala caeli [L.] A ladder to heaven.

scaldino [It.] An earthenware brazier.

scampi [It.] Prawns.

scandale [F.] A scandal.

scandaleux [F.] Scandalous; outrageous.

scandalum magnatum [L.] A scandal of the great; the slander and denunciation of great people; profanation of famous or revered individuals.

scapin [F.] A rascal; a knave; a rogue.

scélérat [F.] A rascal; a villain; a criminal.

scenario [It.] A synopsis or skeleton outline of a play, novel, motion picture, etc., sketching out the plot, situation, and character development.

Schadenfreude [G.] Pleasure felt over the suffering of other people.

scherzando [It.] In music, a direction calling for a humorous or playful rendering.

scherzo [It.] In music, a light, playful composition usually written in triple measure.

Schlafrock [G.] A dressing gown; a night gown.

schlampig [G.] Disordered; unruly; slovenly.

Schloss [G.] A castle.

(der) Schmerz ist die Geburt der höheren Naturen [G.] Grief is the birth of the higher nature.

schnapps [G.] A strong type of whisky.

Schrecklichkeit [G.] Frightfulness.

schrik [Dutch] A panic; sudden fear or terror.

schuss [G.] In skiing, a straight, unobstructed course.

Schwärmerei [G.] Great enthusiasm for something.

schweizerkäse [G.] Swiss cheese.

Schwerpunkt [G.] A military manoeuvre used by the Germans in World War II in which a heavy concentration of men and artillery were sent against a weak spot in the enemy line to effect a breakthrough.

scribendi cacoëthes [L.] The disease of writing; an incurable desire to write; cf. *cacoëthes scribendi.*

scribere jussit amor [L.] Love bade me write.

scriptorium [L.] A room for writing; in the middle ages, a room in a monastery reserved for the copying of sacred texts.

scrutinio [It.] A scrutiny; a close study of something.

sculpsit [L.] He or she sculpted it; used with the signature of a sculptor.

sculpteur [F.] A sculptor; a carver.

scuto bonae voluntatis tuae coronasti nos [L.] Thou hast crowned us with a shield of thy good will; used as the motto of the State of Maryland.

sec [F.] Dry, said of wine.

secchio [It.] A bucket; a pail.

secco [It.] Dry, said of wine.

secondo [It.] In music, the second part of a musical composition.

secours [F.] Aid; help; assistance in time of need.

secrétaire [F.] A writing desk, especially one in which the writing board folds up when not in use.

secret de la comédie [F.] Secret of the comedy, i.e., a secret made ridiculous by the fact that it is actually public knowledge.

secundum [L.] According to.

secundum naturam [L.] According to nature.

secundum usum [L.] According to usage.

secundum veritatem [L.] According to truth.

secundus [L.] The second; added to a person's name to indicate that he is second in seniority or rank.

securus et ebrius [L.] Drunk and without care.

securus judicat orbis terranum [L.] The verdict of the world is conclusive.

se defendendo [L.] In law, done in self-defense.

sed haec hactenus [L.] But so much for this.

sedia [It.] A chair; also, a sedan chair.

segno [It.] In music, the sign or $:S:$ which marks the beginning or end of a repeat.

segue [It.] Follows.

se habla español [Sp.] Spanish is spoken.

se há de usar de esta vida como cosa agena [Sp.] We ought to use this life as a thing not our own.

Sehnsucht [G.] Longing; craving; an ardent desire.

seicento [It.] The seventeenth century.

seigneur [F.] A lord; a nobleman; a seignior (q.v.).

seignior [F.] Sir; lord; in France, a title of nobility; also, a land-owning nobleman.

selamlik [Turkish] In Turkey, a section of a private house reserved for receiving male guests.

selon les règles [F.] According to the rules.

selon lui [F.] According to him.

selon moi [F.] According to me.

selon mon sentiment [F.] According to my sentiment; in my opinion.

semel et simul [L.] At once and together.

semel in anno [L.] Once in the year.

semel insanivimus omnes [L.] Everyone has played the fool once.

séminaire [F.] A seminary.

se moquer de la philosophie, c'est vraiment philosophe [F.] "To ridicule philosophy, that's truly philosophy": *Pascal.*

semper [L.] Always.

semper avarus eget [L.] A greedy man is always in want.

semper bonus homo tiro est [L.] A good man is always a novice in the ways of the world.

semper eadem [L.] Always the same; used as the motto of Queen Elizabeth of England.

semper felix [L.] Always well off; ever fortunate.

semper fidelis [L.] Always faithful; used as the motto of the United States Marine Corps.

semper idem [L.] Always the same.

semper paratus [L.] Always prepared; used as the motto of the United States Coast Guard.

semplice [It.] In music, a direction calling for a simple, unadorned rendering.

sempre il mal non vien per nuoccere [It.] Evil does not always come to do harm.

senatus consult. See *senatus consultum.*

senatus consultum [L.] A decree of the ancient Roman senate.

senectus insanabilis morbus est [L.] Old age is an incurable disease.

seniores priores [L.] Elders come first.

se non è vero, è ben trovato [It.] If it's not true, it's well invented.

señor [Sp.] Mister; sir, used as a title of respect; also, a gentleman; a man.

señora [Sp.] Mrs.; madame; used as a title of respect for a married women; also, a lady; a woman.

señorita [Sp.] Miss; used as a title of respect for an unmarried lady; also, a young lady; a maiden.

(le) sens commun n'est pas si commun [F.] Common sense is not so common.

sens interdit [F.] No entry; do not enter.

sensu bono [L.] In a good sense.

sensu malo [L.] In a bad sense.

sensu stricto [L.] In the strict meaning of the word; literally.

senza ceremonie [It.] Without ceremony.

senza speme vivemo in desio [It.] "Still desiring, we live without hope": *Dante.*

sepoy [Port. from Hindi] In eighteenth- and nineteenth-century India, a native soldier serving in a European army in India.

sept [F.] The number seven.

Septembre [F.] The month of September.

sequiturque patrem, non passibus aequis [L.] And he follows his father, not with equal steps.

sérac [Swiss F.] A large angular block or pinnacle of ice broken off from a glacier and wedged in a crevasse.

seraglio [It. from Turkish] (1.) In Constantinople, a palace of a sultan. (2.) A harem; a place for the keeping of a sultan's wives and concubines.

serai [Turkish] (1.) In the East, an inn; a rest stop along a caravan route. (2.) A harem; a seraglio (q.v.).

sérail [F.] A harem; a seraglio (q.v.).

serape [Sp.] In Spanish American countries, a blanket-shaped shawl.

serdab [Ar.] In ancient Egypt, a hidden chamber in a tomb or pyramid where portraits of the deceased were stored.

serein [F.] A gentle rain or snow that falls from a clear sky; also, a night-dew; a soft evening rain.

serenata [It.] (1.) A cantata written on a secular theme and meant to be performed in a pastoral environment. (2.) A musical composition similar to a symphony but less unified and complex.

serenissimo [It.] Most serene; used as a title for a king.

sérieusement [F.] Seriously; in earnest; gravely.

sermo animi est imago [L.] Speech is a picture of the mind; as a man speaks, so is his mind.

sero, sed serio [L.] Late, but with weight.

sero venientibus ossa [L.] The bones, i.e., the leftovers, to those who come late.

serrement de coeur [F.] Pain of the heart; a pang of grief; great sadness.

serus in caelum redeas [L.] May you return late to heaven, i.e., may you live a long time.

servabo fidem [L.] I will keep faith.

serviette [F.] A napkin.

serviteur [F.] A servant.

serviteur de l'état [F.] A servant of the state.

servum pecus [L.] A servile herd.

sesquipedalia verba [L.] Words a foot and one-half long; unnecessarily long and abstruse words.

settecento [It.] The eighteenth century.

sextodecimo [L.] Having sixteen pages or sheets of a book; also, the size of a book, measuring approximately 4½ x 6¾ inches.

sforzando [It.] In music, a direction calling for a sharp accent on a single note or chord.

sfumato [It.] Smoked; in art, painted with a soft, blurry contour in order to give a hazy effect.

shah [Persian] In many Eastern countries, the title of a king or emperor.

shako [F. from Hung.] A high, stiff military hat with a broad brim and fur plume on top, often worn in the United States by military cadets.

Shakti [Skr.] In Hindu Tantracism, the passive or creative force of the cosmos as personified in the image of a goddess; also, the creative energy itself.

shikar [Hindi and Persian] Sports; games, especially hunting and shooting.

shikaree. See "shikari."

shikari [Persian] A hunter; one who tracks big game; also, a native guide, especially one who leads hunting parties.

shiksa [Yidd.] A non-Jewish girl; usually used disparagingly.

shintaï [Jap.] In Japanese mythology, the residence of the gods.

shmaltz [Yidd.] Colloquially, a maudlin and overly sentimental musical or literary production.

si [Sp.] Yes; yea; indeed.

sic [L.] Thusly; in such a way; often used parenthetically to indicate that an error is native to the quotation and not to the author or printer. (*"The principle* [*sic*] *is arriving tomorrow,"* he wrote.)

sicco pede [L.] With dry feet.

siccum lumen [L.] With dry eyes; without tears; unsentimental, especially at moments when emotion is expected.

sic eunt fata hominum [L.] In such a way follows the fate of men.

sic floret decoro decus [L.] Thus decorum engenders decorum.

sic in originali [L.] Thus in the original.

sic itur ad astra [L.] In such a way one goes to the stars.

sic passim [L.] So everywhere.

sic semper tyrannis [L.] Thus ever to tyrants; used as the motto of the State of Virginia; also, the words cried by John Wilkes Booth at Ford's Theatre immediately after he had assassinated Abraham Lincoln.

sic transit gloria mundi [L.] In such a way passes the glory of the world.

sicut ante [L.] As before.

sicut patribus, sit Deus nobis [L.] As with our fathers, may God be with us.

sic vos non vobis [L.] You did it, but the credit is not yours.

Siddur [Heb.] In Judaism, the daily prayer book.

si Deus pro nobis, quis contra nos [L.] If God is for us, who can be against us?

si dis placet [L.] If it pleases the gods.

siècle [F.] A century; an age; a period of time.

siècle d'or [F.] The golden age.

siècles des ténèbres [F.] The dark ages.

siesta [Sp.] A short nap, usually

taken after lunch or in the early afternoon.

sieur [F.] Sir; in France, used as a title of respect.

si fortuna me tormenta esperança me contenta [Sp.] If fortune torments me, hope contents me.

signe de la croix [F.] The sign of the cross.

signor [It.] Sir; Mr.; in Italy, used as a title of respect for a man; also, a gentleman; a lord; a fine man.

signora [It.] Mrs.; Madame; in Italy, used as a title of respect for a married lady.

signore [It.] Sir; Mr.; in Italy, used as a polite term of address for a gentleman.

si je puis [F.] If I can; if I am able.

si jeunesse savait, si vieillesse pouvait [F.] If the young knew, if the old were able.

sile, et philosophus esto [L.] Keep silent, and be counted a philosopher.

(le) silence du peuple est la leçon des rois [F.] The silence of the people is the lesson of kings.

silentium altum [L.] Profound silence.

silent leges inter arma [L.] The laws are silent in time of war.

si leonina pellis non satis est, assuenda vulpina [L.] If the lion's skin does not suffice, sew the fox's to it; if strength is not enough, add cunning.

si le peuple manque de pain, qu'il mange de la brioche [F.] If the people have no bread let them eat cake; the famous reply of Marie Antoinette when told that her subjects were starving.

si les hommes font les lois, les femmes font les moeurs [F.] If men make the laws, women make the customs.

s'il vous plaît [F.] If you please; please.

simagrée [F.] Pretense; affectation.

similia similibus curantur [L.] Like cures like; the basic theory of homeopathic medicine.

similis simili gaudet [L.] Like takes pleasure in like.

si monumentum requiris circumspice [L.] If you seek his monument look around; used as the epitaph of the British architect, Sir Christopher Wren, in St. Paul's Church, London.

simpatico [It.] Sympathetic; understanding; compassionate.

simplex munditiis [L.] Elegant in simplicity.

simplice [It.] Simple; plain.

Simplicissimus [G.] A simpleton; a carefree fool who is constantly exploited by others, but who never learns from his own mistakes.

(la) simplicité affectée est une imposture délicate [F.] "Affected simplicity is a subtle deception": *La Rochefoucauld.*

sine [L.] Without.

sine anno [L.] Without year; undated.

sine cortice natare [L.] To swim without corks, i.e., to carry one's own weight; without help.

sine cruce, sine luce [L.] Without the cross, without light.

sine dubio [L.] Without doubt.

sine ictu [L.] Without a stroke.

sine invidia [L.] Without envy.

sine loco et anno [L.] Without place and year, as in a book without a publisher's imprint and without a date.

sine mora [L.] Without delay.

sine nomine [L.] Without name.

sine nomine vulgus [L.] The nameless rabble; the vulgar multitude.

sine odio [L.] Without animosity.

sine praejudicio [L.] Without prejudice; impartially.

sine qua non [L.] Without which not, i.e., a necessary thing; something that cannot be dispensed with. (*Intelligence is the* sine qua non *of scholarship.*)

singillatim [L.] One by one; in single file.

sinistre [F.] Sinister; threateningly unpleasant; ominous.

sipahdar [Persian] In Persia, a general; a military governor.

si parla italiano [It.] Italian is spoken.

si quaeris peninsulam amoenam circumspice [L.] If thou seekest a beautiful peninsula, look around; used as the motto of the State of Michigan.

sirdar [Hindi] In India, a leader; a chief.

si replica [It.] To be repeated.

sirocco [It.] A hot south wind originating in the Sahara and prevalent in most Mediterranean countries.

sirvente [F.] In medieval France, a ballad sung by the troubadours, satirizing contemporary customs or political beliefs.

sirwan [Hindi] In India, a camel driver.

si, señor [Sp.] Yes, sir; certainly, mister.

si sic omnia [L.] If only everything had been like this.

siste, viator [L.] Stop, traveler.

sit tibi terra levis [L.] May the earth rest lightly upon thee; used as a tombstone inscription.

Sittlichkeit [G.] Ethics; morality; responsible behavior; that which is appropriate or proper.

si vis pacem, para bellum [L.] If you want peace, prepare for war.

six [F.] The number six.

skias onar anthropos [Gr.] Man is the dream of a shadow.

smalto [It.] In mosaic work, a fragment of enamel or tinted glass inset into mosaic designs.

smörbröd [Nor.] Bread and butter.

smörgåsbord [Sw.] A type of meal in which many different meats, vegetables, cheeses, etc. are placed on a long table; a buffet meal.

soave [It.] Sweet; mild; soft.

sobriquet [F.] A nickname.

société [F.] A society; a gathering of people for a common interest or cause.

société savante [F.] A learned society.

soeur [F.] A sister; also, a nun.

soeur de la charité [F.] A sister of charity; a nun.

soi-disant [F.] Calling one's self; hence, self-styled; put-on; would-be; pretended.

soigné [F.] Well-arranged; wrought or finished in good taste; of a sophisticated design or appearance; also, well-groomed; neat and elegant.

soirée [F.] A party held in the evening; a nighttime celebration.

soirée dansante [F.] An evening party at which dancing is the featured entertainment.

soirée musicale [F.] An evening party in which music is the featured entertainment.

sois juste et tu seras heureux [F.] "Be just and you will be happy": *J. J. Rousseau.*

sol [L.] The sun.

sola [L.] Alone; used as a stage direction; cf. *solus.*

solamen curarum [L.] A solace for cares.

sola nobilitas virtus [L.] Virtue is the only nobility.

solano [Sp.] A hot, dusty and often violent southeasterly wind which blows in the Mediterranean countries.

sola virtus expers sepulchri [L.] Virtue alone escapes the grave.

solco onde, e'n rena fondo, e scrivo in vento [It.] "I plough in water, build upon sand, and write upon the wind": *Petrarch.*

soldat [F.] A soldier.

(le) soldat inconnu [F.] The unknown soldier.

soli Deo gloria [L.] Glory be to God alone.

soliloquium [L.] A soliloquy.

soliste [F.] In ballet, a solo dancer.

solitude à deux [F.] Solitude for two; cf. *à deux.*

sol lucet omnibus [L.] The sun shines for everybody.

solus [L.] Alone; used as a stage direction; cf. *sola.*

solutis curis [L.] With all cares dissipated; without worry.

solutus omni foenere [L.] Free of all debt.

solvuntur risu tabulae [L.] The case is dismissed with laughter.

soma [Skr.] In Hindu Vedic mythology, the drink of the gods; the elixir of life.

sombre [F.] Somber; gloomy; depressed.

sombrero [Sp.] A broad-brimmed hat, popular in Mexico and the American Southwest.

sonata [It. from F.] In music, a composition consisting of three parts —exposition, development and recapitulation—each of which varies from the other in rhythm, key, and mood.

sonatina [It.] A short sonata (q.v.).

Sonnabend [G.] Saturday.

sonner [F.] To ring; to sound a bell or chime.

Sonntag [G.] Sunday.

s'orienter [F.] To orient one's self; to get one's bearings.

sortes virgilianae [L.] A type of divination practiced in ancient Rome where advice was sought by opening a copy of Virgil at random and acting on whatever information appeared.

sostenuto [It.] In music, a direction indicating that the tones of a particular passage are to be sustained; also, the sustained passage itself.

sot [F.] Obtuse; stupid; brainless.

sot à triple étage [F.] A tripledecker fool; a colossally stupid individual.

sottise [F.] Stupidity; dullness.

sotto voce [It.] In low voice; under the breath; thus, in private; to one's self. (*He uttered the complaint sotto voce.*)

soubise [F.] An onion sauce.

soubrette [F.] In theatre, originally the role of a saucy maid or servant; thus, any pert, flirtatious young lady; also, a young girl who plays such a part on the stage.

soubriquet. See "sobriquet."

souci [F.] Sadness; melancholy; worry.

souk [Ar.] In Middle Eastern countries, a bazaar or marketplace; the commercial sector of a city, often characterized by canopied streets and outdoor displays of merchandise.

soulagement [F.] Relief; alleviation; solace.

soupçon [F.] A hint; a suspicion; also, a trace; a tiny amount. (*He mixed in a soupçon of garlic.*)

soupe [F.] Soup.

soupe a l'oignon [F.] Onion soup.

soupe au pistou [F.] A vegetable soup seasoned with garlic, basil, and tomato sauce.

soupe maigre [F.] Meager soup, i.e., vegetable soup, meager because it contains no meat.

souplesse [F.] Flexibility; suppleness; ability to bend.

sourd bruit [F.] A whispered rumor; a hushed piece of gossip.

souris qui n'a qu'un trou est bientôt prise [F.] The mouse with but one hole is soon caught.

sournois [F.] Shrewd; cunning; sneaky.

sous [F.] Under; below; beneath.

sous-officier [F.] In the French army, a noncommissioned officer.

sous tous les rapports [F.] In all respects; in every way.

soutache [F.] A thin, flat, ornamental braid, usually worn on the shoulder of military uniforms.

souteneur [F.] A pimp.

souterrain [F.] A cave; an underground cavern or secret room.

souvent d'un grand dessein un mot nous fait juger [F.] Often one words upsets a grand design.

souvent la peur d'un mal nous conduit dans un pire [F.] Often fear of one evil leads us into one worse.

spada [Sp.] A sword.

sparsim [L.] Here and there; thrown about.

spécialité [F.] A specialty. (*Steak is the* spécialité *of the restaurant.*)

spectatrix [L.] A female observer or spectator.

spectemur agendo [L.] Let us be known by our deeds.

spelunca [L.] A cave; an underground cavern.

(la) speranza e il pan de' miseri [It.] Hope is the bread of the wretched.

sperate miseri, cavete felices [L.] Hope, ye miserable ones, beware, ye fortunate ones.

spero meliora [L.] I hope for better things.

spes [L.] Hope.

spes gregis [L.] The hope of the flock.

spesso da un gran male, nasce un gran bene [It.] Often a great good comes from a great evil.

spiccato [It.] In music, a direction addressed to the player of a stringed instrument, calling for a type of short stroke in rapid tempo produced by bouncing the bow on the strings.

spiegeleisen [G.] A form of pig iron, brittle and hard, containing about 20 per cent manganese and used in the production of steel.

spinaci [It.] Spinach.

spiritoso [It.] In music, a direction calling for a lively and spirited rendering.

spirituel [F.] Spiritual; incorporeal; ethereal; also, witty; lively; ingenious.

splendide [F.] Splendid; magnificent; wonderful.

splendide mendax [L.] Honorably untruthful; splendidly dishonest.

spleuchan [Gael.] A pouch used for holding coins, trinkets, tobacco, etc.

spolia opima [L.] The choicest spoils; the finest booty at the conclusion of a battle, especially that which is reserved for the victorious general.

sponte sua [L.] Of one's own accord; by one's own volition.

spoor [Dutch] A trail; a road; a path through the undergrowth.

sposa [It.] Wife; bride.

Sprechen ist Silber, Schweigen ist Gold [G.] Speech is silver, silence is gold.

Sprechen Sie Deutsch? [G.] Do you speak German?

spretae injuria formae [L.] The insult of beauty slighted.

sproposito [It.] A stupid speech; babble; inappropriate and nonsensical words.

spumone [It.] In Italy, a form of water-ice or ice cream, usually served with fruit and nuts.

squalor carceris [L.] The misery of prison.

staccato [It.] In music, a brief, abrupt striking of notes or chords, designed to produce an uneven, disconnected effect.

Stadthaus [G.] A city house, especially a town hall.

stalag [G.] In Germany, a prison camp for soldiers of low rank.

stans pede in uno [L.] Standing on one foot.

stare super vias antiquas [L.] To stand upon the ways of the ancients.

stat magni nominis [L.] There survives the shadow of a great name; that is all that is left of a once-great reputation.

statua [L.] A statue.

status in quo [L.] The state in which, i.e., the state in which something exists; the way a thing or situation happens to be.

status quo. See "status in quo."

status quo ante bellum [L.] The state of things existing before the war.

sta viator et considera monumentum philos antiqui [L.] Stay, traveler, and contemplate the tomb of the ancient philosopher.

Stein [G.] An earthenware beer mug, especially one decorated with painted designs or low relief.

Stellwagen [G.] A stagecoach.

stet [L.] Let it stand; do not erase or delete.

stet fortuna domus [L.] May the good fortune of the house endure.

stiletto [It.] A small pocket dagger.

stillatim [L.] Drop by drop. (*The water was poured on his head* stillatim.)

stilus virum arguit [L.] The style shows the man.

Strasse [G.] A street; an avenue.

stratum super stratum [L.] Layer on top of layer.

stringendo [It.] In music, a direction indicating that the tempo is to be accelerated.

strudel [G.] A dessert pastry made with sheets of thin dough filled with layers of fruit.

stumrel [Sc.] Stupid; moronic.

stupa [Skr.] In Buddhist countries, a bell-shaped shrine with a pinnacle on top, worshiped as a symbol of divine laws.

stupor mundi [L.] The wonder of the world; one who has gained international fame and praise.

Sturmabteilung [G.] In Nazi Germany, a military force, also known as the Brownshirts and Storm Troopers, organized by Hitler in 1924, noted for the violence of its operations.

Sturm und Drang [G.] Storm and Stress; in eighteenth-century Ger-

many, a romantic literary movement, initiated as a response to
the sterility of neoclassicism and
dedicated to the glorification of
nature and the individual.

(le) style c'est l'homme [F.] The
style is the man.

sua cuique voluptas [L.] To each
his own type of pleasure; cf. *de
gustibus non est disputandum.*

suaviter in modo, fortiter in re [L.]
Gently in manner, strongly in
deed.

subadar. See "subahdar."

subahdar [Hindi and Persian] (1.)
The governor of a state or territory. (2.) An Indian officer serving in the British army and com-
manding an army of Indian
troops.

sub conditione [L.] Under the condition.

sub judice [L.] In law, before the
court; under consideration by a
judge.

sublata causa tollitur effectus [L.]
The cause having been removed
the effect is erased.

sub rosa [L.] In secret; in private;
confidentially. (*When his back
was turned they held a* sub rosa
conference.)

sub sigillo [L.] Under the seal, i.e.,
in strict confidence; in secret.

sub silentio [L.] Under silence; in
silence.

sub specie [L.] Under the appearance of.

sub specie aeternitatis [L.] Under
the aspect of eternity; hence, in
its natural or essential condition.

sub verbo [L.] Under the word; refers to any word or entry in a
dictionary, catalogue, etc.; abbreviated as *s.v.*

sub voce. See *sub verbo.*

succès de circonstance [F.] A success of circumstances; an accidental success.

succès de scandale [F.] A literary
or artistic production which gains
fame through its notoriety rather
than by its genius.

succès d'estime [F.] A success of
esteem; thus, a play or novel that
is well received by the critics and
intelligentsia but not popular with
the public.

succès fou [F.] A mad success; a
success accompanied by wild enthusiasm.

sucre [F.] Sugar.

sudor [L.] Sweat; perspiration.

sufre por saber, y trabaja por tener
[Sp.] Suffer in order to know, toil
in order to have.

suggestio falsi [L.] A suggestion of
what is false.

sui generis [L.] Of its own kind;
in a class all by itself; unique.

sui juris [L.] In law, people of full
legal standing and responsibility,
as opposed to those with legal
disabilities such as insanity.

sukiyaki [Jap.] A Japanese dish
made of diced meat, fresh vegetables, soya sauce, sake (q.v.),
and seasonings, all fried together
in one pan.

summa cum laude [L.] With greatest praise; used as an academic
title of the highest honor, usually
awarded at graduation ceremonies.

summa petit livor [L.] Even the
most noble are attacked by envy.

summum bonum [L.] The highest
good; the absolute good.

summum jus, summa injuria [L.]
Extreme law, extreme justice.

sunt lacrimae rerum [L.] There are
tears for mortal things.

suo jure [L.] In one's own right.

suo loco [L.] In its proper place; in the rightful location.

superbia [L.] Pride; false satisfaction.

suppressio veri [L.] A suppressor of truth.

suppressio veri, suggestio falsi [L.] The withholding of the true is a suggestion of the false; cf. *suggestio falsi*.

supra [L.] Above; as mentioned previously, as in a book or reference.

suprema lex [L.] The highest law.

supremum vale [L.] Farewell for the last time.

sur [F.] On; upon; above.

sur le champ [F.] On the field, i.e., now; immediately.

sur le pavé [F.] On the street.

sursum corda [L.] Lift up your hearts.

surtout [F.] Mainly; above all; chiefly.

surtout, pas de zèle [F.] Above all, no zeal.

sutra [Skr.] In Hinduism, a wise statement; a proverb; also, a collection of such statements.

suttee [Hindi] In India, the practice, outlawed since the nineteenth century, of cremating the wives and concubines of a Hindu man along with the man himself; also, a widow so cremated.

suum cuique [L.] To each his own.

syce [Ar.] In India, a groom; a horse trainer.

syllabatim [L.] Syllable by syllable.

sympathique [F.] Sympathetic; likeable; friendly.

T

tabagie [F.] Smelling of cigarette or cigar smoke; also, a room filled with tobacco smoke.

tabardillo [Sp.] Sunstroke; a fever caused by overexposure to direct sunlight.

tabatière [F.] A snuff box.

table à écrire [F.] A writing table.

tableau [F.] A picture; a vivid image; a scene from life; also, a silent and motionless arrangement of people, the purpose of which being to pictorially dramatize a particular historical or social event.

tableau vivant [F.] A living picture; a group of people standing in frozen positions, dramatizing a particular historical or social event.

table de nuit [F.] A night table.

table des matières [F.] Table of contents.

table d'hôte [F.] In an inn or hotel, a meal served to guests at an appointed hour each day; also, the table where such a meal is eaten.

tabula ex naufragio [L.] A plank in a shipwreck, i.e., the last hope.

tabula rasa [L.] A clean tablet; a blank slate; something which has not been written upon.

tace [L.] Be silent.

tacent, satis laudant [L.] Silence is praise enough.

tacet [L.] It is silent; in music, a direction indicating that a performer should refrain from playing during a particular passage.

tâche [F.] A task; a job.

tâche sans tache [F.] A work without fault.

tacita [L.] Tacit things; things which are implied rather than stated.

taedium vitae [L.] The tedium of life; a weariness with living; existential ennui.

Tag [G.] Day.

täglich [G.] Daily.

taille douce [F.] An engraving printed with a copper plate.

tailleur [F.] A tailor.

tais-toi [F.] Silence; be quiet; used as an exclamation.

tal padrone, tal servitore [It.] Like master, like man.

tal para cual [Sp.] This for that; tit for tat; an eye for an eye and a tooth for a tooth.

tamale [Sp.] In Mexico, a popular dish made of a highly seasoned meat base covered with a crust of cornbread.

tamasha [Ar.] A parade; a spectacle; an extravagant pageant.

tamis [F.] A sieve; a strainer.

tandem aliquando [L.] Now at last. (*The visitor supped, read, spoke, fiddled, and* tandem aliquando, *went to bed.*)

tangere ulcus [L.] To touch a sore spot; to poke at one's vulnerabilities.

tant [F.] So much; so many.

tantaene animis caelestibus irae [L.] Are there such violent passions in heavenly beings?

tant bien que mal [F.] As good as bad; so-so; *comme çi comme ça* (q.v.).

tant de monde [F.] So many people.

tante [F.] Aunt.

tanti paesi, tanti usanze [It.] So many countries, so many customs.

tant mieux [F.] So much the better.

tanto è miser l'uom quant' ei si riputa [It.] A man is only as miserable as he thinks himself so.

tanto uberior [L.] So much the richer.

tant pis [F.] So much the worse.

tant s'en faut [F.] So far from it.

tant soit peu [F.] Ever so little.

tantum non [L.] All but; practically. (*As he himself doth* tantum non *confess.*)

tapis [F.] A rug; a carpet.

tarantella [It.] A spirited Neapolitan folk dance done in six-eighth time.

tard [F.] Late; tardy.

tarde quae credita laedunt credimus [L.] We are slow to believe what hurts when believed.

tarocchi [It.] A deck of tarot cards, used for games and for divination; also, a type of game played with these cards.

tarsia [It.] In art, a process of inlaying pieces of carved and polished wood into mosaic patterns.

tarte [F.] A tart.

tartine [F.] A piece of bread spread with butter or jam.

Tartufe [F.] The hero of a play by Molière, who is characterized by his false religiosity; hence, a sanctimonious hypocrite.

tasse de thé [F.] A cup of tea.

tatsache [G.] Fact.

tat tvam asi [Skr.] That thou art; a mantra (q.v.).

Te Deum Laudamus [L.] Thee God, We Praise; title of a sacred Christian canticle.

te hominem esse memento [L.] Remember thou art a man.

te judice [L.] Thou being the judge; if you were the one to decide.

tel brille au second rang, qui s'éclipse au premier [F.] Some will shine in the second rank who are lost in the first.

tell [Ar.] A hill; a mound.

tel maître, tel valet [F.] Like master, like man.

tel menace, qui a peur [F.] He who threatens is always afraid.

tel père, tel fils [F.] Like father, like son.

tema [It.] In music, a theme.

témoignage [F.] An eyewitness account; an impartial testimony.

temperantia [L.] Temperance.

temperantia est moderatio cupiditatum rationi obediens [L.] Temperance is the moderating of one's desires in obedience to reason.

tempête [F.] A tempest; a storm.

tempête dans un verre d'eau [F.] A tempest in a glass of water.

tempi passati [It.] Times past; time gone by.

tempora mutantur nos et mutamur

in illis [L.] The times change, and we change with them.

tempore [L.] In the time of.

tempori parendum [L.] It is necessary that one yield to the times.

temps [F.] Time; a period; a term.

temps morts [L.] Dead times; hence, long and boring periods of time; uneventful days or hours.

temps perdu [F.] Time lost; the forgotten past.

tempus [L.] Time; the hours.

tempus edax rerum [L.] Time, the devourer of all things.

tempus fugit [L.] Time flies.

tempus omnia revelat [L.] Time reveals everything.

tenaille [F.] A low outwork set in the main ditch between two bastions.

tenax propositi [L.] Tenacious of purpose.

tendre [F.] Tender; affectionate; soft.

tendresse [F.] Tenderness.

tenez bonne table et soignez les femmes [F.] "Keep a good table and flatter the ladies": *Napoleon.*

tenir maison [F.] To keep house; to maintain a household.

tennis de table [F.] Table tennis; ping-pong.

tenore [It.] In opera, a tenor; one who sings in a tenor voice.

tentanda via est [L.] A way must be attempted.

tenue [F.] Deportment; bearing; the way one behaves in public.

tenue de ville [F.] Town clothes; fashions worn in an urban atmosphere.

tenuto [It.] In music, a direction indicating that a note or chord be held to its full value; a tenuto mark is made in this way: ＰＩ.

tequila [Sp.] A plant native to Mexico; also, an intoxicating drink made from the juices of this plant.

terminus ad quem [L.] The terminal point; the finishing point; the end.

terminus a quo [L.] The starting point.

terminus vitae [L.] The end of life; death.

terra [L.] Land; earth; soil.

terra-cotta [It.] (1.) A type of hard-baked earthenware used in ornamental decorations and for the fashioning of vases, jugs, etc. (2.) A brownish-orange color of medium to low brilliance.

terra culta [L.] Cultivated land; earth that has been tilled.

terra damnate [L.] Damned earth; hence, garbage; dross; trash.

terrae filius [L.] A son of the earth; thus, one of low birth; a peasant.

terrae incognita. See "terra incognita."

terrae motus [L.] A movement of the earth, i.e., an earthquake.

terra es, terram ibis [L.] Dust thou art, to dust thou shall return.

terra firma [L.] Firm earth; solid ground, as opposed to swampland, quicksand, the seas, etc.

terra incognita [L.] Unknown land; a territory which has not been charted or explored; hence, any unknown subject or field of study.

terra nova [L.] New land; undiscovered country.

terras irradient [L.] May they illuminate the earth; used as the motto of Amherst College.

terreno [It.] The ground floor.

terreplein [F.] A level platform on the top of a bulwark or rampart where the canons are situated.

terre sainte [F.] Holy earth; consecrated ground.

tertio [L.] Thirdly.

tertium gaudens [L.] A third person who takes advantage of the hostilities between two other people to gain his own ends.

tertium quid [L.] A third something; something which cannot be placed in one category or the other; a third object or element in a situation which differs from both that have come before; also, a medium between two incompatible things.

tertius gaudet. See *tertius gaudens.*

terza rima [It.] A form of rhyming poem in which the second line of one triplet rhymes with the first and third line of the next.

terzetto [It.] In music, a composition written for three performers or vocalists.

terzo [It.] Third.

teskeria [Turkish] A license; a permit.

testatum [L.] It is testified.

testis unus, testis nullus [L.] One witness is no witness; it takes more than one witness to prove a case.

tête [F.] The head.

tête-à-tête [F.] Face to face; hence, a confidential meeting or discussion between two people.

tête-bêche [F.] In philately, the printing of a stamp or series of stamps upside down; also, the stamps so printed, often considered very valuable by collectors.

tête-de-pont [F.] A bridgehead.

tête folie [F.] A superfluous person; one of no substance or depth.

teterrima belli causa [L.] The most dire cause of war; ordinarily used as a satirical reference to women.

tetrum ante omnia vultum [L.] A countenance hideous beyond all conception.

Teufel [G.] The devil.

(der) Teufel ist ein Egoist [G.] "The devil is all for himself": *Goethe.*

texte [F.] A text; a theme; a passage.

thanatos [Gr.] Death.

thé [F.] Tea.

théâtre de verdure [F.] An open-air theater.

thé dansant [F.] A tea dance; a dance given in the afternoon during which tea rather than intoxicating drinks is served.

thèse [F.] A thesis; a proposition; a plan; also, an academic thesis.

tibi seris, tibi metis [L.] For yourself you sow, for yourself you reap.

tiempo ni hora no se ata con soga [Sp.] Time and tide wait for no man.

tiens [F.] Look here; used as an exclamation.

tiens ta foi [F.] Keep thy faith.

tiers état [F.] The third estate; the lower classes.

tigré [F.] Spotted; speckled.

tilak [Hindi] In India, a caste mark worn on the forehead.

timbre-poste [F.] A postage stamp.

timide [F.] Timid; timorous; bashful.

timidi mater non flet [L.] A coward's mother does not weep.

timeo Danaos et dona ferentes [L.] I fear the Greeks even when bearing gifts.

timor [L.] Fear; fright; dread; also, an object that causes fear.

timor addidit alas [L.] Fear gave him wings.

timor belli [L.] Fear of war.

tinaja [Sp.] A large earthen jar for holding water.

tirage [F.] An edition.

tirailleur [F.] A sharpshooter; a sniper; a soldier who is highly trained with a rifle.

tireur [F.] A marksman; a sharpshooter; a good shot with a rifle.

tiroir [F.] A drawer of a bureau, desk, etc.

titre [F.] A title; a heading.

titulado [Sp.] One who is titled.

todo cae en el dedo malo [Sp.] Everything falls on the sore finger.

toga virilis [L.] The robe of virility; in ancient Rome, a toga presented to adolescent males as a symbol of their approaching manhood.

tohu bohu [Heb.] Without form; void; primordial chaos.

toison d'or [F.] The golden fleece.

tollite barbarum morem [L.] Away with such a barborous custom.

tomando ora la espada, ora la pluma [Sp.] Taking now the sword, now the pen.

tombe [F.] A tomb; a grave; also, a gravestone.

ton [F.] The fashion; the vogue; that which is chic; also, style; fashionableness.

tonga [Hindi] In India, a two-wheeled passenger vehicle pulled by horses and occasionally by men.

tonnelle [F.] An arbor.

to pan [Gr.] The all; the cosmos.

tophaike [Turkish] A musket; a rifle.

torero [Sp.] A bullfighter.

torii [Jap.] In Japan, the gateway to a Shinto temple.

Torte [G.] A tart; a fancy layer cake.

tortilla [Sp.] A flat Mexican cake usually made of maize.

tortuga [Sp.] A turtle.

Totentanz [G.] The dance of death.

totidem verbis [L.] In so many words.

totis viribus [L.] With all one's strength.

toto caelo [L.] By the entire heavens, i.e., separated from each other by the distance of all heaven; diametrically opposed.

toto genere [L.] In whole character; in all generic characteristics.

totum [L.] The whole.

totum divisum [L.] A divided whole; an entity which lends itself to division.

totus in se [L.] Wrapped entirely in one's self; drawn into one's self.

totus teres atque rotundus [L.] Whole, smooth, and round; hence, spherical; complete in itself; self-contained.

touché [F.] Touched; in fencing, an exclamation indicating that a swordsman has scored a point over his opponent; hence, in an argument, an utterance admitting that one's adversary has made a clever point.

toucher [F.] To touch; to feel; to handle.

toujours [F.] Always; ever.

toujours amoureux, jamais marié [F.] Always in love, never married.

toujours gai [F.] Always gay.

toujours perdrix [F.] Always partridge; hence, too much of a good thing.

toujours politesse [F.] Always politeness, i.e., manners gain all ends.

toujours prêt [F.] Always ready.

tourbillon [F.] A vortex; a whirl-wind.

tour de force [F.] A feat of strength; an act of great force or power. (*His final speech, a* tour de force, *left the crowd stunned.*)

tour de promenade [F.] A walk; a stroll.

tour d'horizon [F.] A tour of the horizon; hence, a scan; an over-view.

tour d'ivoire [F.] An ivory tower.

tourisme [F.] Tourism.

tous frais faits [F.] All expenses paid.

tous maux sont pareils alors qu'ils sont extrêmes [F.] "All evils are equal when they are ex-treme": *Corneille.*

tout à fait [F.] Completely; en-tirely.

tout à la mort [F.] All to the death; without quarter; to the bloody end.

tout au contraire [F.] Quite to the contrary.

tout au moins [F.] At the very least.

tout à vous [F.] All for you; at your service.

tout bois n'est pris bon à faire flèche [F.] Every kind of wood is not suited for making arrows.

tout comme chez nous [F.] Just as with us.

tout comme vous voudrez [F.] Just as you please.

tout comprendre, c'est tout pardon-ner [F.] To understand every-thing is to pardon everything.

tout court [F.] Quite short; with-out anything added.

tout de bon [F.] All in earnest; sincere; without ulterior motive.

tout de suite [F.] All at once; im-mediately.

tout d'un coup [F.] At one blow; suddenly.

toute eau éteint feu [F.] Any water puts out fire.

tout ensemble [F.] All together; taken as a whole; the entire effect.

tout est bien qui finit bien [F.] All's well that ends well.

tout est dit [F.] All has been said.

toutes têtes ne sont pas coffres à rai-son [F.] All heads are not knowledge boxes.

tout est perdue hors l'honneur [F.] All is lost save our honor; said by Francais I of France to his mother when taken prisoner after the battle of Pavia.

tout homme qui à quarante ans n'est pas misanthrope n'a jamais aimé les hommes [F.] Every man who is not a misanthrope at forty has never loved humanity.

tout le monde [F.] All the world; everyone; everybody.

tout le monde est sage après coup ([F.] Everybody is wise after the event.

tout nu [F.] All naked; stark naked; nude.

tout simplement [F.] Quite simply.

trabajo [Sp.] Work; labor; toil.

trabajo de manos [Sp.] Manual work.

tracasserie [F.] Annoyance; vexa-tion; turmoil.

tractent fabrilia fabri [L.] Let smiths do the work of smiths.

traditus, non victus [L.] Betrayed, not conquered.

traduttori traditori [It.] Transla-tors are traitors.

tragédien [F.] A tragedian; a tragic performer.

tragi-comique [F.] Tragicomic.

tragique [F.] Tragic; mad.

trahison [F.] Treachery; foul play.

trahit sua quemque voluptas [L.] Every man is attached to his concept of pleasure.

traînant [F.] Dragging; trailing.

traîneau [F.] A sledge; a sleigh; a dragnet.

trait de génie [F.] A stroke of genius; a brainstorm.

traité [F.] A tract; a treatise.

traité de paix [F.] A French treaty.

traiteur [F.] An innkeeper; one who owns or maintains a restaurant.

trajet [F.] Passage; distance, a journey.

trampa [Sp.] A trap; a snare; a trapdoor.

tranquillo [It.] In music, a direction calling for a passage to be rendered in a peaceful and tranquil manner.

translateur [F.] A translator.

trattoria [It.] In Italy, a small restaurant.

Traum [G.] A dream.

travail [F.] Work; labor; toil; also, great suffering; pain.

trecentista [It.] An artist of the thirteenth century, especially one in Italy; cf. *trecento.*

trecento [It.] The thirteenth century.

treillage [F.] Trellice work; lattice work.

trek-schuit [Dutch] A passenger boat that travels on canals.

tremolando [It.] In music, a direction indicating that a passage should be rendered in a tremulous and emotional manner.

tremor cordis [L.] A quaking of the heart.

trente et quarante [F.] Thirty and forty; an alternate name for the card game rouge et noir (q.v.).

très [F.] Very; much; most.

très bien [F.] Very well; very good.

très distingué [F.] Very distinguished.

très gentil [F.] Very gentle.

très grande dame [F.] A very great lady; a woman of high position and enormous wealth.

tria juncta in uno [L.] Three joined in one; used as the motto of the Order of the Bath.

tricolore [F.] Three-colored; also, a three-colored flag.

tricorne [F.] A three-cornered hat.

triennium [L.] A period of three years.

trillo [It.] A trill.

triomphe [F.] Triumph; victory.

tripotage [F.] A medley; a mess; a jumble.

triste [F.] Sad; melancholy; dull.

trivium [L.] The three ways; the three nonmathematical disciplines, part of the medieval system of the seven liberal arts, including grammar, rhetoric, and logic; cf. quadrivium.

troika [Russ.] A passenger carriage drawn by a team of three horses riding abreast.

trois [F.] The number three.

trois-temps [F.] A waltz done in three-quarter time.

trompe l'oeil [F.] Fool the eye; in art, any visual trick created by the artist to fool the observer; an intentional optical illusion.

troppo [It.] Too much.

troppo disputare la verità fa errare [It.] Too much dispute leads the truth astray.

trop tard [F.] Too late.

trottoir [F.] The pavement; the sidewalk.

trouvé [F.] Found.

truites à le meunière [F.] Trout cooked in butter.

tu [F.] You; thou.

tumbak [Turkish] Tobacco.

tu ne cede malis, sed contra audentior ito [L.] Yield not thou to misfortune, but confront them the more boldly; cf. *ne cede malis.*

tu quoque [L.] Thou also; you too; a retort accusing one of his own accusations.

türbe [Turkish] In Turkey, a tomb or mausoleum; a burial chamber.

tutor et ultor [L.] Protector and avenger.

tutrix [L.] A female tutor.

tutte le strade conducono a Roma [It.] All roads lead to Rome.

tutti-frutti [It.] Mixed fruits.

tutti i giorni [It.] Every day.

tuum [L.] Thine.

tuum est [L.] It is your own.

U

ua mau ke ea o ka aina i ka pono
[Hawaiian] The life of the land
is established in righteousness;
used as the motto of the State of
Hawaii.

Übermensch [G.] A superman; a
person of superhuman abilities.

uberrima fides [L.] Superabundant
faith.

ubi amor, ibi oculus [L.] Where
there is desire, there is the eye.

ubi bene, ibi patria [L.] Where it
goes well with me, there is my
country.

*ubicumque homo est, ibi beneficio lo-
cus est* [L.] Wherever a man
is, there is a chance to do a kindness.

ubi jus incertum, ibi jus nullum [L.]
Where justice is uncertain, there
justice does not exist.

ubi lapsus, quid feci? [L.] Where
have I slipped, what have I done?

ubi mel, ibi apes [L.] Where there
is honey, there are the bees.

ubique [L.] Everywhere.

*ubi solitudinem faciunt pacem appel-
lant* [L.] Where they make a
devastation, they call it a peace.

ubi supra [L.] Where above mentioned; abbreviated as *u.s.*

uhuru [Swahili] Liberty; freedom.

uitlander [Dutch] In Dutch South
Africa, an outsider; an alien.

ulema [Turkish] In Islam, a group
of learned men trained in law
and in the doctrines of the Koran.

ultima ratio regum [L.] The ultimate argument of kings, i.e., war.

Ultima Thule [L.] The farthest
Thule; a name given by the ancients to the outer limits of the
earth; hence, any distant place
or remote boundary.

ultimo sforzo [It.] A final effort; a
last attempt.

ultimum supplicium [L.] Extreme
punishment, i.e., death.

ultimum vale [L.] The final farewell; the last good-bye.

ultimus regum [L.] Last of the
kings.

ultimus Romanorum [L.] Last of
the Romans, i.e., the classicists;
said of Samuel Johnson, among
others.

ultra licitum [L.] Beyond that
which is allowed; beyond the legal
limits.

ultra mare [L.] Beyond the sea.

ultra modum [L.] Beyond measure;
hence, extravagant; outlandish;
beyond the accepted norm.

ultra posse [L.] Beyond possibility.

ultra vires [L.] Beyond one's power;
beyond the limits of one's capa-
bilities; in law, outside the powers

of the court; beyond judicial authority.

umiak [Eskimo] A wooden frame boat covered with animal skins, used primarily by Eskimo women.

umile e preziosa e casta [It.] Humble and precious and chaste.

um so besser [G.] So much the better.

un [F.] The number one.

una golondrina no hace verano [Sp.] One swallow does not make a summer.

una voce [L.] With one voice; in accord.

una volta furfante è sempre furfante [It.] Once a rascal, always a rascal.

und [G.] And.

und andere [G.] And others.

und so fort [G.] And so forth.

und so weiter [G.] And so forth; and so on; commonly abbreviated as *u.s.w.*

unguento [It.] An unguent; a salve.

unguentum album [L.] White ointment.

unguibus et rostro [L.] With talons and beak.

unguis in ulcere [L.] A claw in the scar; salt in the wound.

unio mystica [L.] Mystical union.

(l') union fait la force [F.] In union there is strength; used as the motto of Belgium.

unitas [L.] Unity.

un mal chiama l'altro [It.] One evil calls up another.

uno animo [L.] With one mind.

uno ictu [L.] With one blow.

uno saltu [L.] In one step; with a single jump.

unrein [G.] In music, out of tune.

Unsinn [G.] Nonsense.

unum necessarium [L.] The one necessary; the one thing on which all others depend.

unum post aliud [L.] One thing at a time.

unus testis oculatus plus valet quam mille auriti [L.] One eyewitness is worth more than a thousand who have heard of it.

uomo universale [It.] A universal man; a Renaissance man.

uova [It.] Eggs.

urbem lateritiam invenit, marmoream reliquit [L.] He found the city brick and left it marble; said of the Roman Emperor Augustus.

urbi et orbi [L.] To the city, Rome, and the world.

urbs [L.] A city; a large community.

Ursprache [G.] A parent language; a mother tongue.

usine [F.] A factory.

uso fa legge [It.] Custom makes the law.

usque ad aras [L.] Even to the altars; hence, acquiescence only up to the point of one's personal religious beliefs; cf. *amicus usque ad aras*.

usque ad nauseam [L.] To the point of nausea; cf. "ad nauseam."

usque haugh [Gael.] The water of life, i.e., whisky.

usurpatrix [L.] A female usurper.

usus loquendi [L.] The current usage of speech.

ut ameris, ama [L.] That thou mays't be loved, love.

ut ameris, amabilis esto [L.] In order to be loved, be loveable.

utcunque placuerit Deo [L.] In whatsoever way it shall please God.

utile dulci [L.] The useful with the pleasant.

utinam noster esset [L.] Would that he were one of us; would that he were on our side.

ut infra [L.] As below.

uti possidetis [L.] As you possess it; used in treaties of war to indicate that opposing sides should retain possession of the territories which they happen to occupy at the moment of signing the treaty.

ut pignus amicitiae [L.] As a pledge of friendship.

ut prosim [L.] In order that I might be of service.

ut saepe [L.] As often.

ut supra [L.] As above; abbreviated as *u.s.*

uxor [L.] Wife.

V

vacantia bona [L.] Goods without an owner; unclaimed belongings.

vache [F.] A cow.

vache de loin a lait assez [F.] A cow in another pasture gives plenty of milk; the grass is always greener on the other side.

vacher [F.] A cowherd.

vacuo [L.] A vacuum; an emptiness; an unfilled space.

vade in pace [L.] Go in peace.

vade mecum [L.] Go with me; used to describe any object which is constantly carried and frequently used. (*The guidebook became my vade mecum.*)

vade retro [L.] Get thee behind!

vae [L.] Alas.

vae soli [L.] Woe to he who is alone, i.e., he who is cut off from his fellow men.

va-et-vient [F.] A coming and going; a hubbub.

vagón [Sp.] A railroad car.

vainqueur [F.] A vanquisher; conqueror; victor.

vale [L.] Farewell.

valeant mendacia vatum [L.] Away with the lies of poets.

valeat quantum valere potest [L.] Let it pass for what it is worth.

vale mas buena esperanza que ruin posesion [Sp.] "A good hope is better than a poor possession": *Cervantes.*

valentia [L.] A prince.

valet [F.] A manservant; a male attendant who looks after the personal and household affairs of his employer.

valet de chambre [F.] A manservant who looks after the private needs of his employer.

valet de place [F.] A manservant whose services are available for short periods of time, especially to travelers.

valeur [F.] Value; price; worth.

valeur en espèces [F.] Cash value.

valide [F.] Valid.

vallum [L.] In ancient Rome, a high embankment built to protect Roman military camps.

valor [L.] Value; worth.

val più un asino vivo, che un dottore morto [It.] A living donkey is better than a dead professor.

valuta [It.] Value; worth, especially of revenues during international exchange.

vámonos [Sp.] Let us go.

van [Dutch] Of; from.

vanille [F.] The liquid extract of the vanilla bean.

vanitas vanitatum [L.] Vanity of vanities.

vaquero [Sp.] In Spanish American

191

countries, a herdsmen; a sheep or cow wrangler.

vargueño [Sp.] A square writing desk, usually decorated and painted.

varia lectio [L.] A variant or alternative reading.

variatio delectat [L.] Variety pleases.

variazioni [It.] In music, variations.

variété [F.] Variety; change; diversity.

variorum notae [L.] Notations by various commentators.

varium et mutabile semper femina [L.] A thing of moods and changes is woman ever.

vas [L.] In anatomy, a vessel; a duct.

vase de nuit [F.] A vase of the night, i.e., a chamber pot.

vaso vuoto suona meglio [It.] An empty barrel makes the loudest sound.

vastator [L.] One who lays to waste; a devastator.

va-t'en [F.] Get away; get out; used as an exclamation.

Vater [G.] Father.

Vater, ich rufe dich [G.] Father, to thee I call.

Vaterland [G.] The fatherland.

Vaterlandsliebe [G.] Love of the fatherland; patriotism.

Vaterunser [G.] The Lord's Prayer.

vates [L.] A fortune teller; a prophet; a soothsayer.

vates sacer [L.] A sacred prophet or poet.

vaticinator [L.] A prophet; one endowed with powers of divination.

vaurien [F.] A good-for-nothing; a worthless person.

vaya con Dios [Sp.] Go with God; used as a farewell.

veau [F.] A calf; also veal.

vedi Napoli e poi mori [It.] See Naples and die.

veilleuse [F.] A night lamp.

veld [Dutch] A wild prairie covered with shrubs and tall grass.

veldt. See "veld."

velho amador, Inverno com flor [Port.] An old man in love is like a flower in winter.

velis et remis [L.] With sails and oars; thus, with all haste; with all possible effort.

velites [L.] Foot soldiers in the ancient Roman army.

velouté [F.] Velvetlike; soft; also, in wine testing, smooth to the palate.

vel prece, vel pretio [L.] For love or money.

velut aegri somnia [L.] Like the dreams of a sick man.

veluti in speculum [L.] As in the mirror.

vena [L.] In anatomy, a vein.

ven aca [Sp.] Come here.

venaison [F.] Venison.

venda [Port.] An inn.

vendetta [It.] In Corsica and Italy, a blood feud; the inevitable violent retaliation which takes place when the honor of one family or individual is offended by another.

vendeur [F.] A vendor; a salesman.

vendeuse [F.] A salesgirl.

vendidit hic auro patriam [L.] This man sold his country for gold.

Vendredi [F.] Friday.

venez au fait [F.] Come to the point.

venia sit dicto [L.] Pardon the expression.

Veni Creator Spiritus [L.] Come, Creator Spirit; the title of a medieval hymn.

venienti occurrite morbo [L.] Apply the remedies while the sickness is coming.

venire facias [L.] Cause to come; in law, a writ issued a sheriff directing him to summon a jury.

venite [L.] O, come.

veni, vidi, vici [L.] I came, I saw, I conquered; the words of Julius Caesar to the Roman senate after his defeat of Pharnaces.

vent [F.] A wind; a breeze.

venta [Sp.] (1.) A roadside inn; a small hotel . (2.) A marketplace; a small shop.

ventana [Sp.] A window; a window frame; also, the shutter of a window.

vent de mer [F.] A sea breeze.

vente [F.] A sale; an auction.

venter non habet aures [L.] The stomach does not have ears, i.e., words mean nothing to a starving man.

ventis secundis [L.] With prosperous winds; with good luck.

vento e ventura pouco dura [Port.] Wind and fortune quickly change.

ventre affamé n'a point d'oreilles [F.] An empty belly has no ears.

ventre à terre [F.] With belly to the ground, i.e., at full speed.

ventura [Sp.] Felicity; happiness; good fortune.

vera causa [L.] A true cause; something which produces an objective and observable result.

vera incessu patuit dea [L.] The true goddess was revealed by her step.

vera pro gratis [L.] True things rather than pleasant things.

vera prosperità è non aver necessità [It.] True wealth is to have no want.

verba facit emortuo [L.] He is talking to a dead man; i.e., he is wasting his breath.

verbatim et litteratim [L.] Word for word and letter for letter.

verbi gratia [L.] For the sake of a word; for instance; by example.

verbis ad verbera [L.] From words to blows.

verbosa et grandis epistola [L.] A huge and wordy letter.

verboten [G.] Forbidden; prohibited; against the law.

verbum [L.] A word.

verbum sapienti sat est [L.] For a wise man a word is enough.

verbum non amplius addam [L.] I will not add another word.

verdad [Sp.] Truth; accuracy; veracity.

verdad es amarga [Sp.] Truth is a bitter herb.

verde [Sp.] Green; verdant; also, unripe; immature; undeveloped.

Verderben, gehe deinen Gang [G.] "Destruction, take thy course!": *Schiller.*

verdeur [F.] Tartness; also, of wines, harshness; bitterness.

vere adeptus [L.] A true adept; a genuine initiate; an individual well-versed in the arcane arts and sciences.

Verein [G.] An association; an organization; a society or club.

vere scire est per causas scire [L.] True knowledge consists of knowing causes.

Verfasser [G.] Author; writer.

(la) véritable éloquence consiste à dire tout ce qu'il faut et à ne dire que ce qu'il faut [F.] True eloquence consists in saying all that is necessary and nothing more than is necessary.

veritas [L.] Truth.

veritas: Christo et ecclesiae [L.]

Truth: for Christ and for the Church; used as the motto of Harvard University.

veritas et virtus [L.] Truth and virtue; used as the motto of Pittsburgh University.

veritas liberabit vos [L.] Truth shall make you free.

veritas nihil veretur nisi abscondi [L.] Truth fears nothing but concealment.

veritas nunquam perit [L.] The truth never dies.

veritas praevalebit [L.] Truth will prevail.

veritas temporis filia [L.] Truth is the daughter of time.

veritas victrix [L.] Truth the conqueror.

veritas vos liberabit [L.] Truth shall make you free; used as the motto of Johns Hopkins University.

veritatem dilexi [L.] I have loved the truth; used as the motto of Bryn Mawr College.

veritatis cultores, fraudis inimici [L.] Devotees of truth, enemies of error.

veritatis simplex oratio est [L.] The language of truth is simple.

vérité [F.] Truth; verity.

vérité sans peur [F.] Truth without fear.

(la) vérité sort de la couche des enfants [F.] From the mouths of children comes the truth.

Verlag [G.] A publishing company.

Verlagsbuchhändler [G.] A book publisher.

Verlust will Vorwand [G.] Bad luck is ever ready to make excuses.

vermicelli [It.] A thin spaghetti-shaped pasta.

vermoulu [F.] Worm-eaten.

ver perpetuum [L.] Perpetual spring.

verre [F.] A glass; a drinking glass.

verre à vin [F.] A wine glass.

vers [F.] Verse; poetry.

Versammlung [G.] A meeting; an assembly.

vers blancs [F.] Blank verse.

vers de société [F.] The verse of society; light and witty poetry dealing with fashionable topics.

verse libre [F.] Free verse; unrhymed lines of poetry.

verser des larmes de crocodile [F.] To cry big crocodile tears.

Verstand [G.] Understanding; discrimination; intelligence.

vert [F.] The color green.

vertigine [It.] Vertigo.

vertù [It.] Virtue; also, taste.

(la) vertu n'irait pas si loin si la vanité ne lui tenait compagnie [F.] "Virtue would not go so far if vanity did not keep her company": *La Rochefoucauld.*

verum et falsum [L.] True and false.

verus et fidelis semper [L.] Always true and loyal.

verweile doch ! du bist so schön [G.] "Stay, thou art so fair": *Goethe.*

verworren [G.] Confused; muddled.

vespertilio [L.] A bat.

vestido [Sp.] Costume; clothing; garb.

vestido de corte [Sp.] Court dress; a costume worn in royal surroundings.

vestigia [L.] Footprints; tracks; remaining traces; vestiges.

vestigia nulla retrorsum [L.] No footsteps backwards; cf. *vestigia terrent.*

vestigia terrent [L.] The footsteps frighten me; said by the fox in

Aesop's fable *The Lion and the Fox* when he saw tracks leading into the lion's den but none coming out.

vestigium [L.] A footprint; a vestige; the remains.

vetera extollimus, recentium incuriosi [L.] We extol the old things, regardless of the productions of our own time.

vettura [It.] A carriage.

veuf [F.] A widower.

vexata quaestio [L.] A vexed question that has not been solved; a dilemma.

via [L.] Road; way; path.

via [It.] Come; come along; used as an exclamation.

via ad vitam [L.] The road to life.

via amicabili [L.] In a friendly way.

via dolorosa [L.] The way of sorrow; specifically, the path tread by Christ to the Cross.

via lactea [L.] The milky way.

via media [L.] The middle way; the moderate course through all extremes.

viande [F.] Meat.

via trita, via tuta [L.] Beaten path, safe path.

via, veritas, vita [L.] The way, the truth, the life.

vibrato [It.] In music, a tremulous or pulsating sound produced vocally or instrumentally.

vicerè [It.] A viceroy.

vice versa [L.] Conversely; the terms of the case or situation being reversed.

vichyssoise [F.] Potato soup.

victoria Pyrrhica [L.] A Pyrrhic victory, i.e., one in which the conqueror loses more than the conquered.

victor ludorum [L.] The winner of the games; the champion of an athletic competition.

victrix fortunae sapientia [L.] Wisdom is the conqueror of fortune.

(la) vida es sueño [Sp.] Life is a dream.

vide [L.] See; consult; check with.

vide ante [L.] See before; see previously.

vide et crede [L.] See and believe.

video meliora proboque, deteriora sequor [L.] I know and approve the better course, I follow the worse.

vide post [L.] See the following.

vide supra [L.] See above.

videtur [L.] It seems; it appears.

vide ut supra [L.] See as above.

vie amoureuse [F.] Love life; an intimate narrative describing one's romantic and sexual affairs.

vieille barbe [F.] An old beard; hence, an old man; an elderly gentleman.

vieille cour [F.] The old court, i.e., the French monarchy as it existed before the Revolution.

vieille moustache [F.] An old mustache, i.e., an old soldier.

viejo [Sp.] An old man.

viele Kinder, viele Segen [G.] Many children, many blessings.

viele Köpfe, viele Sinne [G.] So many men, so many minds.

Vieles wünscht sich der Mensch, und doch bedarf er nur wenig [G.] "Man desires many things, yet has need of but little": *Goethe.*

viellard [F.] An old man.

vien dietro a me, e lascia dir le genti [It.] "Come, follow me, and leave the world to its babblings": *Dante.*

vierge [F.] A virgin; a maiden.

vi et armis [L.] By force of arms.

vieux [F.] Old; aged.

(les) vieux fous sont plus fous que les jeunes [F.] Old fools are greater fools than young ones.

vieux garçon [F.] An old bachelor.

vieux jeu [F.] An old game; something which is long out of fashion; a style that is now outdated.

vieux marcheur [F.] An old walker, i.e., an elderly man who still pursues women; a roué (q.v.).

vieux militaire [F.] An old soldier.

vieux style [F.] The old style; the old manner of doing things.

vigilante et orate [L.] Watch and pray.

vigne [F.] A vine; also, a vineyard.

vignette [F.] In book illustration, a small design or drawing, ordinarily placed at the beginning and end of each chapter; also, any small sketch or illustration.

vignoble [F.] A vineyard.

vigoroso [It.] In music, a direction calling for a passage to be played with vigor.

vigueur de dessus [F.] Strength from on high.

viis et modis [L.] By all possible ways and means; by any methods possible.

villa [L. and It.] A large and ostentatious country residence; an estate.

ville [F.] Town; city.

ville lumière [F.] The city of light, i.e., Paris.

ville qui parlemente est moitié rendue [F.] The man who parleys is half-surrendered.

vin [F.] Wine.

viña [Sp.] A vineyard.

vinaigre [F.] Vinegar.

vinata [It.] A drinking song; a tune that is sung while drinking wine.

vin blanc [F.] White wine.

vincam aut moriar [L.] I will conquer or die.

vin chaud [F.] Mulled wine.

vincit qui patitur [L.] He who can endure overcometh.

vincit veritas [L.] Truth conquers.

vin coupé [F.] Mixed wine.

vinculum matrimonii [L.] Matrimonial ties; the bonds of marriage.

vin de marque [F.] Vintage wine.

vin de table [F.] Table wine; an undistinguished wine ordinarily served with the daily meal.

vindex injuriae [L.] An avenger of injustice.

vindicta [L.] Revenge.

vin doux [F.] Sweet wine.

vin du pays [F.] A wine of the country; hence, a local wine, usually a *vin ordinaire* (q.v.).

vingt-et-un [F.] Twenty-one; name of a popular card game.

vin léger [F.] Light wine.

vino [It.] Wine.

vin ordinaire [F.] Ordinary wine; hence, common table wine, as opposed to vintage wine.

vin pur [F.] Pure wine; wine that has not been adulterated.

vin rosé [F.] Light red wine; a popular light red wine from France.

vin rouge [F.] Red wine.

vires acquirit eundo [L.] It grows in strength by moving forward.

vir et uxor [L.] Man and wife.

virginibus puerisque [L.] For boys and girls.

virgo [L.] A virgin.

virgo intacta [L.] An undefiled virgin.

virgule [F.] A comma.

viridarium [L.] A large and meticulously kept garden such as one located within the walls of a palace or large estate.

viritim [L.] Man by man; one by one; in single file.

vir sapit qui pauca loquitur [L.] The man who talks little is wise.

virtu [It.] Virtue.

virtuosamente [It.] Virtuously; wonderfully; without flaw.

virtus [L.] Virtue; strength; an exalted personal quality.

virtus est vitium fugere [L.] It is a virtue to shun vice.

virtus in actione consistit [L.] Virtue consists in action.

virtus in usu sui tota posita est [L.] The whole of virtue consists in practice.

virtus millia scuta [L.] Virtue is a thousand shields.

virtus non stemma [L.] Virtue, not pedigree.

virtus post nummos [L.] Money before virtue.

virtute et armis [L.] By valor and arms; used as the motto of the State of Mississippi.

virtute et fide [L.] By virtue and faith.

virtute fideque [L.] By virtue and faith.

virtute mea me involvo [L.] I wrap myself up in my virtue.

virtute, non astutia [L.] By virtue, not by cunning.

virtute, non verbis [L.] By virtue, not by words.

virtute officii [L.] By virtue of the office held.

virtute quies [L.] In virtue there is peace.

virtute securus [L.] Secure through virtue.

virtuti, non armis, fido [L.] In virtue, not in arms, I trust.

virtutis amore [L.] For love of virtue.

virtutum viva imago [L.] A living embodiment of the virtues.

vis [L.] Power; strength; force.

visage fardé [F.] A painted face, i.e., a face painted with a hypocritical expression; hence, a false front; a dissembling appearance.

vis anima [L.] Power of soul; strength.

vis armata [L.] Armed force.

vis a tergo [L.] A force from behind.

vis-à-vis [F.] (1.) Face to face; opposite; facing, especially in dancing, during a conversation, across a table, etc. (2.) Compared with.

vis cogitativa [L.] The force or faculty of thinking; the intellect.

vis comica [L.] Comic powers; a talent for comedy.

vis divina [L.] The divine force; the power of God.

vis inertiae [L.] The force of inertia.

visionario [Sp.] A visionary; one who sees visions; a dreamer.

visitador [Sp.] A visitor; a frequent caller.

vis major [L.] A supreme power; an irresistible force.

vis medicatrix naturae [L.] A natural means of recovery from disease; the tendency of a sick organism to heal itself.

vis mortua [L.] In physics, a dead force; hence, a force that performs no work.

vis motiva [L.] Moving force; that force which animates or produces motion.

vis unita fortior [L.] Union is strength.

vis vitae [L.] Vital force.

vis viva [L.] A living force; in physics, a force equal to the mass of a body in motion times the square of its velocity.

vita [L.] (1.) Life. (2.) A short biography.

vita brevis, ars longa [L.] Life is short, art long.

vitae via virtus [L.] Virtue is the way of life.

vita humana [L.] Human life.

vita patris [L.] In the father's lifetime.

vita sine litteris mors est [L.] To live without literature is death.

vite [F.] In music, a direction calling for the swift rendering of a passage.

vitello [It.] Veal.

vitesse [F.] Quickness; speed.

vite, vite [F.] Quickly, quickly.

vitia erunt, donec homines [L.] As long as men live, there will be vices.

vitiosum est ubique, quod nimium est [L.] Excess in anything is a mistake.

viva [It.] Long live; used as an exclamation preceding a name.

vivace [It.] In music, a direction calling for a passage to be rendered in a gay and lively manner.

viva il papa [It.] Long live the pope.

viva il rè! [It.] Long live the king.

viva la reine [F.] Long live the queen.

vive le roi [F.] Long live the king.

vivamus atque amemus [L.] Let us live and love.

vivant [F.] Living; alive; animated.

vivat [L.] May he or she live.

vivat regina [L.] Long live the queen.

vivat respublica [L.] Long live the republic.

vivat rex [L.] Long live the king.

viva voce [L.] By the living voice, i.e., orally; by the word of mouth.

vive la bagatelle [F.] Long live frivolity.

vive la différence [F.] Long live the difference; said of the differences between the sexes.

vive memor leti [L.] Live mindful of death.

vivere est cogitare [L.] To think is to live.

viveur [F.] One who lives well; a rake; a bon vivant (q.v.).

vive ut vivas [L.] Live, in order that you may live (hereafter).

vive, vale [L.] Farewell, be happy.

vive, valeque [L.] Farewell, and be happy.

vivit post funera virtus [L.] Virtue lives on after the grave.

vivre [F.] To live; to exist; to be alive.

vizier [Turkish] In Moslem countries, a minister or high state official, usually second in command to the king.

vizré [Port.] A viceroy.

voce [It.] Voice.

Vogel [G.] A bird.

vogue la galère [F.] Row the galley, i.e., come what may; whatever may pass; despite the obstacles.

(la) voie lactée [F.] The Milky Way.

voie royale [F.] The royal way.

voies de fait [F.] Ways of action, especially violent methods of making things happen.

voilà [F.] Here; here it is.

voilà le malheur [F.] That is the problem; therein lies the difficulty.

voilà tout [F.] That is all.

voir dire [F.] To speak the truth;

in law, the ability of a witness to give impartial testimony.

voir le dessous des cartes [F.] To see the underside of the cards, i.e., to be in on a secret.

voiture [F.] A vehicle; a carriage; a coach.

voix [F.] The voice.

voix larmoyante [F.] A teary voice.

volage [F.] Fickle; inconstant.

volat hora per orbem [L.] The hours fly along in a circle.

vol-au-vent [F.] A small puff pastry usually stuffed with meat or fowl.

volée [F.] Flight of birds.

volens et potens [L.] Willing and able.

voleur [F.] A thief; a robber.

Volkslied [G.] A folk song.

Volsmärchen [G.] A folk tale.

Volkssturm [G.] The people's army.

Volkstanz [G.] A folk dance.

volkstümlich [G.] Unsophisticated.

volo [L.] I fly.

volo, non valeo [L.] I am willing but unable.

volte-face [F.] A change of front; thus, a reversal of plans; a change in policy.

volti [It.] In music, a direction indicating that the page should be turned.

volto sciolto con pensieri stretti [It.] An open countenance with thoughts concealed.

voluptates corporis [L.] The pleasures of the body.

volupté [F.] Voluptuousness.

von [G.] Of; from.

von oben [G.] From the top.

von unten [G.] From the bottom.

vorago [L.] A pit; an abyss.

Vorlage [G.] In skiing, the posture of leaning far forward without lifting the heels from the skiis.

Vorspiel [G.] In music, an overture.

Vorstellung [G.] A presentation; a performance of a drama, film, etc.

vorwärts [G.] Forward.

vos valete et plaudite [L.] Goodbye, and give us your applause; traditional closing lines of the ancient Roman comedy; also, reputed last words spoken by the Roman Emperor Augustus.

votum castitatis [L.] A vow of chastity.

vouloir, c'est pouvoir [F.] Will is power.

vouloir prendre la lune avec les dents [F.] To wish to seize the moon by the teeth; to desire the impossible.

vouloir rompre l'anguille au genou [F.] To wish to break an eel on the knee.

voulu [F.] Wished; needed; desired.

vous [F.] You.

vous aurez toujours des voisins [F.] You will always have neighbors; remarks made by a peasant to Louis XIV while the gardens of Versailles were being constructed.

vous autres [F.] You others.

vous l'avez voulu [F.] You have desired it; it is your doing.

vous-mêmes [F.] Yourselves.

vox [L.] The voice.

vox clamantis in deserto [L.] The voice of one crying in the wilderness; used as the motto of Dartmouth University.

vox cycnea [L.] The swan song.

vox et praeterea nihil [L.] A voice and nothing else.

vox faucibus haesit [L.] His voice struck in his throat.

vox humana [L.] (1.) The human voice. (2.) The name of a reed stop on an organ.

vox litterata et articulata debito modo pronuntiata [L.] The word correct in spelling and form and properly pronounced.

vox nihili [L.] A word of nothing; a string of meaningless words.

vox populi [L.] The voice of the people; public opinion.

vox populi, vox Dei [L.] The voice of the people is the voice of God.

vox stellarum [L.] The voice of the stars; the music of the spheres.

voyager à pied [F.] To travel on foot.

voyageur [F.] A traveler; a voyager.

voyez [F.] See; see here; used as an exclamation.

vrai [F.] True; real; genuine.

vraiment [F.] Truly; really; actually.

vrai noblesse nul ne blesse [F.] True nobility can suffer no hurt.

vraisemblance [F.] Likelihood; probability.

vrouw [Dutch] A woman; a housewife.

vue d'oiseau [F.] A bird's eye view; a superficial acquaintance.

vulgo concepti [L.] Vulgar conceptions, i.e., bastard children.

vulgus [L.] The common people; the crowds.

vulneratus, non victus [L.] Wounded, not conquered.

vulpes [L.] The wolf.

vultus est index animi [L.] The countenance is the index of the soul.

W

Wächterlied [G.] In music, a watch-man's song.

wadi [Ar.] In the Middle East, a river valley; a river bed.

Waffe [G.] Weapon; arms.

waffie [Sc.] A vagabond; a wan-derer.

wagon-lit [F.] A sleeping car on a train.

Wahrheit [G.] Truth.

Wahrheit und Dichtung [G.] Truth and poetry.

Wald [G.] Forest; woods.

wali [Ar.] In Islam, a saint; a holy man.

Wanderjahr [G.] A year of wan-dering, especially one spent dur-ing youth.

wanderlust [G.] A lust to wander; a yearning to constantly travel and visit new places.

Wandervogel [G.] A wander bird, i.e., a young traveler in a foreign land; a youthful wanderer.

warum nicht [G.] Why not?

was gibt es [G.] What is the trou-ble?

Wasser [G.] Water.

weder gehauen noch gestochen [G.] Neither fish nor flesh.

Weinstube [G.] A wine house; an inn where a variety of wines are served.

Wein, Weib und Gesang [G.] Wine, woman, and song.

Weltanschauung [G.] A world view; an overall view of the world and its history as seen individually or collectively.

Weltansicht [G.] A world view; an overall conception of the world and temporal existence.

Weltbürger [G.] A citizen of the world.

Weltgeschichte [G.] History of the world.

Weltliteratur [G.] World literature; universal literature.

Weltpolitik [G.] World politics; the politics of international di-plomacy.

Weltschmerz [G.] World sorrow; a melancholy view of the world and its evils; a romantic gloomi-ness over mankind and its sor-rows.

Weltweisheit [G.] World wisdom.

wer dem Pöbel dient, hat einen schlechten Herrn [G.] The servant of the masses has a bad master.

wer hängen soll, ersäuft nicht [G.] He who was born to be hanged is never drowned.

wer ist da [G.] Who goes there?

wer nicht liebt Wein, Weib und Gesang, der bleibt ein Narr sein

Leben lang [G.] Who loves not wine, woman, and song, remains a fool his whole life long.

wer oft schiesst, trifft endlich [G.] He who shoots often, finally hits his mark.

wer rastet rostet [G.] Who rests rusts.

wesoly [Pol.] Merry; gay; extraordinarily happy.

wie der Herr, so der Diener [G.] Like master, like servant.

wie Einer ist, so ist sein Gott [G.] As is the man, so is his God.

wie geht's? [G.] How are you?

Wiegendruck [G.] Books printed before the year 1500; incunabula (q.v.).

Wiegenlied [G.] A cradle song.

wienerwurst [G.] A thin sausage made of beef and pork.

wieviel Uhr ist es? [G.] What time is it?

Willkom [G.] A cylindrical drinking glass popular in sixteenth and seventeenth century Europe.

Wirtshaus [G.] A tavern.

wohlfeil [G.] Cheap; inexpensive.

wollt ihr immer leben? [G.] Do you wish to live forever?; asked by Frederick the Great of cowardly members of his guard.

Wörterbuch [G.] A dictionary.

wozu das? [G.] What is the use of that?

Wunderkind [G.] A wonder child; a remarkable youth; a prodigy.

Wurst [G.] Sausage.

Y

y á Roma por todo [Sp.] And to Rome for everything.

yashmak [Ar.] A cloth veil worn in public by Moslem women to conceal their faces.

yatsushiro [Jap.] A form of Japanese ceramic work from the province of Higo.

yeseria [Sp.] A technique of decorative plaster work, popular in Renaissance Spain.

yeux [F.] Eyes.

yeux doux [F.] Sweet eyes; amorous glances; loving looks.

yi-dam [Tibetan] In Lamaism, a series of tutelary divinities said to participate in the spiritual education of humanity.

yōdansu [Jap.] A decorative lacquered chest with many drawers.

yoga [Skr.] In Hinduism, a system of philosophy and physical exercises designed to spiritually elevate the devotee.

yogi [Skr.] One who practices yoga (q.v.).

yuz-bashi [Turkish] In Turkey, an officer in command of a troop of soldiers.

Z

zabeta [Ar.] A rule; a law; a regulation; also, a tariff.

zacatón [Sp.] A dry, wiry prairie grass found in Mexico and the Southwestern United States.

zaftra [Russ.] Tomorrow.

zaibatsu [Jap.] A small group of families in feudal Japan who controlled the wealth and government of the state.

zamarra [Sp.] In Spain, a sheepskin coat worn by sheepherders.

zamindar [Hindi and Persian] In India and Persia, a landowner; a landlord; also, one who collects land taxes.

zampogna [It.] A bagpipe.

zapatero á tu zapato [Sp.] Shoemaker, attend to your shoe.

zapato [Sp.] A shoe.

zareba [Ar.] A shelter; a pen; a small stockade.

zareeba. See "zareba."

zärtlich [G.] Tender; fondly.

Zauber [G.] Magic.

Zeitgeist [G.] The spirit of the times; the social or intellectual ethos of an age.

Zeitschrift [G.] Magazine; periodical.

Zeitung [G.] Newspaper.

Zeitvertreib [G.] Pastime.

zélateur [F.] A zealous person; a zealot.

zelator [L.] A zealot.

zemindar. See "zamindar."

zenana [Hindi] A harem; the woman's section of a home or palace.

Zeus lui-même était soumis au destin [F.] Zeus himself was subject to fate.

zhená [Russ.] Wife; lady; woman.

ziggurat [Assyrian-Babylonian] In ancient Babylonia, a large spiral stone tower capped with a temple, built for the purposes of mathematical calculation and divination by the stars.

zingano. See zingaro.

zingaro [It.] A gypsy.

zoe [Gr.] Life; existence.

zoe, mou, sas agapo [Gr.] My life, I love thee.

Zollverein [G.] A custom's union.

zonam perdidit [L.] He has lost his purse, i.e., he is brought to ruin.

zoon politikon [Gr.] A political animal; Aristotle's definition of man.

zonam solvere [L.] To lose the virgin parts; to be deflowered; also, to marry a virgin.

zucca [It.] Squash.

zucchetto [It.] A round colored cap worn by priests in the Roman Catholic Church.

zum Beispiel [G.] For example; for instance; commonly abbreviated as *z. B.*

zum ersten [G.] In the first place.

zum Teil [G.] In part.

zuppa di pollo [It.] Chicken soup.

zu viel Demut ist Hochmut G.] Too much humility is pride.

zwei Seelen und ein Gedanke, zwei Herzen und ein Schlag [G.] Two souls and one thought, two hearts and one beat.

zwei Seelen wohnen, ach in meiner Brust [G.] "Two souls, alas, dwell in my breast": *Goethe.*

Zwieback [G.] A form of toasted biscuit.

Zwischengoldglas [G.] In art, a technique of pressing and fixing gold between two layers of glass.

Abbreviations of Foreign Terms Commonly Used in the English Language

A

A.A.C (*anno ante Christum*) [L.] The year before Christ.

a.a.O. (*am angeführten Orte*) [G.] In the place cited.

A.B. (*Artium Baccalaureus*) [L.] Bachelor of arts.

ab ex. (*ab extra*) [L.] From without.

ab init. (*ab initio*) [L.] From the beginning.

abs. re. (*absente reo*) [L.] In law, the defendant being absent.

A.C. (*Ante Christum*) [L.] Before Christ.

a.c. (*ante cibum*) [L.] In pharmacy, before food; before eating.

A.D. (*Anno Domini*) [L.] In the year of our Lord.

A.D.C. (*aide-de-camp*) [F.] An aide-de-camp.

add. (*addatur*) [L.] In pharmacy, let there be added.

ad ex. (*ad extremum*) [L.] To the extreme; to the end.

ad inf. (*ad infinitum*) [L.] To infinity; to eternity.

ad int. (*ad interim*) [L.] In the interim.

aet. (*aetas*) [L.] Age.

A.H. (*Anno Hegirae*) [L.] In Islam, in the year of the Hegira.

Alt. dieb. (*alternis diebus*) [L.] Medicine: every other day.

A.M. (*ante meridiem*) [L.] Before noon; (*Anno Mundi*) [L.] In the year of the world; (*Artium Magister*) [L.] Master of arts.

A.N.C. (*Ante Nativitatem Christi*) [L.] Before the birth of Christ.

a.p. (*anni praesentis*) [L.] In the present year.

aq. (*aqua*) [L.] Water.

A.R. (*Anno Regni*) [L.] In the year of the king.

A.U.C. (*ab urbe condita*) [L.] From the founding of the city Rome, 753 B.C.

B

bacc. en dr. (*baccalaureat en droit*) [F.] Baccalaureate in law.

bacc. es l. (*baccaulauréat ès lettres*) [F.] Baccalaureate in literature.

bacc. ès sc. (*baccaulauréat ès sc.*) [F.] Baccalaureate in science.

B. Ch. D. (*Baccalaureus Chirurgiae Dentium*) [L.] Bachelor of dental surgery.

b.d.s. (*bis die sumendum*) [L.] In medicine, to be taken twice.

B. ès A. (*Bachelier ès Arts*) [F.] Bachelor of arts.

B. ès L. (*Bachelier ès Lettres*) [F.] Bachelor of literature.

B. ès S. (*Bachelier ès Sciences*) [F.] Bachelor of sciences.

B.L.L. (*Baccalaureus Legum*) [L.] Bachelor of law.

B.P. (*Baccalaureus Pharmaciae*) [L.] Bachelor of pharmacy.

B.V.M. (*Beata Virgo Maria*) [L.] The Blessed Virgin Mary.

b.w. (*bitte wenden*) [G.] Please turn the page.

b.z.g.l. (*bezüglich*) [G.] In regard to.

C

ca. (*circa*) [L.] Around; during the period of.

c.-a.-d. (*c'est-à-dire*) [F.] That is to say.

cantab. (*Cantabrigiensis*) [L.] Of Cambridge.

c.d.v. (*carte de viste*) [F.] A visiting card.

cf. (*confer*) [L.] Consult; see; refer to.

C.J.Can. (*Corpus Juris Canonici*) [L.] The body of canon law.

C.L.H. (*croix de la légion d'honneur*) [F.] The cross of the Legion of Honor.

con. (*contra*) [L.] Against.

c.o.q.b. (*cum omnibus bonis quiescat*) [L.] May he rest with all good souls.

D

D. (*Deus*) [L.] God.

D.C. (*Da capo*) [It.] In music, from the beginning.

D. ès L. (*Docteur ès Lettres*) [F.] Doctor of letters.

D.F. (*Defensor Fidei*) [L.] Defender of the Faith.

D.G. (*Dei gratia*) [L.] By the grace of God.

dig. (*digeratur*) [L.] Let it be digested.

d.s. (*dal segno*) [It.] In music, from the sign.

d.t. (*delirium tremens*) [L.] The delirium tremens.

E

e.g. (*exempli gratia*) [L.] For example.

et al. (*et alibi*) [L.] And elsewhere.

etc. (*et cetera*) [L.] And so forth.

et seq. (*et sequens*) [L.] And the following.

et seq. (*et sequentes*) [L.] And the following.

ex. off. (*ex officio*) [L.] From the authority of the office.

F

f. (*forte*) [It.] In music, loud.

f.c. (*fidei commissum*) [L.] He bequeathed in trust.

F.D. (*Fidei Defensor*) [L.] Defender of the Faith.

fel. mem. (*felicis memoriae*) [L.] Of happy memory.

fha. (*fecha*) [Sp.] Date.

fi. fa. (*fieri facias*) [L.] In law, cause to be done (a legal writ).

fin. (*finis*) [L.] Finished.

Frl. (*Fräulein*) [G.] Miss.

f.v. (*folio verso*) [L.] On the back of the page.

G

garg. (*gargarisma*) [L.] In pharmacy, gargle.

geb. (*geboren*) [G.] Born.

G.F.P. (*Geheime Feldpolizei*) [G.] The secret police.

G.P. (*Gloria Patri*) [L.] Glory to the Father.

gt. (*gutta*) [L.] A drop.

H

h.a. (*hoc anno*) [L.] In the present year.

h.d. (*hora decubitus*) [L.] In medicine, take at bedtime.

h.e. (*hic est*) [L.] That is; this is.

H.J. (*Hic Jacet*) [L.] Here lies.

H Maj:t (*Hans Majestät*) [Swedish] His majesty.

h.t. (*hoc tempore*) [L.] At this time.

I

I. (*Imperator*) [L.] Emperor.

i.A. (*im Auftrage*) [G.] By the order of.

ib. (*ibidem*) [L.] In the same place.

ibid. (*ibidem*) [L.] In the same place.

i.c. (*inter cibos*) [L.] Between meals.

id. (*idem*) [L.] The same.

i.e. (*id est*) [L.] That is; that is to say.

igla. (*iglesia*) [Sp.] Church.

ign. (*ignotus*) [L.] Unknown.

i.J.d.W. (*im Jahre der Welt*) [G.] In the year of the world.

Ind. Imp. (*Indiae Imperator*) [L.] Emperor of India.

in init. (*in initio*) [L.] In the beginning.

in pr. (*in principio*) [L.] In the beginning.

I.N.R.I. (*Iesus Nazarenus Rex Iudaeorum*) [L.] Jesus of Nazareth, King of the Jews.

in trans. (*in transitu*) [L.] In transit.

inv. (*invenit*) [L.] He designed it.

i.q. (*idem quod*) [L.] The same as.

J

J.D.C. (*Juris Civilis Doctor*) [L.] Doctor of civil law.

jr. (*jour*) [F.] Year.

K

K.K. (*Kaiserlich-Königlich*) [G.] Imperial-Royal.

Konz. (*Konzentriert*) [G.] Concentrated.

k.t.l. (*kai ta loipa*) [Gr.] And so forth.

L

lb. (*libra*) [L.] A pound.

l.c. (*loco citato*) [L.] In the place cited.

L.H.D. (*Litterarum Humaniorum Doctor*) [L.] Doctor of humanities.

l.J. (*im laufen den Jahre*) [G.] The current year.

LL.D. (*Legum Doctor*) [L.] Doctor of laws.

loc. cit. (*loco citato*) [L.] In the place cited.

l.s. (*locus sigilli*) [L.] In the place of the seal.

lx. (*lux*) [L.] Light.

M

M. (*Monsieur*) [F.] Mister.

M.A. (*Magister Artium*) [L.] Master of arts.

m.E. (*meines Erachtens*) [G.] In my opinion.

M. ès A. (*Maitre ès Arts*) [F.] Master of arts.

Messrs. (*Messieurs*) [F.] Misters.

mf. (*mezzo forte*) [It.] Moderately loud.

Mlle. (*Mademoiselle*) [F.] Miss.

Mme. (*Madame*) [F.] Mrs.

m/n (*moneda nacional*) [Sp.] National money.

mod. praescript. (*modo praescripto*) [L.] In the manner prescribed.

monsig. (*Monseigneur*) [F.] Lord; sir.

N

n. (*natus*) [L.] Born.

n.b. (*nota bene*) [L.] Note well.

nem. con. (*nemine contradicente*) [L.] No one opposing.

no. (*numero*) [L.] By number.

nol. pros. (*nolle prosequi*) [L.] In law, not wishing to prosecute.

non seq. (*non sequitur*) [L.] It does not follow.

N.S.I.C. (*Noster Salvator Iesus Christus*) [L.] Our Savior Jesus Christ.

O

ob. (*obiit*) [L.] He died.

o.d. (*omni die*) [L.] Every day.

ol. (*oleum*) [L.] Oil.

omn. hor. (*omni hora*) [L.] Every hour.

o.n. (*omni nocte*) [L.] Every night.

op. cit. (*opere citato*) [L.] In the work cited.

o.p.m. (*ora pro nobis*) [L.] Pray for us.

Oxon. (*Oxonia*) [L.] From Oxford University.

P

P. (*Pater*) [L.] Father.

p. (*piano*) [It.] In music, softly.

p. ae. (*partes aequales*) [L.] In equal parts.

p.c. (*post cibum*) [L.] After food; after eating.

p.e. (*partes aequales*) [L.] In equal parts.

p. ex. (*par exemple*) [F.] For example.

Ph.B. (*Philosophiae Baccalaureus*) [L.] Bachelor of philosophy.

Ph.D. (*Philosophiae Doctor*) [L.] Doctor of philosophy.

pinx. (*pinxit*) [L.] He painted it.

P.M. (*post meridiem*) [L.] From afternoon to midnight.

post-obit. (*post-obitum*) [L.] After death.

p.p. (*praemissis praemittendis*) [L.] Omitting preliminaries.

pro tem. (*pro tempore*) [L.] For the time being.

prox. (*proximo*) [L.] Next; of the next month.

p.s. (*postscriptum*) [L.] Postscript.

Q

Q.B.S.M. (*que besa su mano*) [Sp.] Salutation: who kisses your hand.

q.d. (*quaque die*) [L.] Every day.

Q.D.G. (*que Dios guarde*) [Sp.] May God keep him.

q.e. (*quod est*) [L.] Which is.

Q.E.D. (*quod erat demonstrandum*) [L.] That which was to be demonstrated.

Q.E.F. (*quod erat faciendum*) [L.] That thing which was to be done.

q.h. (*quaque hora*) [L.] In medicine, every hour.

q.i.d. (*quarter in die*) [L.] In medicine, four times a day.

q.l. (*quantum libet*) [L.] In medicine, as much as you please.

q. pl. (*quantum placet*) [L.] As much as you please.

q.q. (*qualitate qua*) [L.] In the capacity of.

qr. (*quadrans*) [L.] A farthing.

q.s. (*quantum satis*) [L.] In medicine, as much as is sufficient.

qu. (*quaere*) [L.] Inquire; question.

q.v. (*quod vide*) [L.] Which see; which the reader should refer to.

R

R. (*Rex*) [L.] King; (*Regina*) [L.] Queen; (Recipe) [L.] In medicine, take.

repet. (*repetatur*) [L.] Let it be repeated.

R.I.P. (*requiescat in pace*) [L.] May he rest in peace.

rit. (*ritardando*) [It.] In music, retarding.

R.S.V.P. (*répondez s'il vous plâit*) [F.] Please reply.

R.V.S.V.P. (*répondez vite, s'il vous plâit*) [F.] Reply quickly, please.

S

s.a. (*sine anno*) [L.] Without the year or date.

s.c. (*scilicet*) [L.] In law, namely.

Sc. B. (*Scientiae Baccalaureus*) [L.] Bachelor of science.

s/cta. (*su cuenta*) [Sp.] Your account.

s.d. (*sans date*) [F.] Without date; (*sine die*) [L.] Without appointing a day.

sec. (*secundum*) [L.] According to.

s.e.o.o. (*sauf erreur ou omission*) [F.] Errors or omissions excepted.

seq. (*sequens*) [L.] The following.

seqq. (*sequens*) [L.] The following.

s.i.d. (*semel in die*) [L.] Once a day.

s.l.n.d. (*sans lieu ni date*) [F.] Without place or date.

S.M. (*Sa Majesté*) [F.] His or Her Majesty.

s.p. (*sine parole*) [L.] Without issue.

S.P.Q.R. (*Senatus Populusque Romanus*) [L.] The Senate of the Roman People.

sq. (*sequens*) [L.] The following.

S.S.S. (*Su Seguro Servidor*) [Sp.] Your faithful servant.

s.s.s. (*stratum super stratum*) [L.] Layer upon layer.

S.T.B. (*Sacrae Theologiae Baccalaureus*) [L.] Bachelor of sacred theology.

S.T.D. (*Sacrae Theologiae Doctor*) [L.] Doctor of sacred theology.

sup. (*supra*) [L.] Above.

sus. per col. (*suspensio per collum*) [L.] Suspension by the neck, i.e., hanging.

S.V. (*Sancta Virgo*) [L.] The Holy Virgin.

s.v. (*sub verbo*) [L.] Under the word; (*sub voco*) [L.] Under the title.

s.v.p. (*s'il vous plâit*) [F.] If you please.

T

t.a. (*testantibus actis*) [L.] As the records show.

Th. D. (*Theologiae Doctor*) [L.] Doctor of theology.

T.S.V.P. (*tournez s'il vous plâit*) [F.] Please turn the page.

U

u. (*und*) [G.] And.

U.A.w.g. (*Um Antwort wird gebeten*) [G.] An answer is expected.

u.s. (*ubi supra*) [L.] Where above cited.

u.s.w. (*und so weiter*) [G.] And so forth.

ut dict. (*ut dictum*) [L.] As directed.

V

v. (*vide*) [L.] See; refer to; (*von*) [G.] Of.

v.a. (*vixit annos*) [L.] He lived.

v.g. (*verbi gratia*) [L.] For example.